THE WHO'S BUYING SERIES
BY THE NEW STRATEGIST EDITORS

Who's Buying
Executive Summary of Household Spending

5th EDITION

New Strategist Publications, Inc.
P.O. Box 242, Ithaca, New York 14851
800/848-0842; 607/273-0913
www.newstrategist.com

ISBN 978-1-935114-32-1
ISBN 1-935114-32-8
ISSN 1933-2009

Printed in the United States of America

Contents

Introduction

Welcome to the fifth edition of *Who's Buying: Executive Summary of Household Spending*. This report presents a broad overview of household spending in the year 2007. With this report in hand, students and researchers can gain important insights into consumer spending patterns and how those patterns differ by age, race, household type, region of residence, and other significant demographic characteristics.

Consumer spending is the result of a complex mix of wants and needs, hopes and fears. This mix determines the success of individual businesses and the health of our economy. Knowing how consumers spend their dollars is key to understanding where our economy is headed. *Who's Buying: Executive Summary of Household Spending* is for those who want to know the big picture of who does what with their money.

Who's Buying: Executive Summary of Household Spending is based on data collected by the Bureau of Labor Statistics' Consumer Expenditure Survey, an ongoing, nationwide survey of household spending. This report presents the average spending figures collected and published by the Bureau of Labor Statistics. It also presents indexed spending figures, showing at a glance which households spend the most on products and services. This report analyzes spending for the following demographic segments: age of householder, household income, high-income households, age by income, household type, region, region by income, metropolitan area, race and Hispanic origin of householder, educational attainment of householder, household size, housing tenure, earners in the household, and occupation of householder.

The Bureau of Labor Statistics' Consumer Expenditure Survey is a complete accounting of household expenditures. It includes everything from big-ticket items such as homes and cars to small purchases like laundry detergent and videogames. The survey does not include expenditures by government, business, or institutions. The lag time between data collection and publication is about two years. The data in this book are from the 2007 Consumer Expenditure Survey, unless otherwise noted. For more information about the Consumer Expenditure survey, see the appendix at the end of this report.

The data in *Who's Buying: Executive Summary of Household Spending* reveal how American households allocate their spending. The starting point for all calculations are the average household spending data collected by the Consumer Expenditure Survey. These are shown in the average spending tables. New Strategist's statisticians produced the indexed spending tables based on the average figures. The indexed spending tables reveal whether households in a given segment spend more or less than the average household (or the average household in that segment), and by how much. These two types of tables are described below.

• **Average Spending Tables** The average spending tables show the average annual spending of households on each major product and service category in 2007. The Consumer Expenditure Survey produces average spending data for all households in a segment, e.g., all households with a householder aged 25 to 34, not just for those who purchased an item. When reviewing the spending data, it is important to remember that by including both purchasers and nonpurchasers in the calculation, the average is diluted—especially for infrequently purchased items. For universally purchased items, such as food, the average spending figures give a fairly accurate account of actual spending. But for infrequently purchased items, such as new cars and trucks, the average spending figures are less revealing than the indexes.

Average spending figures are useful for determining the market potential of a product or service in a local area. By multiplying the average amount households in Dallas spend on women's clothing, for example, businesses can estimate the size of the women's clothing market in Dallas. The Dallas media could show those figures to potential advertisers as evidence of the local demand for women's clothes.

Note that because of sampling errors, average values can vary—especially for infrequently purchased items. To examine the standard errors for these data, visit: http://www.bls.gov/cex/csx-stnderror.htm.

• **Indexed Spending Tables** The indexed spending tables compare the spending of each household segment with that of the average household. To compute the indexes, New Strategist's statisticians divide the average amount each household segment spends on a particular category by how much the average household spends on the category and multiply the resulting figure by 100.

An index of 100 is the average for all households. An index of 125 means the spending of a household segment is 25 percent above average (100 plus 25). An index of 75 indicates spending that is 25 percent below the average for all households (100 minus 25). Indexed spending figures identify the best customers for a product or service category. Households with an index of 177 for furniture, for example, are a strong market for that product. They spend 77 percent more than the average household on furniture. Those with an index below 100 are either a weak or an underserved market.

Spending indexes reveal the household segments with a high propensity to buy a particular product or service. Householders aged 55 to 74, for example, spend 28 percent more than the average household on reading material. This is a higher index than that of any other age group, which makes householders aged 55 to 74 the best customers for reading material. Married couples with school-aged children at home spend 64 percent more than the average household on fresh milk and cream, which makes them the best customers of this category. Researchers can use the indexed spending tables to target their best customers.

Note that because of sampling errors, small differences in index values are usually insignificant. But the broader patterns revealed by indexes can guide researchers to their best customers.

For more information

To find out more about the Consumer Expenditure Survey, contact the specialists at the Bureau of Labor Statistics at (202) 691-6900 or visit the Consumer Expenditure Survey home page at http://www.bls.gov/cex/. The web site includes news releases, technical documentation, and current and historical summary-level survey data.

For a comprehensive look at detailed household spending data for all products and services, see the 14th edition of *Household Spending: Who Spends How Much on What.* Each of Strategist's books is available in hardcopy or as a download with links to the Excel version of each table. Find out more by visiting http://www.newstrategist.com or by calling 1-800-848-0842.

Household Spending Trends: 2000 to 2007

Between 2000 and 2007, spending by the average household rose by 8 percent, after adjusting for inflation—to $49,638. The 8 percent rise is substantial, but it masks the onset of the recession that officially began in December of that year. Households were grappling with the economic downturn even as the government was collecting the 2007 spending data. In fact, between 2006 and 2007 spending by the average household fell by several hundred dollars, after adjusting for inflation—a sign that recession was imminent.

An examination of the 2000 to 2007 spending trends reveals two opposing forces. On the one hand, the numbers show that some households were awash in the easy money that resulted from surging housing prices and the abuse of home equity loans. On the other hand, the cost of necessities soared between 2000 and 2007, and many households were forced to trim their spending well before the official start of the recession.

Average household spending on mortgage interest grew by an enormous 22 percent between 2000 and 2007, after adjusting for inflation, as the rate of homeownership reached a record high and some families bought larger homes than they could afford. Entertainment spending grew by 20 percent as some spent their home equity on big-screen TVs and other electronic toys. Average household spending on food away from home, other lodging (mostly hotel and motel expenses), alcoholic beverages, and public transportation (mostly airfares) also grew during those years.

Ominously, however, the cost of necessities was rising sharply. The average household spent 53 percent more on gasoline in 2007 than in 2000, after adjusting for inflation. Health insurance spending rose 31 percent, and education spending was up 24 percent. The middle class was being squeezed, and consumers were cutting back. Spending on used vehicles plummeted by 26 percent between 2000 and 2007. Spending on new vehicles fell by 19 percent. Spending on women's clothes fell 14 percent, and spending on shoes was down 21 percent. Despite the record high homeownership rate, spending on household furnishings and equipment fell by 4 percent.

Then the recession hit. Those who track the government's Consumer Expenditure Survey statistics would not have been surprised by the sharp decline in household spending that followed. For years, spending trends have suggested that American households are struggling. In 2007, they finally threw in the towel and spent less than in 2006, cutting back on a growing number of items, such as food away from home. American consumers are proving once again to be cautious spenders, with enormous consequences for our economy.

Households are being squeezed by the rising cost of necessities

(percent change in spending by the average household on selected products and services, 2000–07; in 2007 dollars)

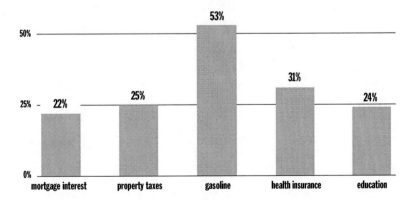

Table 2. Household spending trends, 2000 to 2007

(average annual spending of consumer units, 2000, 2006, and 2007; percent change, 2006–07 and 2000–07; in 2007 dollars)

	2007	2006	2000	percent change 2006–07	percent change 2000–07
Number of consumer units (in 000s)	120,171	118,843	109,367	1.1%	9.9%
Average before-tax income of consumer units	$63,091	$62,257	$53,761	1.3	17.4
Average annual spending of consumer units	49,638	49,776	45,809	−0.3	8.4
FOOD	6,133	6,285	6,211	−2.4	−1.2
Food at home	3,465	3,514	3,638	−1.4	−4.7
Cereals and bakery products	460	459	545	0.3	−15.7
Cereals and cereal products	143	147	188	−2.8	−23.9
Bakery products	317	313	358	1.4	−11.4
Meats, poultry, fish, and eggs	777	820	957	−5.2	−18.8
Beef	216	243	287	−11.0	−24.6
Pork	150	161	201	−7.1	−25.4
Other meats	104	108	122	−3.7	−14.5
Poultry	142	145	175	−2.1	−18.7
Fish and seafood	122	125	132	−2.8	−7.9
Eggs	43	38	41	13.0	5.0
Dairy products	387	378	391	2.3	−1.1
Fresh milk and cream	154	144	158	7.0	−2.4
Other dairy products	234	234	232	−0.2	0.7
Fruits and vegetables	600	609	627	−1.5	−4.4
Fresh fruits	202	201	196	0.7	2.9
Fresh vegetables	190	198	191	−4.3	−0.8
Processed fruits	112	112	138	−0.1	−19.1
Processed vegetables	96	98	101	−1.7	−5.1
Other food at home	1,241	1,247	1,116	−0.4	11.2
Sugar and other sweets	124	129	141	−3.5	−12.0
Fats and oils	91	88	100	2.9	−8.9
Miscellaneous foods	650	645	526	0.8	23.5
Nonalcoholic beverages	333	341	301	−2.5	10.6
Food prepared by consumer unit on trips	43	44	48	−2.8	−10.7
Food away from home	2,668	2,771	2,573	−3.7	3.7
ALCOHOLIC BEVERAGES	457	511	448	−10.6	2.0
HOUSING	16,920	16,832	14,833	0.5	14.1
Shelter	10,023	9,949	8,566	0.7	17.0
Owned dwellings	6,730	6,702	5,541	0.4	21.5
Mortgage interest and charges	3,890	3,860	3,178	0.8	22.4
Property taxes	1,709	1,696	1,371	0.8	24.6
Maintenance, repair, insurance, other expenses	1,131	1,147	993	−1.4	13.9
Rented dwellings	2,602	2,664	2,449	−2.3	6.2
Other lodging	691	583	576	18.5	20.1
Utilities, fuels, and public services	3,477	3,494	2,997	−0.5	16.0
Natural gas	480	523	370	−8.3	29.9
Electricity	1,303	1,302	1,097	0.1	18.8
Fuel oil and other fuels	151	142	117	6.4	29.3
Telephone services	1,110	1,118	1,056	−0.7	5.1
Water and other public services	434	408	356	6.3	21.8
Household services	984	975	824	0.9	19.5
Personal services	415	404	393	2.7	5.7
Other household services	569	571	431	−0.3	32.0
Housekeeping supplies	639	658	580	−2.9	10.1
Laundry and cleaning supplies	140	155	158	−9.9	−11.2
Other household products	347	339	272	2.2	27.5
Postage and stationery	152	164	152	−7.0	0.2

	2007	2006	2000	percent change 2006–07	percent change 2000–07
Household furnishings and equipment	$1,797	$1,757	$1,865	2.3%	–3.7%
Household textiles	133	158	128	–16.0	4.2
Furniture	446	476	471	–6.3	–5.3
Floor coverings	46	49	53	–6.8	–13.2
Major appliances	231	248	228	–6.8	1.5
Small appliances and miscellaneous housewares	101	112	105	–9.9	–3.6
Miscellaneous household equipment	840	713	880	17.9	–4.6
APPAREL AND RELATED SERVICES	**1,881**	**1,927**	**2,235**	**–2.4**	**–15.8**
Men and boys	**435**	**457**	**530**	**–4.7**	**–17.9**
Men, aged 16 or older	351	363	414	–3.3	–15.3
Boys, aged 2 to 15	84	94	116	–10.2	–27.3
Women and girls	**749**	**772**	**873**	**–3.0**	**–14.2**
Women, aged 16 or older	627	647	731	–3.1	–14.2
Girls, aged 2 to 15	122	125	142	–2.8	–14.1
Children under age 2	**93**	**99**	**99**	**–5.8**	**–5.8**
Footwear	**327**	**313**	**413**	**4.6**	**–20.8**
Other apparel products and services	**276**	**288**	**320**	**–4.2**	**–13.8**
TRANSPORTATION	**8,758**	**8,750**	**8,931**	**0.1**	**–1.9**
Vehicle purchases	**3,244**	**3,518**	**4,116**	**–7.8**	**–21.2**
Cars and trucks, new	1,572	1,849	1,933	–15.0	–18.7
Cars and trucks, used	1,567	1,613	2,131	–2.8	–26.5
Other vehicles	105	54	52	94.4	102.8
Gasoline and motor oil	**2,384**	**2,290**	**1,554**	**4.1**	**53.4**
Other vehicle expenses	**2,592**	**2,422**	**2,746**	**7.0**	**–5.6**
Vehicle finance charges	305	306	395	–0.5	–22.8
Maintenance and repairs	738	708	751	4.3	–1.8
Vehicle insurance	1,071	911	937	17.5	14.3
Vehicle rentals, leases, licenses, other charges	478	496	663	–3.6	–28.0
Public transportation	**538**	**519**	**514**	**3.6**	**4.6**
HEALTH CARE	**2,853**	**2,845**	**2,488**	**0.3**	**14.7**
Health insurance	1,545	1,507	1,184	2.5	30.5
Medical services	709	689	684	2.9	3.7
Drugs	481	529	501	–9.0	–4.0
Medical supplies	118	120	119	–1.9	–1.0
ENTERTAINMENT	**2,698**	**2,444**	**2,243**	**10.4**	**20.3**
Fees and admissions	658	623	620	5.6	6.1
Audio and visual equipment and services	987	932	749	5.9	31.8
Pets, toys, and playground equipment	560	424	402	32.2	39.2
Other entertainment products and services	493	464	473	6.3	4.2
PERSONAL CARE PRODUCTS AND SERVICES	**588**	**602**	**679**	**–2.3**	**–13.4**
READING	**118**	**120**	**176**	**–1.9**	**–32.9**
EDUCATION	**945**	**913**	**761**	**3.5**	**24.2**
TOBACCO PRODUCTS AND SMOKING SUPPLIES	**323**	**336**	**384**	**–4.0**	**–15.9**
MISCELLANEOUS	**808**	**870**	**934**	**–7.1**	**–13.5**
CASH CONTRIBUTIONS	**1,821**	**1,922**	**1,435**	**–5.3**	**26.9**
PERSONAL INSURANCE AND PENSIONS	**5,336**	**5,420**	**4,052**	**–1.6**	**31.7**
Life and other personal insurance	309	331	480	–6.7	–35.7
Pensions and Social Security*	5,027	5,089	3,571	–1.2	–
PERSONAL TAXES	**2,233**	**2,501**	**3,753**	**–10.7**	**–40.5**
Federal income taxes	1,569	1,760	2,901	–10.8	–45.9
State and local income taxes	468	534	677	–12.3	–30.8
Other taxes	196	208	176	–5.7	11.5
GIFTS FOR PEOPLE IN OTHER HOUSEHOLDS	**1,198**	**1,187**	**1,304**	**0.9**	**–8.1**

* Spending on pensions and Social Security in 2000 is not comparable with 2006 or 2007 numbers because of changes in methodology.

Note: Average spending is rounded to the nearest dollar, but the percent change calculation is based on unrounded figures. Spending by category does not add to total spending because gift spending is also included in the preceding product and service categories and personal taxes are not included in the total.

Source: Bureau of Labor Statistics, 2000, 2006, and 2007 Consumer Expenditure Surveys, Internet site http://www.bls.gov/cex/; calculations by New Strategist

Spending by Age, 2007

The average household spent $49,638 in 2007, but some spent more and others less. Because spending rises with income, affluent householders spend the most. Householders aged 35 to 54 are in their peak earning years, which explains why they spent 18 to 19 percent more than the average household in 2007, the highest level of spending among all age groups.

Households headed by people under age 25 or aged 75 or older spend the least because their incomes are lowest. Householders under age 25 spend just 59 percent as much as the average household, while householders aged 75 or older spend 61 percent as much as the average.

Householders aged 35 to 44 spend the most overall, but only because of their steep mortgage interest payments—60 percent higher than the average household. Householders aged 45 to 54 spend just slightly less than householders aged 35 to 44, mostly because their spending on mortgage interest is only 31 percent more than the average household. Other age groups spend more in some categories. Householders under age 25 spend much more than average on rented dwellings, for example. Householders aged 25 to 34, also avid renters, spend the most on clothes for children under age 2. Spending on women's apparel and on tobacco products and smoking supplies is highest in the 45-to-54 age group. Households headed by people aged 65 to 74 spend the most on health care, including the individual category of health insurance. Americans aged 55 to 64 spend more on cash contributions than any other age group.

With millions of baby boomers postponing retirement because of the recession, the two-earner couples of the baby-boom generation may boost the spending of householders aged 55 to 64 in the years ahead.

Table 2. Average spending by age of householder, 2007

(average annual spending of consumer units (CUs) by product and service category and age of consumer unit reference person, 2007)

	total consumer units	under 25	25 to 34	35 to 44	45 to 54	55 to 64	aged 65 or older total	65 to 74	75 or older
Number of consumer units (in 000s)	120,171	8,150	20,499	23,416	25,245	19,462	23,400	12,011	11,390
Average number of persons per CU	2.5	2.0	2.8	3.2	2.7	2.1	1.7	1.8	1.5
Average before-tax income of CUs	$63,091	$31,443	$57,256	$76,540	$80,560	$71,048	$40,305	$47,708	$32,499
Average annual spending of consumer units	49,638	29,457	47,510	58,934	58,331	53,786	36,530	42,262	30,414
FOOD	6,133	4,141	6,000	7,393	7,181	6,241	4,515	5,226	3,738
Food at home	3,465	2,265	3,210	4,125	4,003	3,457	2,905	3,348	2,419
Cereals and bakery products	460	274	427	548	522	456	405	459	346
Cereals and cereal products	143	93	144	177	161	129	116	137	94
Bakery products	317	180	282	371	361	327	289	322	252
Meats, poultry, fish, and eggs	777	491	692	976	907	758	634	738	520
Beef	216	155	197	284	243	200	174	190	156
Pork	150	84	127	185	173	147	135	166	102
Other meats	104	71	89	127	125	107	83	93	72
Poultry	142	90	138	179	173	134	101	125	73
Fish and seafood	122	64	99	152	146	127	103	122	81
Eggs	43	27	41	49	47	44	39	42	36
Dairy products	387	238	368	459	442	384	332	376	284
Fresh milk and cream	154	103	157	187	172	142	126	136	115
Other dairy products	234	136	211	271	271	242	206	240	169
Fruits and vegetables	600	340	529	677	684	640	557	628	479
Fresh fruits	202	112	168	227	232	219	193	212	172
Fresh vegetables	190	103	163	220	217	207	175	205	142
Processed fruits	112	66	111	125	123	113	106	113	99
Processed vegetables	96	58	87	105	112	102	84	99	67
Other food at home	1,241	922	1,194	1,465	1,447	1,219	976	1,147	789
Sugar and other sweets	124	69	100	151	150	119	118	136	99
Fats and oils	91	53	76	101	107	95	89	97	80
Miscellaneous foods	650	528	683	781	729	599	489	569	403
Nonalcoholic beverages	333	255	305	382	411	343	247	297	192
Food prepared by consumer unit on trips	43	17	30	50	50	63	33	49	16
Food away from home	2,668	1,876	2,790	3,268	3,178	2,784	1,610	1,878	1,319
ALCOHOLIC BEVERAGES	457	461	514	469	498	533	285	346	218
HOUSING	16,920	9,598	17,329	20,952	19,195	17,223	12,396	13,547	11,173
Shelter	10,023	6,220	10,536	12,758	11,617	9,763	6,656	7,271	6,009
Owned dwellings	6,730	1,398	5,985	9,232	8,626	7,063	4,414	5,329	3,448
Mortgage interest and charges	3,890	919	4,286	6,239	5,093	3,421	1,320	2,049	550
Property taxes	1,709	325	1,076	1,950	2,178	2,127	1,651	1,767	1,529
Maintenance, repair, insurance, other expenses	1,131	154	623	1,043	1,356	1,515	1,443	1,513	1,369
Rented dwellings	2,602	4,649	4,288	2,849	2,055	1,539	1,639	1,277	2,020
Other lodging	691	173	263	677	936	1,161	604	664	540
Utilities, fuels, and public services	3,477	1,813	3,063	3,928	4,053	3,754	3,117	3,392	2,828
Natural gas	480	169	379	534	539	557	497	522	470
Electricity	1,303	706	1,148	1,479	1,499	1,403	1,175	1,289	1,055
Fuel oil and other fuels	151	28	85	132	192	171	208	185	232
Telephone services	1,110	744	1,094	1,295	1,330	1,135	806	946	659
Water and other public services	434	166	357	487	493	488	431	451	411
Household services	984	363	1,175	1,422	867	860	825	715	941
Personal services	415	174	780	844	193	159	205	83	334
Other household services	569	189	394	579	674	701	620	632	607
Housekeeping supplies	639	278	522	646	724	902	562	661	453
Laundry and cleaning supplies	140	84	129	178	161	134	115	138	90
Other household products	347	134	265	343	365	572	296	348	240
Postage and stationery	152	60	127	125	198	197	150	175	123

	total consumer units	under 25	25 to 34	35 to 44	45 to 54	55 to 64	aged 65 or older total	65 to 74	75 or older
Household furnishings and equipment	**$1,797**	**$925**	**$2,034**	**$2,198**	**$1,933**	**$1,944**	**$1,235**	**$1,508**	**$943**
Household textiles	133	65	120	169	120	170	117	145	86
Furniture	446	281	537	625	461	437	235	308	159
Floor coverings	46	4	48	50	54	48	48	58	37
Major appliances	231	122	213	251	285	266	180	205	152
Small appliances and miscellaneous housewares	101	59	103	110	115	92	98	115	79
Miscellaneous household equipment	840	394	1,013	993	898	931	558	678	429
APPAREL AND RELATED SERVICES	**1,881**	**1,477**	**2,106**	**2,335**	**2,191**	**1,888**	**1,040**	**1,323**	**732**
Men and boys	**435**	**323**	**508**	**582**	**514**	**402**	**209**	**255**	**160**
Men, aged 16 or older	351	290	396	403	428	367	187	220	152
Boys, aged 2 to 15	84	33	112	178	87	35	22	36	8
Women and girls	**749**	**535**	**729**	**855**	**952**	**793**	**487**	**636**	**325**
Women, aged 16 or older	627	510	570	604	822	723	460	590	316
Girls, aged 2 to 15	122	25	158	251	130	70	28	46	8
Children under age 2	**93**	**145**	**206**	**119**	**54**	**55**	**23**	**32**	**14**
Footwear	**327**	**237**	**383**	**399**	**383**	**351**	**160**	**209**	**106**
Other apparel products and services	**276**	**237**	**281**	**381**	**287**	**286**	**160**	**190**	**128**
TRANSPORTATION	**8,758**	**5,708**	**9,065**	**10,558**	**9,943**	**9,608**	**5,785**	**7,669**	**3,784**
Vehicle purchases	**3,244**	**2,273**	**3,930**	**4,183**	**3,223**	**3,348**	**1,977**	**2,701**	**1,213**
Cars and trucks, new	1,572	1,058	1,541	1,955	1,645	1,700	1,209	1,721	668
Cars and trucks, used	1,567	1,126	2,256	2,106	1,404	1,582	740	925	545
Other vehicles	105	89	133	122	174	66	29	56	–
Gasoline and motor oil	**2,384**	**1,760**	**2,446**	**2,870**	**2,846**	**2,504**	**1,461**	**1,862**	**1,039**
Other vehicle expenses	**2,592**	**1,365**	**2,293**	**2,966**	**3,213**	**2,993**	**1,928**	**2,536**	**1,270**
Vehicle finance charges	305	221	384	400	335	325	122	197	43
Maintenance and repairs	738	437	609	809	941	885	543	693	384
Vehicle insurance	1,071	492	802	1,173	1,382	1,214	975	1,321	597
Vehicle rentals, leases, licenses, other charges	478	216	498	584	555	569	287	325	247
Public transportation	**538**	**310**	**396**	**540**	**661**	**763**	**420**	**569**	**262**
HEALTH CARE	**2,853**	**800**	**1,740**	**2,315**	**2,792**	**3,476**	**4,631**	**4,967**	**4,275**
Health insurance	1,545	397	918	1,269	1,386	1,751	2,770	2,821	2,716
Medical services	709	267	556	651	772	883	844	1,027	651
Drugs	481	103	203	303	498	674	859	935	777
Medical supplies	118	34	64	93	135	168	159	184	132
ENTERTAINMENT	**2,698**	**1,448**	**2,462**	**3,551**	**3,163**	**2,730**	**1,966**	**2,636**	**1,255**
Fees and admissions	658	290	500	967	823	645	450	575	318
Audio and visual equipment and services	987	726	1,034	1,196	1,126	965	694	812	570
Pets, toys, and playground equipment	560	243	480	730	711	653	338	429	239
Other entertainment products and services	493	189	448	658	504	468	484	821	128
PERSONAL CARE PRODUCTS AND SERVICES	**588**	**337**	**512**	**662**	**686**	**632**	**528**	**599**	**451**
READING	**118**	**51**	**72**	**107**	**137**	**151**	**143**	**151**	**136**
EDUCATION	**945**	**1,787**	**604**	**819**	**1,687**	**929**	**292**	**245**	**341**
TOBACCO PRODUCTS AND SMOKING SUPPLIES	**323**	**290**	**331**	**379**	**388**	**353**	**176**	**243**	**106**
MISCELLANEOUS	**808**	**368**	**589**	**845**	**1,008**	**1,084**	**672**	**787**	**548**
CASH CONTRIBUTIONS	**1,821**	**549**	**1,027**	**1,569**	**1,972**	**2,746**	**2,282**	**1,923**	**2,661**
PERSONAL INSURANCE AND PENSIONS	**5,336**	**2,440**	**5,159**	**6,980**	**7,489**	**6,193**	**1,819**	**2,600**	**996**
Life and other personal insurance	309	39	164	286	402	461	329	375	279
Pensions and Social Security	5,027	2,401	4,995	6,694	7,087	5,732	1,491	2,225	716
PERSONAL TAXES	**2,233**	**641**	**1,491**	**2,489**	**3,485**	**3,083**	**1,126**	**1,374**	**864**
Federal income taxes	1,569	433	982	1,741	2,490	2,234	760	1,003	505
State and local income taxes	468	191	413	561	754	551	143	139	147
Other taxes	196	17	96	188	241	298	223	232	212
GIFTS FOR PEOPLE IN OTHER HOUSEHOLDS	**1,198**	**427**	**582**	**806**	**1,847**	**1,948**	**1,085**	**1,265**	**889**

Note: Spending by category does not add to total spending because gift spending is also included in the preceding product and service categories and personal taxes are not included in the total.

Source: Bureau of Labor Statistics, 2007 Consumer Expenditure Survey, Internet site http://www.bls.gov/cex/

Table 3. Indexed spending by age of householder, 2007

(indexed average annual spending of consumer units by product and service category and age of consumer unit reference person, 2007; index definition: an index of 100 is the average for all consumer units; an index of 132 means that spending by consumer units in that group is 32 percent above the average for all consumer units; an index of 68 indicates spending that is 32 percent below the average for all consumer units)

	total consumer units	under 25	25 to 34	35 to 44	45 to 54	55 to 64	aged 65 or older		
							total	65 to 74	75 or older
Average spending of consumer units, total	$49,638	$29,457	$47,510	$58,934	$58,331	$53,786	$36,530	$42,262	$30,414
Average spending of consumer units, index	100	59	96	119	118	108	74	85	61
FOOD	100	68	98	121	117	102	74	85	61
Food at home	100	65	93	119	116	100	84	97	70
Cereals and bakery products	100	60	93	119	113	99	88	100	75
Cereals and cereal products	100	65	101	124	113	90	81	96	66
Bakery products	100	57	89	117	114	103	91	102	79
Meats, poultry, fish, and eggs	100	63	89	126	117	98	82	95	67
Beef	100	72	91	131	113	93	81	88	72
Pork	100	56	85	123	115	98	90	111	68
Other meats	100	68	86	122	120	103	80	89	69
Poultry	100	63	97	126	122	94	71	88	51
Fish and seafood	100	52	81	125	120	104	84	100	66
Eggs	100	63	95	114	109	102	91	98	84
Dairy products	100	61	95	119	114	99	86	97	73
Fresh milk and cream	100	67	102	121	112	92	82	88	75
Other dairy products	100	58	90	116	116	103	88	103	72
Fruits and vegetables	100	57	88	113	114	107	93	105	80
Fresh fruits	100	55	83	112	115	108	96	105	85
Fresh vegetables	100	54	86	116	114	109	92	108	75
Processed fruits	100	59	99	112	110	101	95	101	88
Processed vegetables	100	60	91	109	117	106	88	103	70
Other food at home	100	74	96	118	117	98	79	92	64
Sugar and other sweets	100	56	81	122	121	96	95	110	80
Fats and oils	100	58	84	111	118	104	98	107	88
Miscellaneous foods	100	81	105	120	112	92	75	88	62
Nonalcoholic beverages	100	77	92	115	123	103	74	89	58
Food prepared by consumer unit on trips	100	40	70	116	116	147	77	114	37
Food away from home	100	70	105	122	119	104	60	70	49
ALCOHOLIC BEVERAGES	100	101	112	103	109	117	62	76	48
HOUSING	100	57	102	124	113	102	73	80	66
Shelter	100	62	105	127	116	97	66	73	60
Owned dwellings	100	21	89	137	128	105	66	79	51
Mortgage interest and charges	100	24	110	160	131	88	34	53	14
Property taxes	100	19	63	114	127	124	97	103	89
Maintenance, repair, insurance, other expenses	100	14	55	92	120	134	128	134	121
Rented dwellings	100	179	165	109	79	59	63	49	78
Other lodging	100	25	38	98	135	168	87	96	78
Utilities, fuels, and public services	100	52	88	113	117	108	90	98	81
Natural gas	100	35	79	111	112	116	104	109	98
Electricity	100	54	88	114	115	108	90	99	81
Fuel oil and other fuels	100	19	56	87	127	113	138	123	154
Telephone services	100	67	99	117	120	102	73	85	59
Water and other public services	100	38	82	112	114	112	99	104	95
Household services	100	37	119	145	88	87	84	73	96
Personal services	100	42	188	203	47	38	49	20	80
Other household services	100	33	69	102	118	123	109	111	107
Housekeeping supplies	100	44	82	101	113	141	88	103	71
Laundry and cleaning supplies	100	60	92	127	115	96	82	99	64
Other household products	100	39	76	99	105	165	85	100	69
Postage and stationery	100	39	84	82	130	130	99	115	81

	total consumer units	under 25	25 to 34	35 to 44	45 to 54	55 to 64	aged 65 or older		
							total	65 to 74	75 or older
Household furnishings and equipment	100	51	113	122	108	108	69	84	52
Household textiles	100	49	90	127	90	128	88	109	65
Furniture	100	63	120	140	103	98	53	69	36
Floor coverings	100	9	104	109	117	104	104	126	80
Major appliances	100	53	92	109	123	115	78	89	66
Small appliances and miscellaneous housewares	100	58	102	109	114	91	97	114	78
Miscellaneous household equipment	100	47	121	118	107	111	66	81	51
APPAREL AND RELATED SERVICES	100	79	112	124	116	100	55	70	39
Men and boys	100	74	117	134	118	92	48	59	37
Men, aged 16 or older	100	83	113	115	122	105	53	63	43
Boys, aged 2 to 15	100	39	133	212	104	42	26	43	10
Women and girls	100	71	97	114	127	106	65	85	43
Women, aged 16 or older	100	81	91	96	131	115	73	94	50
Girls, aged 2 to 15	100	20	130	206	107	57	23	38	7
Children under age 2	100	156	222	128	58	59	25	34	15
Footwear	100	72	117	122	117	107	49	64	32
Other apparel products and services	100	86	102	138	104	104	58	69	46
TRANSPORTATION	100	65	104	121	114	110	66	88	43
Vehicle purchases	100	70	121	129	99	103	61	83	37
Cars and trucks, new	100	67	98	124	105	108	77	109	42
Cars and trucks, used	100	72	144	134	90	101	47	59	35
Other vehicles	100	85	127	116	166	63	28	53	–
Gasoline and motor oil	100	74	103	120	119	105	61	78	44
Other vehicle expenses	100	53	88	114	124	115	74	98	49
Vehicle finance charges	100	72	126	131	110	107	40	65	14
Maintenance and repairs	100	59	83	110	128	120	74	94	52
Vehicle insurance	100	46	75	110	129	113	91	123	56
Vehicle rentals, leases, licenses, other charges	100	45	104	122	116	119	60	68	52
Public transportation	100	58	74	100	123	142	78	106	49
HEALTH CARE	100	28	61	81	98	122	162	174	150
Health insurance	100	26	59	82	90	113	179	183	176
Medical services	100	38	78	92	109	125	119	145	92
Drugs	100	21	42	63	104	140	179	194	162
Medical supplies	100	29	54	79	114	142	135	156	112
ENTERTAINMENT	100	54	91	132	117	101	73	98	47
Fees and admissions	100	44	76	147	125	98	68	87	48
Audio and visual equipment and services	100	74	105	121	114	98	70	82	58
Pets, toys, and playground equipment	100	43	86	130	127	117	60	77	43
Other entertainment products and services	100	38	91	133	102	95	98	167	26
PERSONAL CARE PRODUCTS AND SERVICES	100	57	87	113	117	107	90	102	77
READING	100	43	61	91	116	128	121	128	115
EDUCATION	100	189	64	87	179	98	31	26	36
TOBACCO PRODUCTS AND SMOKING SUPPLIES	100	90	102	117	120	109	54	75	33
MISCELLANEOUS	100	46	73	105	125	134	83	97	68
CASH CONTRIBUTIONS	100	30	56	86	108	151	125	106	146
PERSONAL INSURANCE AND PENSIONS	100	46	97	131	140	116	34	49	19
Life and other personal insurance	100	13	53	93	130	149	106	121	90
Pensions and Social Security	100	48	99	133	141	114	30	44	14
PERSONAL TAXES	100	29	67	111	156	138	50	62	39
Federal income taxes	100	28	63	111	159	142	48	64	32
State and local income taxes	100	41	88	120	161	118	31	30	31
Other taxes	100	9	49	96	123	152	114	118	108
GIFTS FOR PEOPLE IN OTHER HOUSEHOLDS	100	36	49	67	154	163	91	106	74

Note: "–" means sample is too small to make a reliable estimate.
Source: Calculations by New Strategist based on the Bureau of Labor Statistics' 2007 Consumer Expenditure Survey

Spending by Income, 2007

The average household spent $49,638 in 2007. Not surprisingly, households with incomes of $70,000 or more spend the most, 69 percent more than the average household. The highest income group spends the most on almost every product and service category, with a few exceptions such as rented dwellings and tobacco.

Households with incomes below $50,000 spend less than the average household on most categories. One of the few exceptions is rent. Households with incomes below $30,000 spend more money than they make. The income they report to government interviewers is less than their reported expenditures. These households make up the difference through borrowing, the use of savings, and unreported income.

Income makes a bigger difference in the purchasing of some products than others. Everyone has to buy food, but only those who can afford to do so will buy a new car. Households with incomes of $70,000 or more spend close to the average on items such as eggs, drugs, and tobacco. They spend over twice what the average household spends on other lodging (a category that includes hotel and motel expenses as well as housing for children in college dorms), mortgage interest, and fees and admissions to entertainment events, among other items.

Table 4. Average spending by household income, 2007

(average annual spending of consumer units (CUs) by product and service category and before-tax income of consumer unit, 2007)

	total consumer units	under $10,000	$10,000–$19,999	$20,000–$29,999	$30,000–$39,999	$40,000–$49,999	$50,000–$69,999	$70,000 or more
Number of consumer units (in 000s)	120,171	9,590	15,114	14,720	13,211	11,824	18,390	37,322
Average number of persons per CU	2.5	1.5	1.8	2.2	2.3	2.4	2.7	3.1
Average before-tax income of CUs	$63,091	$4,095	$14,993	$24,893	$34,751	$44,555	$59,527	$130,455
Average annual spending of consumer units	49,638	17,964	22,360	29,704	34,739	41,083	50,428	84,072
FOOD	**6,133**	**2,708**	**3,201**	**4,071**	**4,645**	**5,689**	**6,371**	**9,464**
Food at home	**3,465**	**1,765**	**2,128**	**2,648**	**2,913**	**3,368**	**3,630**	**4,853**
Cereals and bakery products	460	234	289	347	384	440	495	638
Cereals and cereal products	143	80	95	119	121	137	149	192
Bakery products	317	154	194	229	263	303	346	446
Meats, poultry, fish, and eggs	777	409	502	647	664	777	822	1,038
Beef	216	101	147	177	189	217	233	287
Pork	150	83	99	138	131	156	171	183
Other meats	104	58	68	79	93	98	113	141
Poultry	142	77	87	118	126	136	138	197
Fish and seafood	122	62	67	96	85	127	124	178
Eggs	43	28	34	39	41	42	43	52
Dairy products	387	185	237	288	326	370	412	548
Fresh milk and cream	154	85	104	124	140	151	159	204
Other dairy products	234	100	133	164	186	219	253	344
Fruits and vegetables	600	316	362	454	504	580	615	850
Fresh fruits	202	103	121	146	155	204	198	296
Fresh vegetables	190	101	115	144	156	180	198	270
Processed fruits	112	59	67	90	99	103	117	157
Processed vegetables	96	53	58	74	94	93	102	127
Other food at home	1,241	621	737	911	1,035	1,200	1,286	1,779
Sugar and other sweets	124	60	75	90	101	119	133	178
Fats and oils	91	48	63	77	83	93	96	119
Miscellaneous foods	650	310	379	473	534	631	674	939
Nonalcoholic beverages	333	192	208	256	290	329	339	459
Food prepared by consumer unit on trips	43	11	14	15	28	29	43	84
Food away from home	**2,668**	**942**	**1,073**	**1,423**	**1,731**	**2,321**	**2,741**	**4,611**
ALCOHOLIC BEVERAGES	**457**	**149**	**174**	**257**	**305**	**423**	**489**	**768**
HOUSING	**16,920**	**7,346**	**8,925**	**10,994**	**12,389**	**13,997**	**17,014**	**27,408**
Shelter	**10,023**	**4,424**	**5,296**	**6,456**	**7,365**	**8,180**	**9,908**	**16,363**
Owned dwellings	6,730	1,383	1,964	3,016	3,701	4,655	6,698	13,245
Mortgage interest and charges	3,890	623	716	1,273	1,935	2,555	4,004	8,106
Property taxes	1,709	510	672	891	1,058	1,209	1,547	3,228
Maintenance, repair, insurance, other expenses	1,131	250	576	852	708	891	1,147	1,911
Rented dwellings	2,602	2,933	3,221	3,286	3,389	3,195	2,659	1,501
Other lodging	691	107	111	154	275	331	551	1,617
Utilities, fuels, and public services	**3,477**	**1,750**	**2,326**	**2,748**	**3,072**	**3,282**	**3,697**	**4,772**
Natural gas	480	215	317	352	405	427	481	709
Electricity	1,303	725	937	1,079	1,193	1,256	1,363	1,712
Fuel oil and other fuels	151	58	100	125	130	122	159	217
Telephone services	1,110	551	705	868	984	1,071	1,231	1,510
Water and other public services	434	201	268	324	361	407	464	623
Household services	**984**	**218**	**390**	**437**	**496**	**640**	**890**	**1,966**
Personal services	415	53	124	130	181	227	400	890
Other household services	569	166	266	306	314	414	490	1,076
Housekeeping supplies	**639**	**252**	**301**	**427**	**482**	**544**	**632**	**1,035**
Laundry and cleaning supplies	140	62	93	111	128	150	150	184
Other household products	347	119	138	209	205	292	342	606
Postage and stationery	152	71	69	107	149	102	140	245

	total consumer units	under $10,000	$10,000– $19,999	$20,000– $29,999	$30,000– $39,999	$40,000– $49,999	$50,000– $69,999	$70,000 or more
Household furnishings and equipment	$1,797	$703	$613	$926	$974	$1,350	$1,887	$3,272
Household textiles	133	31	55	76	83	108	146	231
Furniture	446	142	147	194	202	294	424	889
Floor coverings	46	15	14	14	43	20	37	95
Major appliances	231	103	97	147	138	140	222	418
Small appliances and miscellaneous housewares	101	36	49	55	77	93	104	164
Miscellaneous household equipment	840	378	249	440	430	695	954	1,475
APPAREL AND RELATED SERVICES	1,881	807	755	1,016	1,274	1,517	1,856	3,275
Men and boys	435	199	156	244	263	323	435	777
Men, aged 16 or older	351	167	114	199	193	252	349	638
Boys, aged 2 to 15	84	32	42	45	70	71	86	139
Women and girls	749	268	310	386	514	585	781	1,301
Women, aged 16 or older	627	235	269	317	415	494	670	1,083
Girls, aged 2 to 15	122	33	41	69	99	91	111	218
Children under age 2	93	81	40	62	80	84	90	140
Footwear	327	155	147	194	277	297	317	525
Other apparel products and services	276	106	101	131	140	228	232	532
TRANSPORTATION	8,758	2,632	3,764	5,434	6,503	7,346	9,828	14,362
Vehicle purchases	3,244	678	1,404	1,887	2,233	2,149	3,840	5,595
Cars and trucks, new	1,572	213	632	619	788	901	1,508	3,199
Cars and trucks, used	1,567	450	741	1,220	1,359	1,226	2,216	2,187
Other vehicles	105	–	31	48	86	22	117	209
Gasoline and motor oil	2,384	907	1,152	1,695	1,999	2,335	2,788	3,486
Other vehicle expenses	2,592	916	1,008	1,644	1,971	2,514	2,788	4,167
Vehicle finance charges	305	53	84	139	217	267	400	522
Maintenance and repairs	738	231	304	464	564	688	769	1,212
Vehicle insurance	1,071	498	482	840	936	1,213	1,179	1,480
Vehicle rentals, leases, licenses, other charges	478	134	137	200	255	346	439	953
Public transportation	538	133	202	208	300	348	412	1,115
HEALTH CARE	2,853	1,003	1,825	2,481	2,493	2,800	3,066	3,928
Health insurance	1,545	574	1,126	1,418	1,439	1,502	1,643	2,017
Medical services	709	160	289	532	514	664	809	1,125
Drugs	481	206	370	451	445	515	488	604
Medical supplies	118	62	40	81	95	119	126	182
ENTERTAINMENT	2,698	862	996	1,375	1,766	2,029	2,660	4,927
Fees and admissions	658	124	124	177	321	378	539	1,466
Audio and visual equipment and services	987	462	533	688	764	886	1,062	1,497
Pets, toys, and playground equipment	560	138	191	300	412	427	584	995
Other entertainment products and services	493	138	148	211	269	338	475	969
PERSONAL CARE PRODUCTS AND SERVICES	588	202	270	350	414	505	573	998
READING	118	42	64	71	70	96	110	205
EDUCATION	945	1,017	344	382	285	501	632	1,921
TOBACCO PRODUCTS AND SMOKING SUPPLIES	323	253	267	319	380	361	405	293
MISCELLANEOUS	808	209	415	410	685	648	836	1,354
CASH CONTRIBUTIONS	1,821	368	684	794	1,052	1,737	1,468	3,534
PERSONAL INSURANCE AND PENSIONS	5,336	367	676	1,749	2,478	3,435	5,120	11,635
Life and other personal insurance	309	61	118	216	166	184	254	606
Pensions and Social Security	5,027	306	558	1,534	2,312	3,251	4,866	11,030
PERSONAL TAXES	2,233	78	–53	184	427	927	1,691	5,842
Federal income taxes	1,569	40	–130	17	188	500	1,093	4,325
State and local income taxes	468	–1	19	81	121	257	397	1,148
Other taxes	196	39	59	87	117	170	201	369
GIFTS FOR PEOPLE IN OTHER HOUSEHOLDS	1,198	422	302	466	634	676	1,132	2,443

Note: Spending by category does not add to total spending because gift spending is also included in the preceding product and service categories and personal taxes are not included in the total. "–" means sample is too small to make a reliable estimate.
Source: Bureau of Labor Statistics, 2007 Consumer Expenditure Survey, Internet site http://www.bls.gov/cex/; calculations by New Strategist

Table 5. Indexed spending by household income, 2007

(indexed average annual spending of consumer units by product and service category and before-tax income of consumer unit reference person, 2007; index definition: an index of 100 is the average for all consumer units; an index of 132 means that spending by consumer units in that group is 32 percent above the average for all consumer units; an index of 68 indicates spending that is 32 percent below the average for all consumer units)

	total consumer units	under $10,000	$10,000–$19,999	$20,000–$29,999	$30,000–$39,999	$40,000–$49,999	$50,000–$69,999	$70,000 or more
Average spending of consumer units, total	$49,638	17,964	22,360	$29,704	$34,739	$41,083	$50,428	$84,072
Average spending of consumer units, index	100	36	45	60	70	83	102	169
FOOD	100	44	52	66	76	93	104	154
Food at home	100	51	61	76	84	97	105	140
Cereals and bakery products	100	51	63	75	83	96	108	139
Cereals and cereal products	100	56	66	83	85	96	104	134
Bakery products	100	49	61	72	83	96	109	141
Meats, poultry, fish, and eggs	100	53	65	83	85	100	106	134
Beef	100	47	68	82	88	100	108	133
Pork	100	55	66	92	87	104	114	122
Other meats	100	56	65	76	89	94	109	136
Poultry	100	54	61	83	89	96	97	139
Fish and seafood	100	51	55	79	70	104	102	146
Eggs	100	66	79	91	95	98	100	121
Dairy products	100	48	61	74	84	96	106	142
Fresh milk and cream	100	55	68	81	91	98	103	132
Other dairy products	100	43	57	70	79	94	108	147
Fruits and vegetables	100	53	60	76	84	97	103	142
Fresh fruits	100	51	60	72	77	101	98	147
Fresh vegetables	100	53	61	76	82	95	104	142
Processed fruits	100	53	60	80	88	92	104	140
Processed vegetables	100	55	61	77	98	97	106	132
Other food at home	100	50	59	73	83	97	104	143
Sugar and other sweets	100	48	60	73	81	96	107	144
Fats and oils	100	53	69	85	91	102	105	131
Miscellaneous foods	100	48	58	73	82	97	104	144
Nonalcoholic beverages	100	58	62	77	87	99	102	138
Food prepared by consumer unit on trips	100	25	31	35	65	67	100	195
Food away from home	100	35	40	53	65	87	103	173
ALCOHOLIC BEVERAGES	100	33	38	56	67	93	107	168
HOUSING	100	43	53	65	73	83	101	162
Shelter	100	44	53	64	73	82	99	163
Owned dwellings	100	21	29	45	55	69	100	197
Mortgage interest and charges	100	16	18	33	50	66	103	208
Property taxes	100	30	39	52	62	71	91	189
Maintenance, repair, insurance, other expenses	100	22	51	75	63	79	101	169
Rented dwellings	100	113	124	126	130	123	102	58
Other lodging	100	15	16	22	40	48	80	234
Utilities, fuels, and public services	100	50	67	79	88	94	106	137
Natural gas	100	45	66	73	84	89	100	148
Electricity	100	56	72	83	92	96	105	131
Fuel oil and other fuels	100	38	66	83	86	81	105	144
Telephone services	100	50	64	78	89	96	111	136
Water and other public services	100	46	62	75	83	94	107	144
Household services	100	22	40	44	50	65	90	200
Personal services	100	13	30	31	44	55	96	214
Other household services	100	29	47	54	55	73	86	189
Housekeeping supplies	100	40	47	67	75	85	99	162
Laundry and cleaning supplies	100	44	67	79	91	107	107	131
Other household products	100	34	40	60	59	84	99	175
Postage and stationery	100	47	45	70	98	67	92	161

	total consumer units	under $10,000	$10,000–$19,999	$20,000–$29,999	$30,000–$39,999	$40,000–$49,999	$50,000–$69,999	$70,000 or more
Household furnishings and equipment	100	39	34	52	54	75	105	182
Household textiles	100	23	41	57	62	81	110	174
Furniture	100	32	33	43	45	66	95	199
Floor coverings	100	32	30	30	93	43	80	207
Major appliances	100	45	42	64	60	61	96	181
Small appliances and miscellaneous housewares	100	35	49	54	76	92	103	162
Miscellaneous household equipment	100	45	30	52	51	83	114	176
APPAREL AND RELATED SERVICES	100	43	40	54	68	81	99	174
Men and boys	100	46	36	56	60	74	100	179
Men, aged 16 or older	100	48	33	57	55	72	99	182
Boys, aged 2 to 15	100	38	50	54	83	85	102	165
Women and girls	100	36	41	52	69	78	104	174
Women, aged 16 or older	100	37	43	51	66	79	107	173
Girls, aged 2 to 15	100	27	34	57	81	75	91	179
Children under age 2	100	87	43	67	86	90	97	151
Footwear	100	47	45	59	85	91	97	161
Other apparel products and services	100	38	37	47	51	83	84	193
TRANSPORTATION	100	30	43	62	74	84	112	164
Vehicle purchases	100	21	43	58	69	66	118	172
Cars and trucks, new	100	14	40	39	50	57	96	203
Cars and trucks, used	100	29	47	78	87	78	141	140
Other vehicles	100	–	29	46	82	21	111	199
Gasoline and motor oil	100	38	48	71	84	98	117	146
Other vehicle expenses	100	35	39	63	76	97	108	161
Vehicle finance charges	100	17	28	46	71	88	131	171
Maintenance and repairs	100	31	41	63	76	93	104	164
Vehicle insurance	100	46	45	78	87	113	110	138
Vehicle rentals, leases, licenses, other charges	100	28	29	42	53	72	92	199
Public transportation	100	25	37	39	56	65	77	207
HEALTH CARE	100	35	64	87	87	98	107	138
Health insurance	100	37	73	92	93	97	106	131
Medical services	100	23	41	75	72	94	114	159
Drugs	100	43	77	94	93	107	101	126
Medical supplies	100	53	34	69	81	101	107	154
ENTERTAINMENT	100	32	37	51	65	75	99	183
Fees and admissions	100	19	19	27	49	57	82	223
Audio and visual equipment and services	100	47	54	70	77	90	108	152
Pets, toys, and playground equipment	100	25	34	54	74	76	104	178
Other entertainment products and services	100	28	30	43	55	69	96	197
PERSONAL CARE PRODUCTS AND SERVICES	100	34	46	60	70	86	97	170
READING	100	36	54	60	59	81	93	174
EDUCATION	100	108	36	40	30	53	67	203
TOBACCO PRODUCTS AND SMOKING SUPPLIES	100	78	83	99	118	112	125	91
MISCELLANEOUS	100	26	51	51	85	80	103	168
CASH CONTRIBUTIONS	100	20	38	44	58	95	81	194
PERSONAL INSURANCE AND PENSIONS	100	7	13	33	46	64	96	218
Life and other personal insurance	100	20	38	70	54	60	82	196
Pensions and Social Security	100	6	11	31	46	65	97	219
PERSONAL TAXES	100	3	–	8	19	42	76	262
Federal income taxes	100	3	–	1	12	32	70	276
State and local income taxes	100	0	4	17	26	55	85	245
Other taxes	100	20	30	44	60	87	103	188
GIFTS FOR PEOPLE IN OTHER HOUSEHOLDS	100	35	25	39	53	56	94	204

Note: "–" means sample is too small to make a reliable estimate or not applicable.
Source: Calculations by New Strategist based on the Bureau of Labor Statistics' 2007 Consumer Expenditure Survey

Spending by High-Income Consumer Units, 2007

The higher the income, the greater the spending. Households with incomes of $100,000 or more spent an average of $101,041 in 2007, more than double the $49,638 spending of the average household. The Consumer Expenditure Survey examines the spending of households with incomes up to $150,000 or more. The highest-income households spent over $126,000 in 2007. Spending surges as income rises, in part because affluent households have more earners—and consequently more expenses—than the average household.

On some products and services, the most affluent households spend four or even five times as much as the average household. On other lodging (motels, hotels, vacation homes, college dorms), households with incomes of $150,000 or more spend more than five times as much as the average household. They spend three-and-one-half times the average household on personal services (mostly day care) and more than four times the average on fees and admissions to entertainment events and education. The most-affluent households spend less than average on only two items: rent and tobacco.

Table 6. Average spending by high-income consumer units, 2007

(average annual spending of consumer units (CUs) by product and service category and before-tax income of consumer unit, 2007)

	total consumer units	less than $70,000	$70,000–$79,999	$80,000–$99,999	$100,000 or more total	$100,000–$119,999	$120,000–$149,999	$150,000 or more
Number of consumer units (in 000s)	120,171	82,849	6,957	9,777	20,588	6,651	5,708	8,229
Average number of persons per CU	2.5	2.2	2.9	3.0	3.2	3.1	3.2	3.2
Average before-tax income of CUs	$63,091	$32,745	$74,679	$88,830	$169,072	$108,502	$132,523	$243,376
Average annual spending of consumer units	49,638	34,109	58,005	67,640	101,041	77,838	91,864	126,443
FOOD	**6,133**	**4,625**	**7,541**	**8,128**	**10,890**	**8,856**	**10,567**	**12,849**
Food at home	**3,465**	**2,836**	**4,080**	**4,335**	**5,428**	**4,550**	**5,433**	**6,178**
Cereals and bakery products	460	379	536	598	699	571	733	784
Cereals and cereal products	143	120	167	179	208	176	223	226
Bakery products	317	258	369	419	490	395	510	558
Meats, poultry, fish, and eggs	777	658	874	922	1,165	1,007	1,168	1,300
Beef	216	184	258	281	300	253	300	339
Pork	150	134	168	166	199	197	188	209
Other meats	104	88	121	120	162	139	152	188
Poultry	142	117	145	170	232	220	243	234
Fish and seafood	122	97	133	139	216	147	227	268
Eggs	43	39	49	46	56	50	56	61
Dairy products	387	315	469	496	606	513	628	671
Fresh milk and cream	154	131	185	194	217	194	229	227
Other dairy products	234	184	284	302	390	319	399	444
Fruits and vegetables	600	487	682	710	990	791	985	1,166
Fresh fruits	202	159	234	232	355	279	326	443
Fresh vegetables	190	154	207	227	318	243	338	367
Processed fruits	112	92	131	138	177	138	174	213
Processed vegetables	96	81	110	113	140	132	147	142
Other food at home	1,241	998	1,520	1,609	1,967	1,669	1,920	2,257
Sugar and other sweets	124	100	142	167	197	161	206	222
Fats and oils	91	79	95	107	134	119	138	143
Miscellaneous foods	650	518	815	867	1,026	871	1,012	1,170
Nonalcoholic beverages	333	276	411	411	505	442	478	578
Food prepared by consumer unit on trips	43	25	58	57	106	75	87	144
Food away from home	**2,668**	**1,789**	**3,461**	**3,793**	**5,462**	**4,307**	**5,134**	**6,671**
ALCOHOLIC BEVERAGES	**457**	**316**	**463**	**586**	**979**	**628**	**871**	**1,357**
HOUSING	**16,920**	**12,193**	**19,178**	**21,703**	**32,965**	**24,952**	**30,391**	**41,294**
Shelter	**10,023**	**7,166**	**11,396**	**12,850**	**19,710**	**15,064**	**18,543**	**24,274**
Owned dwellings	6,730	3,795	8,793	10,313	16,141	12,230	15,542	19,718
Mortgage interest and charges	3,890	1,991	5,375	6,557	9,765	7,770	9,554	11,523
Property taxes	1,709	1,025	2,052	2,327	4,053	2,891	3,632	5,285
Maintenance, repair, insurance, other expenses	1,131	780	1,367	1,430	2,323	1,570	2,357	2,910
Rented dwellings	2,602	3,098	1,971	1,771	1,214	1,413	1,342	965
Other lodging	691	273	631	765	2,354	1,420	1,658	3,592
Utilities, fuels, and public services	**3,477**	**2,894**	**4,129**	**4,256**	**5,234**	**4,657**	**5,077**	**5,809**
Natural gas	480	377	590	610	796	668	772	917
Electricity	1,303	1,118	1,468	1,523	1,885	1,643	1,846	2,107
Fuel oil and other fuels	151	121	176	157	260	231	224	309
Telephone services	1,110	929	1,374	1,406	1,605	1,494	1,579	1,712
Water and other public services	434	348	521	559	688	621	654	765
Household services	**984**	**542**	**1,120**	**1,440**	**2,501**	**1,527**	**2,143**	**3,537**
Personal services	415	202	525	704	1,101	714	1,088	1,423
Other household services	569	340	596	736	1,400	813	1,055	2,115
Housekeeping supplies	**639**	**459**	**747**	**836**	**1,254**	**875**	**1,094**	**1,700**
Laundry and cleaning supplies	140	120	152	167	205	196	209	210
Other household products	347	229	403	441	775	451	638	1,154
Postage and stationery	152	110	193	228	275	227	247	336

	total consumer units	less than $70,000	$70,000– $79,999	$80,000– $99,999	$100,000 or more total	$100,000– $119,999	$120,000– $149,999	$150,000 or more
Household furnishings and equipment	**$1,797**	**$1,131**	**$1,785**	**$2,321**	**$4,266**	**$2,830**	**$3,535**	**$5,973**
Household textiles	133	89	132	216	272	181	264	354
Furniture	446	246	401	500	1,242	746	931	1,859
Floor coverings	46	25	42	44	137	43	79	252
Major appliances	231	147	284	324	508	404	433	645
Small appliances and miscellaneous housewares	101	72	148	141	182	155	221	176
Miscellaneous household equipment	840	552	778	1,096	1,924	1,301	1,606	2,686
APPAREL AND RELATED SERVICES	**1,881**	**1,250**	**2,189**	**2,470**	**4,096**	**2,819**	**3,373**	**5,698**
Men and boys	**435**	**281**	**497**	**580**	**985**	**747**	**736**	**1,368**
Men, aged 16 or older	351	221	394	455	826	614	577	1,188
Boys, aged 2 to 15	84	60	103	124	159	133	159	180
Women and girls	**749**	**499**	**946**	**992**	**1,601**	**1,059**	**1,462**	**2,167**
Women, aged 16 or older	627	421	804	785	1,352	897	1,191	1,859
Girls, aged 2 to 15	122	78	142	208	250	163	271	308
Children under age 2	**93**	**72**	**154**	**141**	**135**	**126**	**103**	**167**
Footwear	**327**	**238**	**349**	**413**	**653**	**480**	**551**	**877**
Other apparel products and services	**276**	**160**	**243**	**344**	**722**	**406**	**521**	**1,119**
TRANSPORTATION	**8,758**	**6,232**	**10,886**	**13,039**	**16,163**	**13,892**	**16,050**	**18,074**
Vehicle purchases	**3,244**	**2,185**	**4,046**	**5,386**	**6,217**	**5,626**	**6,198**	**6,708**
Cars and trucks, new	1,572	839	1,856	3,138	3,681	3,042	3,465	4,347
Cars and trucks, used	1,567	1,288	1,907	2,051	2,346	2,378	2,549	2,178
Other vehicles	105	58	283	197	190	206	183	182
Gasoline and motor oil	**2,384**	**1,887**	**3,041**	**3,243**	**3,751**	**3,600**	**3,772**	**3,859**
Other vehicle expenses	**2,592**	**1,882**	**3,329**	**3,705**	**4,666**	**3,837**	**4,857**	**5,201**
Vehicle finance charges	305	208	457	503	553	524	534	588
Maintenance and repairs	738	524	1,040	1,061	1,337	1,275	1,233	1,460
Vehicle insurance	1,071	886	1,234	1,515	1,548	1,201	2,053	1,473
Vehicle rentals, leases, licenses, other charges	478	264	598	626	1,229	837	1,037	1,680
Public transportation	**538**	**278**	**470**	**704**	**1,528**	**829**	**1,223**	**2,307**
HEALTH CARE	**2,853**	**2,368**	**3,136**	**3,619**	**4,348**	**3,794**	**4,297**	**4,836**
Health insurance	1,545	1,332	1,720	1,971	2,139	1,872	2,183	2,324
Medical services	709	522	773	930	1,337	1,168	1,287	1,509
Drugs	481	425	500	558	667	563	636	776
Medical supplies	118	89	144	161	205	191	191	226
ENTERTAINMENT	**2,698**	**1,692**	**2,913**	**3,722**	**6,225**	**5,382**	**5,220**	**7,632**
Fees and admissions	658	294	654	956	1,994	1,244	1,625	2,870
Audio and visual equipment and services	987	757	1,043	1,345	1,721	1,382	1,650	2,049
Pets, toys, and playground equipment	560	363	763	847	1,157	1,174	1,079	1,196
Other entertainment products and services	493	278	453	575	1,353	1,582	867	1,518
PERSONAL CARE PRODUCTS AND SERVICES	**588**	**402**	**701**	**860**	**1,172**	**888**	**1,239**	**1,358**
READING	**118**	**78**	**141**	**168**	**244**	**195**	**226**	**296**
EDUCATION	**945**	**506**	**841**	**997**	**2,725**	**1,580**	**2,227**	**3,996**
TOBACCO PRODUCTS AND SMOKING SUPPLIES	**323**	**336**	**356**	**350**	**245**	**280**	**275**	**196**
MISCELLANEOUS	**808**	**561**	**958**	**1,110**	**1,601**	**1,217**	**1,179**	**2,206**
CASH CONTRIBUTIONS	**1,821**	**1,050**	**2,047**	**2,481**	**4,537**	**2,640**	**3,106**	**7,064**
PERSONAL INSURANCE AND PENSIONS	**5,336**	**2,499**	**6,655**	**8,406**	**14,852**	**10,715**	**12,843**	**19,588**
Life and other personal insurance	309	176	333	482	756	542	676	984
Pensions and Social Security	5,027	2,322	6,321	7,924	14,096	10,173	12,168	18,604
PERSONAL TAXES	**2,233**	**608**	**2,550**	**3,192**	**8,213**	**5,005**	**5,731**	**12,527**
Federal income taxes	1,569	328	1,665	2,294	6,189	3,587	4,179	9,685
State and local income taxes	468	162	648	667	1,545	1,060	1,192	2,182
Other taxes	196	118	237	231	480	358	360	661
GIFTS FOR PEOPLE IN OTHER HOUSEHOLDS	**1,198**	**636**	**1,500**	**1,498**	**3,226**	**1,929**	**2,587**	**4,743**

Note: Spending by category does not add to total spending because gift spending is also included in the preceding product and service categories and personal taxes are not included in the total.

Source: Bureau of Labor Statistics, 2007 Consumer Expenditure Survey, Internet site http://www.bls.gov/cex/

Table 7. Indexed spending by high-income consumer units, 2007

(indexed average annual spending of consumer units by product and service category and before-tax income of consumer unit reference person, 2007; index definition: an index of 100 is the average for all consumer units; an index of 132 means that spending by consumer units in that group is 32 percent above the average for all consumer units; an index of 68 indicates spending that is 32 percent below the average for all consumer units)

	total consumer units	less than $70,000	$70,000–$79,999	$80,000–$99,999	$100,000 or more total	$100,000–$119,999	$120,000–$149,999	$150,000 or more
Average spending of consumer units, total	$49,638	$34,109	$58,005	$67,640	$101,041	$77,838	$91,864	$126,443
Average spending of consumer units, index	100	69	117	136	204	157	185	255
FOOD	100	75	123	133	178	144	172	210
Food at home	100	82	118	125	157	131	157	178
Cereals and bakery products	100	82	117	130	152	124	159	170
Cereals and cereal products	100	84	117	125	145	123	156	158
Bakery products	100	81	116	132	155	125	161	176
Meats, poultry, fish, and eggs	100	85	112	119	150	130	150	167
Beef	100	85	119	130	139	117	139	157
Pork	100	89	112	111	133	131	125	139
Other meats	100	85	116	115	156	134	146	181
Poultry	100	82	102	120	163	155	171	165
Fish and seafood	100	80	109	114	177	120	186	220
Eggs	100	91	114	107	130	116	130	142
Dairy products	100	81	121	128	157	133	162	173
Fresh milk and cream	100	85	120	126	141	126	149	147
Other dairy products	100	79	121	129	167	136	171	190
Fruits and vegetables	100	81	114	118	165	132	164	194
Fresh fruits	100	79	116	115	176	138	161	219
Fresh vegetables	100	81	109	119	167	128	178	193
Processed fruits	100	82	117	123	158	123	155	190
Processed vegetables	100	84	115	118	146	138	153	148
Other food at home	100	80	122	130	159	134	155	182
Sugar and other sweets	100	81	115	135	159	130	166	179
Fats and oils	100	87	104	118	147	131	152	157
Miscellaneous foods	100	80	125	133	158	134	156	180
Nonalcoholic beverages	100	83	123	123	152	133	144	174
Food prepared by consumer unit on trips	100	58	135	133	247	174	202	335
Food away from home	100	67	130	142	205	161	192	250
ALCOHOLIC BEVERAGES	100	69	101	128	214	137	191	297
HOUSING	100	72	113	128	195	147	180	244
Shelter	100	71	114	128	197	150	185	242
Owned dwellings	100	56	131	153	240	182	231	293
Mortgage interest and charges	100	51	138	169	251	200	246	296
Property taxes	100	60	120	136	237	169	213	309
Maintenance, repair, insurance, other expenses	100	69	121	126	205	139	208	257
Rented dwellings	100	119	76	68	47	54	52	37
Other lodging	100	40	91	111	341	205	240	520
Utilities, fuels, and public services	100	83	119	122	151	134	146	167
Natural gas	100	79	123	127	166	139	161	191
Electricity	100	86	113	117	145	126	142	162
Fuel oil and other fuels	100	80	117	104	172	153	148	205
Telephone services	100	84	124	127	145	135	142	154
Water and other public services	100	80	120	129	159	143	151	176
Household services	100	55	114	146	254	155	218	359
Personal services	100	49	127	170	265	172	262	343
Other household services	100	60	105	129	246	143	185	372
Housekeeping supplies	100	72	117	131	196	137	171	266
Laundry and cleaning supplies	100	86	109	119	146	140	149	150
Other household products	100	66	116	127	223	130	184	333
Postage and stationery	100	72	127	150	181	149	163	221

	total consumer units	less than $70,000	$70,000–$79,999	$80,000–$99,999	$100,000 or more total	$100,000–$119,999	$120,000–$149,999	$150,000 or more
Household furnishings and equipment	100	63	99	129	237	157	197	332
Household textiles	100	67	99	162	205	136	198	266
Furniture	100	55	90	112	278	167	209	417
Floor coverings	100	54	91	96	298	93	172	548
Major appliances	100	64	123	140	220	175	187	279
Small appliances and miscellaneous housewares	100	71	147	140	180	153	219	174
Miscellaneous household equipment	100	66	93	130	229	155	191	320
APPAREL AND RELATED SERVICES	100	66	116	131	218	150	179	303
Men and boys	100	65	114	133	226	172	169	314
Men, aged 16 or older	100	63	112	130	235	175	164	338
Boys, aged 2 to 15	100	71	123	148	189	158	189	214
Women and girls	100	67	126	132	214	141	195	289
Women, aged 16 or older	100	67	128	125	216	143	190	296
Girls, aged 2 to 15	100	64	116	170	205	134	222	252
Children under age 2	100	77	166	152	145	135	111	180
Footwear	100	73	107	126	200	147	169	268
Other apparel products and services	100	58	88	125	262	147	189	405
TRANSPORTATION	100	71	124	149	185	159	183	206
Vehicle purchases	100	67	125	166	192	173	191	207
Cars and trucks, new	100	53	118	200	234	194	220	277
Cars and trucks, used	100	82	122	131	150	152	163	139
Other vehicles	100	55	270	188	181	196	174	173
Gasoline and motor oil	100	79	128	136	157	151	158	162
Other vehicle expenses	100	73	128	143	180	148	187	201
Vehicle finance charges	100	68	150	165	181	172	175	193
Maintenance and repairs	100	71	141	144	181	173	167	198
Vehicle insurance	100	83	115	141	145	112	192	138
Vehicle rentals, leases, licenses, other charges	100	55	125	131	257	175	217	351
Public transportation	100	52	87	131	284	154	227	429
HEALTH CARE	100	83	110	127	152	133	151	170
Health insurance	100	86	111	128	138	121	141	150
Medical services	100	74	109	131	189	165	182	213
Drugs	100	88	104	116	139	117	132	161
Medical supplies	100	75	122	136	174	162	162	192
ENTERTAINMENT	100	63	108	138	231	199	193	283
Fees and admissions	100	45	99	145	303	189	247	436
Audio and visual equipment and services	100	77	106	136	174	140	167	208
Pets, toys, and playground equipment	100	65	136	151	207	210	193	214
Other entertainment products and services	100	56	92	117	274	321	176	308
PERSONAL CARE PRODUCTS AND SERVICES	100	68	119	146	199	151	211	231
READING	100	66	119	142	207	165	192	251
EDUCATION	100	54	89	106	288	167	236	423
TOBACCO PRODUCTS AND SMOKING SUPPLIES	100	104	110	108	76	87	85	61
MISCELLANEOUS	100	69	119	137	198	151	146	273
CASH CONTRIBUTIONS	100	58	112	136	249	145	171	388
PERSONAL INSURANCE AND PENSIONS	100	47	125	158	278	201	241	367
Life and other personal insurance	100	57	108	156	245	175	219	318
Pensions and Social Security	100	46	126	158	280	202	242	370
PERSONAL TAXES	100	27	114	143	368	224	257	561
Federal income taxes	100	21	106	146	394	229	266	617
State and local income taxes	100	35	138	143	330	226	255	466
Other taxes	100	60	121	118	245	183	184	337
GIFTS FOR PEOPLE IN OTHER HOUSEHOLDS	100	53	125	125	269	161	216	396

Source: Calculations by New Strategist based on the Bureau of Labor Statistics' 2007 Consumer Expenditure Survey

Spending by Age and Income, 2006–07

Within age groups, spending on most categories of products and services rises with income. There are some interesting exceptions, however. Among householders under age 25, those with incomes below $10,000 spend the most on education—$2,512 on average in 2006–07. These young adults are attending college. Their incomes should rise when their schooling is complete and they embark on a career.

Only 13 percent of householders aged 65 or older have incomes of $70,000 or more. The proportion is a much larger 41 percent among householders aged 35 to 44 and peaks at 43 percent among those aged 45 to 54. Thirty-four percent of householders aged 55 to 64 have incomes of $70,000 or more.

Householders aged 45 to 54 with incomes of $70,000-plus spent the most in 2006–07, fully $87,610 on average. Close behind are affluent householders aged 35 to 44, who spent an average of $87,296 in 2006–07. Householders aged 45 to 54 with incomes of $70,000 or more spent 94 percent as much eating out as they did on groceries in 2006–07. For the average household, the ratio is 78 percent. Affluent householders aged 45 to 54 spent $4,960 on entertainment in 2006–07 compared with $2,637 spent by the average household on entertainment during the time period. Affluent householders aged 65 or older spend two-and-one-half times the average for their age group on alcoholic beverages.

Table 8. Under age 25: Average spending by income, 2006–07

(average annual spending of consumer units headed by people under age 25 by product and service category and before-tax income of consumer unit, 2006–07)

	total consumer units under age 25	under $10,000	$10,000– $19,999	$20,000– $29,999	$30,000– $39,999	$40,000 or more
Number of consumer units (in 000s)	8,158	2,504	1,490	1,140	898	2,125
Average number of persons per consumer unit	2.0	1.3	1.7	2.1	2.3	2.8
Average before-tax income of consumer units	$30,249	$4,820	$14,770	$24,454	$34,237	$72,498
Average annual spending of consumer units	28,881	14,390	19,893	27,068	35,292	49,543
FOOD	**4,033**	**2,185**	**2,959**	**4,023**	**4,714**	**6,189**
Food at home	**2,111**	**1,002**	**1,694**	**2,247**	**2,574**	**3,117**
Cereals and bakery products	257	128	212	257	295	390
Cereals and cereal products	94	52	77	99	101	137
Bakery products	164	76	134	158	194	254
Meats, poultry, fish, and eggs	464	207	322	571	575	681
Beef	143	66	106	185	157	207
Pork	87	38	56	104	112	129
Other meats	66	26	45	72	128	83
Poultry	85	40	59	108	83	131
Fish and seafood	59	24	35	74	61	97
Eggs	25	14	20	27	34	34
Dairy products	229	109	197	230	298	329
Fresh milk and cream	98	48	86	102	130	134
Other dairy products	131	60	111	129	168	194
Fruits and vegetables	330	130	295	355	380	497
Fresh fruits	106	34	108	113	115	160
Fresh vegetables	101	36	87	117	112	155
Processed fruits	67	34	54	70	95	93
Processed vegetables	55	26	47	55	58	88
Other food at home	831	428	669	835	1,026	1,221
Sugar and other sweets	69	40	69	79	74	88
Fats and oils	50	26	39	51	65	72
Miscellaneous foods	467	253	384	471	522	693
Nonalcoholic beverages	229	94	163	224	349	344
Food prepared by consumer unit on trips	17	15	13	10	17	24
Food away from home	**1,922**	**1,183**	**1,266**	**1,776**	**2,141**	**3,071**
ALCOHOLIC BEVERAGES	**467**	**280**	**370**	**282**	**553**	**779**
HOUSING	**9,474**	**4,749**	**7,241**	**9,193**	**11,570**	**15,769**
Shelter	**6,072**	**3,325**	**4,880**	**5,669**	**7,276**	**9,852**
Owned dwellings	1,401	294	284	439	1,322	4,040
Mortgage interest and charges	915	116	126	249	713	2,851
Property taxes	342	170	73	117	335	856
Maintenance, repair, insurance, other expenses	145	8	85	73	273	334
Rented dwellings	4,482	2,851	4,465	5,115	5,771	5,532
Other lodging	188	179	131	114	184	279
Utilities, fuels, and public services	**1,797**	**726**	**1,342**	**1,946**	**2,263**	**3,101**
Natural gas	177	78	102	207	211	318
Electricity	699	289	591	788	874	1,138
Fuel oil and other fuels	29	5	14	42	42	58
Telephone services	733	306	551	765	942	1,259
Water and other public services	158	51	83	144	195	328
Household services	**368**	**142**	**240**	**400**	**484**	**658**
Personal services	193	44	139	232	296	343
Other household services	175	99	101	168	189	315
Housekeeping supplies	**286**	**132**	**201**	**262**	**332**	**481**
Laundry and cleaning supplies	83	42	68	82	82	133
Other household products	141	56	89	129	192	241
Postage and stationery	62	35	44	52	57	107

	total consumer units under age 25	under $10,000	$10,000–$19,999	$20,000–$29,999	$30,000–$39,999	$40,000 or more
Household furnishings and equipment	**$952**	**$424**	**$577**	**$917**	**$1,214**	**$1,677**
Household textiles	61	29	25	57	124	91
Furniture	316	96	164	396	256	664
Floor coverings	14	9	2	2	24	31
Major appliances	115	47	77	65	165	225
Small appliances, miscellaneous housewares	56	23	52	43	94	78
Miscellaneous household equipment	390	220	258	353	552	587
APPAREL AND RELATED SERVICES	**1,465**	**649**	**913**	**1,623**	**1,836**	**2,407**
Men and boys	**307**	**125**	**149**	**407**	**484**	**463**
Men, aged 16 or older	279	112	132	384	433	417
Boys, aged 2 to 15	28	12	17	22	51	46
Women and girls	**546**	**282**	**350**	**615**	**564**	**891**
Women, aged 16 or older	515	271	339	592	514	830
Girls, aged 2 to 15	31	11	11	22	50	61
Children under age 2	**138**	**60**	**115**	**138**	**244**	**179**
Footwear	**244**	**72**	**137**	**248**	**255**	**472**
Other apparel products and services	**231**	**111**	**162**	**216**	**289**	**402**
TRANSPORTATION	**5,724**	**2,113**	**3,252**	**5,275**	**8,283**	**10,762**
Vehicle purchases	**2,334**	**632**	**1,049**	**2,186**	**4,025**	**4,608**
Cars and trucks, new	1,001	276	150	387	2,076	2,375
Cars and trucks, used	1,266	355	836	1,769	1,809	2,142
Other vehicles	68	–	134	31	140	91
Gasoline and motor oil	**1,699**	**816**	**1,273**	**1,732**	**2,114**	**2,843**
Other vehicle expenses	**1,426**	**517**	**755**	**1,174**	**1,825**	**2,825**
Vehicle finance charges	210	37	77	177	282	493
Maintenance and repairs	418	200	280	438	531	706
Vehicle insurance	556	133	258	400	725	1,179
Vehicle rentals, leases, licenses, other charges	241	146	140	159	287	447
Public transportation	**265**	**148**	**175**	**182**	**319**	**487**
HEALTH CARE	**753**	**202**	**405**	**884**	**896**	**1,504**
Health insurance	382	82	191	376	482	830
Medical services	230	72	109	376	236	419
Drugs	100	34	85	91	126	176
Medical supplies	41	14	21	41	53	79
ENTERTAINMENT	**1,431**	**790**	**989**	**1,414**	**1,793**	**2,329**
Fees and admissions	283	197	232	224	344	426
Audio and visual equipment and services	716	382	512	647	871	1,221
Pets, toys, and playground equipment	248	80	163	346	367	373
Other entertainment products and services	184	131	81	197	211	309
PERSONAL CARE PRODUCTS AND SERVICES	**342**	**215**	**237**	**280**	**436**	**540**
READING	**48**	**36**	**50**	**44**	**45**	**65**
EDUCATION	**1,522**	**2,512**	**1,637**	**1,101**	**783**	**809**
TOBACCO PRODUCTS AND SMOKING SUPPLIES	**288**	**98**	**243**	**372**	**487**	**414**
MISCELLANEOUS	**378**	**145**	**282**	**280**	**661**	**638**
CASH CONTRIBUTIONS	**591**	**170**	**322**	**459**	**550**	**1,363**
PERSONAL INSURANCE AND PENSIONS	**2,365**	**244**	**994**	**1,838**	**2,684**	**5,976**
Life and other personal insurance	41	4	18	43	37	99
Pensions and Social Security	2,325	240	975	1,795	2,647	5,877
PERSONAL TAXES	**581**	**–73**	**64**	**396**	**370**	**1,905**
Federal income taxes	382	–69	14	196	127	1,380
State and local income taxes	178	–6	48	189	211	467
Other taxes	21	1	2	10	32	59
GIFTS FOR PEOPLE IN OTHER HOUSEHOLDS	**416**	**244**	**364**	**294**	**641**	**608**

Note: Spending by category does not add to total spending because gift spending is also included in the preceding product and service categories and personal taxes are not included in the total. "–" means sample is too small to make a reliable estimate.
Source: Bureau of Labor Statistics, 2006 and 2007 Consumer Expenditure Surveys, Internet site http://www.bls.gov/cex/; calculations by New Strategist

Table 9.   Under age 25: Indexed spending by income, 2006–07

(indexed average annual spending of consumer units headed by people under age 25 by product and service category and before-tax income of consumer unit, 2006–07; index definition: an index of 100 is the average for all consumer units; an index of 132 means that spending by consumer units in that group is 32 percent above the average for all consumer units; an index of 68 indicates spending that is 32 percent below the average for all consumer units)

	total consumer units under age 25	under $10,000	$10,000– $19,999	$20,000– $29,999	$30,000– $39,999	$40,000 or more
Average spending of consumer units, total	$28,881	$14,390	$19,893	$27,068	$35,292	$49,543
Average spending of consumer units, index	100	50	69	94	122	172
FOOD	**100**	**54**	**73**	**100**	**117**	**153**
Food at home	**100**	**47**	**80**	**106**	**122**	**148**
Cereals and bakery products	100	50	82	100	115	152
Cereals and cereal products	100	55	82	105	107	146
Bakery products	100	46	82	96	118	155
Meats, poultry, fish, and eggs	100	45	69	123	124	147
Beef	100	46	74	129	110	145
Pork	100	44	65	120	129	148
Other meats	100	39	69	109	194	126
Poultry	100	47	70	127	98	154
Fish and seafood	100	41	60	125	103	164
Eggs	100	54	80	108	136	136
Dairy products	100	47	86	100	130	144
Fresh milk and cream	100	49	88	104	133	137
Other dairy products	100	46	85	98	128	148
Fruits and vegetables	100	39	89	108	115	151
Fresh fruits	100	32	101	107	108	151
Fresh vegetables	100	36	86	116	111	153
Processed fruits	100	50	80	104	142	139
Processed vegetables	100	47	85	100	105	160
Other food at home	100	51	81	100	123	147
Sugar and other sweets	100	58	99	114	107	128
Fats and oils	100	53	77	102	130	144
Miscellaneous foods	100	54	82	101	112	148
Nonalcoholic beverages	100	41	71	98	152	150
Food prepared by consumer unit on trips	100	87	77	59	100	141
Food away from home	**100**	**62**	**66**	**92**	**111**	**160**
ALCOHOLIC BEVERAGES	**100**	**60**	**79**	**60**	**118**	**167**
HOUSING	**100**	**50**	**76**	**97**	**122**	**166**
Shelter	**100**	**55**	**80**	**93**	**120**	**162**
Owned dwellings	100	21	20	31	94	288
Mortgage interest and charges	100	13	14	27	78	312
Property taxes	100	50	21	34	98	250
Maintenance, repair, insurance, other expenses	100	6	58	50	188	230
Rented dwellings	100	64	100	114	129	123
Other lodging	100	95	70	61	98	148
Utilities, fuels, and public services	**100**	**40**	**75**	**108**	**126**	**173**
Natural gas	100	44	57	117	119	180
Electricity	100	41	85	113	125	163
Fuel oil and other fuels	100	17	50	145	145	200
Telephone services	100	42	75	104	129	172
Water and other public services	100	32	53	91	123	208
Household services	**100**	**39**	**65**	**109**	**132**	**179**
Personal services	100	23	72	120	153	178
Other household services	100	57	58	96	108	180
Housekeeping supplies	**100**	**46**	**70**	**92**	**116**	**168**
Laundry and cleaning supplies	100	50	82	99	99	160
Other household products	100	39	63	91	136	171
Postage and stationery	100	56	72	84	92	173

	total consumer units under age 25	under $10,000	$10,000– $19,999	$20,000– $29,999	$30,000– $39,999	$40,000 or more
Household furnishings and equipment	100	45	61	96	128	176
Household textiles	100	47	41	93	203	149
Furniture	100	30	52	125	81	210
Floor coverings	100	64	11	14	171	221
Major appliances	100	41	67	57	143	196
Small appliances, miscellaneous housewares	100	42	93	77	168	139
Miscellaneous household equipment	100	56	66	91	142	151
APPAREL AND RELATED SERVICES	100	44	62	111	125	164
Men and boys	100	41	49	133	158	151
Men, aged 16 or older	100	40	47	138	155	149
Boys, aged 2 to 15	100	42	60	79	182	164
Women and girls	100	52	64	113	103	163
Women, aged 16 or older	100	53	66	115	100	161
Girls, aged 2 to 15	100	35	37	71	161	197
Children under age 2	100	43	84	100	177	130
Footwear	100	29	56	102	105	193
Other apparel products and services	100	48	70	94	125	174
TRANSPORTATION	100	37	57	92	145	188
Vehicle purchases	100	27	45	94	172	197
Cars and trucks, new	100	28	15	39	207	237
Cars and trucks, used	100	28	66	140	143	169
Other vehicles	100	–	196	46	206	134
Gasoline and motor oil	100	48	75	102	124	167
Other vehicle expenses	100	36	53	82	128	198
Vehicle finance charges	100	18	37	84	134	235
Maintenance and repairs	100	48	67	105	127	169
Vehicle insurance	100	24	46	72	130	212
Vehicle rentals, leases, licenses, other charges	100	61	58	66	119	185
Public transportation	100	56	66	69	120	184
HEALTH CARE	100	27	54	117	119	200
Health insurance	100	21	50	98	126	217
Medical services	100	31	47	163	103	182
Drugs	100	34	85	91	126	176
Medical supplies	100	34	52	100	129	193
ENTERTAINMENT	100	55	69	99	125	163
Fees and admissions	100	70	82	79	122	151
Audio and visual equipment and services	100	53	72	90	122	171
Pets, toys, and playground equipment	100	32	66	140	148	150
Other entertainment products and services	100	71	44	107	115	168
PERSONAL CARE PRODUCTS AND SERVICES	100	63	69	82	127	158
READING	100	75	104	92	94	135
EDUCATION	100	165	108	72	51	53
TOBACCO PRODUCTS AND SMOKING SUPPLIES	100	34	84	129	169	144
MISCELLANEOUS	100	38	75	74	175	169
CASH CONTRIBUTIONS	100	29	54	78	93	231
PERSONAL INSURANCE AND PENSIONS	100	10	42	78	113	253
Life and other personal insurance	100	10	45	105	90	241
Pensions and Social Security	100	10	42	77	114	253
PERSONAL TAXES	100	–	11	68	64	328
Federal income taxes	100	–	4	51	33	361
State and local income taxes	100	–	27	106	119	262
Other taxes	100	5	11	48	152	281
GIFTS FOR PEOPLE IN OTHER HOUSEHOLDS	100	59	87	71	154	146

Note: "–" means sample is too small to make a reliable estimate or not applicable.
Source: Calculations by New Strategist based on the Bureau of Labor Statistics' 2006 and 2007 Consumer Expenditure Surveys

Table 10. Aged 25 to 34: Average spending by income, 2006–07

(average annual spending of consumer units (CUs) headed by people aged 25 to 34 by product and service category and before-tax income of consumer unit, 2006–07)

	total consumer units aged 25 to 34	under $10,000	$10,000–$19,999	$20,000–$29,999	$30,000–$39,999	$40,000–$49,999	$50,000–$69,999	$70,000 or more
Number of consumer units (in 000s)	20,285	1,255	1,913	2,527	2,650	2,291	3,720	5,928
Average number of persons per CU	2.8	2.4	2.7	2.7	2.7	2.7	2.9	3.1
Average before-tax income of CUs	$57,232	$4,514	$15,287	$25,210	$34,675	$44,256	$59,180	$109,453
Average annual spending of consumer units	47,869	20,199	24,226	29,430	35,782	40,592	51,284	74,253
FOOD	**6,051**	**3,017**	**4,000**	**4,256**	**4,864**	**5,608**	**6,374**	**8,165**
Food at home	**3,198**	**1,914**	**2,537**	**2,445**	**2,701**	**3,118**	**3,276**	**4,002**
Cereals and bakery products	416	264	324	319	339	398	446	516
Cereals and cereal products	144	100	124	117	119	140	143	176
Bakery products	273	164	201	202	219	259	304	341
Meats, poultry, fish, and eggs	719	457	649	589	606	700	735	858
Beef	213	130	174	158	190	208	233	253
Pork	134	95	149	117	115	148	127	147
Other meats	91	65	81	74	71	85	95	109
Poultry	140	97	119	120	107	133	137	175
Fish and seafood	104	41	82	86	91	89	104	134
Eggs	37	30	43	33	32	38	39	40
Dairy products	360	237	259	264	302	344	387	452
Fresh milk and cream	150	104	122	117	138	139	161	177
Other dairy products	210	133	136	147	163	205	225	275
Fruits and vegetables	533	299	424	416	442	494	548	678
Fresh fruits	166	83	130	126	136	164	170	212
Fresh vegetables	170	101	148	137	139	146	171	218
Processed fruits	110	69	81	79	94	103	120	138
Processed vegetables	87	48	66	73	74	81	86	110
Other food at home	1,169	656	881	858	1,012	1,181	1,159	1,498
Sugar and other sweets	97	64	76	76	83	87	99	123
Fats and oils	76	56	63	62	69	70	82	90
Miscellaneous foods	653	340	488	457	554	719	628	842
Nonalcoholic beverages	310	185	235	246	280	276	315	393
Food prepared by consumer unit on trips	32	9	19	17	26	29	35	51
Food away from home	**2,853**	**1,103**	**1,463**	**1,811**	**2,164**	**2,490**	**3,098**	**4,163**
ALCOHOLIC BEVERAGES	**585**	**214**	**258**	**260**	**520**	**552**	**566**	**903**
HOUSING	**17,282**	**8,454**	**9,454**	**11,051**	**12,838**	**14,413**	**18,600**	**26,424**
Shelter	**10,630**	**5,613**	**5,565**	**6,795**	**8,186**	**8,950**	**11,342**	**16,255**
Owned dwellings	6,058	978	846	1,574	3,069	3,869	6,492	12,636
Mortgage interest and charges	4,284	509	463	1,015	2,106	2,715	4,698	9,030
Property taxes	1,132	338	243	330	581	718	1,132	2,337
Maintenance, repair, insurance, other expenses	641	131	140	230	383	437	662	1,268
Rented dwellings	4,287	4,459	4,663	5,146	4,987	4,951	4,556	3,024
Other lodging	285	175	57	75	129	129	295	595
Utilities, fuels, and public services	**3,078**	**1,934**	**2,136**	**2,523**	**2,746**	**2,809**	**3,357**	**3,938**
Natural gas	400	223	214	308	345	336	435	564
Electricity	1,141	780	879	980	1,053	1,066	1,231	1,382
Fuel oil and other fuels	79	28	30	46	33	70	106	126
Telephone services	1,111	712	822	947	1,014	1,051	1,206	1,366
Water and other public services	347	190	191	242	300	286	379	500
Household services	**1,152**	**213**	**549**	**443**	**592**	**781**	**1,146**	**2,246**
Personal services	743	88	344	237	345	467	752	1,506
Other household services	409	125	205	206	247	314	394	740
Housekeeping supplies	**526**	**228**	**365**	**341**	**370**	**531**	**547**	**724**
Laundry and cleaning supplies	142	59	123	111	124	121	170	167
Other household products	265	123	149	156	162	330	265	372
Postage and stationery	119	47	92	74	84	79	113	184

	total consumer units aged 25 to 34	under $10,000	$10,000– $19,999	$20,000– $29,999	$30,000– $39,999	$40,000– $49,999	$50,000– $69,999	$70,000 or more
Household furnishings and equipment	**$1,896**	**$466**	**$839**	**$950**	**$944**	**$1,343**	**$2,208**	**$3,262**
Household textiles	121	25	86	102	95	66	137	174
Furniture	531	90	234	215	260	397	509	1,036
Floor coverings	42	8	11	5	22	16	43	92
Major appliances	196	70	49	113	118	88	207	374
Small appliances, miscellaneous housewares	120	58	95	61	62	114	140	171
Miscellaneous household equipment	885	215	364	453	387	662	1,172	1,416
APPAREL AND RELATED SERVICES	**2,201**	**1,465**	**1,186**	**1,428**	**1,548**	**1,935**	**2,013**	**3,383**
Men and boys	**531**	**184**	**339**	**349**	**366**	**428**	**581**	**779**
Men, aged 16 or older	409	118	225	242	272	319	457	626
Boys, aged 2 to 15	122	66	114	107	94	108	124	153
Women and girls	**735**	**543**	**346**	**456**	**544**	**702**	**598**	**1,147**
Women, aged 16 or older	575	338	225	298	395	585	448	952
Girls, aged 2 to 15	161	204	121	158	149	118	151	195
Children under age 2	**196**	**269**	**112**	**126**	**143**	**182**	**210**	**262**
Footwear	**377**	**294**	**247**	**304**	**284**	**380**	**357**	**498**
Other apparel products and services	**361**	**175**	**142**	**192**	**211**	**242**	**266**	**697**
TRANSPORTATION	**9,135**	**3,127**	**4,488**	**6,097**	**7,440**	**7,593**	**10,377**	**13,715**
Vehicle purchases	**3,921**	**932**	**1,820**	**2,605**	**3,042**	**2,614**	**4,569**	**6,284**
Cars and trucks, new	1,748	684	303	404	1,012	1,123	1,691	3,744
Cars and trucks, used	2,071	624	1,616	2,147	2,027	1,422	2,600	2,429
Other vehicles	102	–	89	54	3	69	279	110
Gasoline and motor oil	**2,397**	**1,051**	**1,499**	**1,832**	**2,084**	**2,394**	**2,744**	**3,134**
Other vehicle expenses	**2,396**	**924**	**997**	**1,468**	**2,019**	**2,320**	**2,683**	**3,512**
Vehicle finance charges	392	66	127	191	247	342	485	659
Maintenance and repairs	616	208	379	399	502	585	760	840
Vehicle insurance	891	476	352	590	965	1,001	981	1,095
Vehicle rentals, leases, licenses, other charges	496	172	140	287	305	393	456	918
Public transportation	**422**	**219**	**171**	**192**	**295**	**264**	**381**	**785**
HEALTH CARE	**1,697**	**447**	**582**	**865**	**1,272**	**1,742**	**1,951**	**2,682**
Health insurance	900	230	265	430	654	865	1,174	1,400
Medical services	513	103	187	249	372	610	482	862
Drugs	222	87	98	139	194	198	236	335
Medical supplies	61	26	33	47	52	69	59	84
ENTERTAINMENT	**2,476**	**906**	**1,049**	**1,454**	**1,621**	**2,084**	**2,514**	**4,123**
Fees and admissions	513	82	167	217	305	379	465	1,001
Audio and visual equipment and services	1,003	492	619	793	760	883	969	1,497
Pets, toys, and playground equipment	525	201	172	268	360	464	568	843
Other entertainment products and services	435	132	91	176	197	359	513	782
PERSONAL CARE PRODUCTS AND SERVICES	**529**	**181**	**336**	**303**	**387**	**435**	**536**	**823**
READING	**77**	**35**	**43**	**37**	**49**	**64**	**73**	**133**
EDUCATION	**657**	**839**	**655**	**491**	**612**	**560**	**663**	**741**
TOBACCO PRODUCTS AND SMOKING SUPPLIES	**325**	**398**	**284**	**373**	**331**	**373**	**362**	**257**
MISCELLANEOUS	**602**	**374**	**326**	**267**	**451**	**521**	**736**	**890**
CASH CONTRIBUTIONS	**1,048**	**357**	**503**	**603**	**815**	**802**	**1,077**	**1,741**
PERSONAL INSURANCE AND PENSIONS	**5,205**	**384**	**1,060**	**1,945**	**3,035**	**3,912**	**5,443**	**10,273**
Life and other personal insurance	168	54	47	54	78	118	168	340
Pensions and Social Security	5,037	331	1,013	1,891	2,957	3,793	5,275	9,933
PERSONAL TAXES	**1,511**	**–330**	**–550**	**–90**	**311**	**1,082**	**1,757**	**3,797**
Federal income taxes	986	–326	–563	–224	88	707	1,133	2,698
State and local income taxes	428	–11	–2	100	171	335	498	907
Other taxes	97	8	15	34	53	40	126	193
GIFTS FOR PEOPLE IN OTHER HOUSEHOLDS	**771**	**278**	**345**	**340**	**401**	**407**	**1,339**	**1,096**

Note: Spending by category does not add to total spending because gift spending is also included in the preceding product and service categories and personal taxes are not included in the total. "–" means sample is too small to make a reliable estimate.
Source: Bureau of Labor Statistics, 2006 and 2007 Consumer Expenditure Surveys, Internet site http://www.bls.gov/cex/; calculations by New Strategist

Table 11. Aged 25 to 34: Indexed spending by income, 2006–07

(indexed average annual spending of consumer units headed by people aged 25 to 34 by product and service category and before-tax income of consumer unit, 2006–07; index definition: an index of 100 is the average for all consumer units; an index of 132 means that spending by consumer units in that group is 32 percent above the average for all consumer units; an index of 68 indicates spending that is 32 percent below the average for all consumer units)

	total consumer units aged 25 to 34	under $10,000	$10,000–$19,999	$20,000–$29,999	$30,000–$39,999	$40,000–$49,999	$50,000–$69,999	$70,000 or more
Average spending of consumer units, total	$47,869	$20,199	$24,226	$29,430	$35,782	$40,592	$51,284	$74,253
Average spending of consumer units, index	100	42	51	61	75	85	107	155
FOOD	**100**	**50**	**66**	**70**	**80**	**93**	**105**	**135**
Food at home	**100**	**60**	**79**	**76**	**84**	**97**	**102**	**125**
Cereals and bakery products	100	64	78	77	81	96	107	124
Cereals and cereal products	100	70	86	81	83	97	99	122
Bakery products	100	60	74	74	80	95	111	125
Meats, poultry, fish, and eggs	100	64	90	82	84	97	102	119
Beef	100	61	82	74	89	98	109	119
Pork	100	71	111	87	86	110	95	110
Other meats	100	71	89	81	78	93	104	120
Poultry	100	69	85	86	76	95	98	125
Fish and seafood	100	40	79	83	88	86	100	129
Eggs	100	81	116	89	86	103	105	108
Dairy products	100	66	72	73	84	96	108	126
Fresh milk and cream	100	69	81	78	92	93	107	118
Other dairy products	100	63	65	70	78	98	107	131
Fruits and vegetables	100	56	80	78	83	93	103	127
Fresh fruits	100	50	79	76	82	99	102	128
Fresh vegetables	100	59	87	81	82	86	101	128
Processed fruits	100	63	73	72	85	94	109	125
Processed vegetables	100	55	75	84	85	93	99	126
Other food at home	100	56	75	73	87	101	99	128
Sugar and other sweets	100	66	79	78	86	90	102	127
Fats and oils	100	73	83	82	91	92	108	118
Miscellaneous foods	100	52	75	70	85	110	96	129
Nonalcoholic beverages	100	60	76	79	90	89	102	127
Food prepared by consumer unit on trips	100	29	58	53	81	91	109	159
Food away from home	**100**	**39**	**51**	**63**	**76**	**87**	**109**	**146**
ALCOHOLIC BEVERAGES	**100**	**37**	**44**	**44**	**89**	**94**	**97**	**154**
HOUSING	**100**	**49**	**55**	**64**	**74**	**83**	**108**	**153**
Shelter	**100**	**53**	**52**	**64**	**77**	**84**	**107**	**153**
Owned dwellings	100	16	14	26	51	64	107	209
Mortgage interest and charges	100	12	11	24	49	63	110	211
Property taxes	100	30	21	29	51	63	100	206
Maintenance, repair, insurance, other expenses	100	20	22	36	60	68	103	198
Rented dwellings	100	104	109	120	116	115	106	71
Other lodging	100	61	20	26	45	45	104	209
Utilities, fuels, and public services	**100**	**63**	**69**	**82**	**89**	**91**	**109**	**128**
Natural gas	100	56	53	77	86	84	109	141
Electricity	100	68	77	86	92	93	108	121
Fuel oil and other fuels	100	36	38	58	42	89	134	159
Telephone services	100	64	74	85	91	95	109	123
Water and other public services	100	55	55	70	86	82	109	144
Household services	**100**	**19**	**48**	**38**	**51**	**68**	**99**	**195**
Personal services	100	12	46	32	46	63	101	203
Other household services	100	31	50	50	60	77	96	181
Housekeeping supplies	**100**	**43**	**69**	**65**	**70**	**101**	**104**	**138**
Laundry and cleaning supplies	100	41	87	78	87	85	120	118
Other household products	100	46	56	59	61	125	100	140
Postage and stationery	100	39	78	62	71	66	95	155

	total consumer units aged 25 to 34	under $10,000	$10,000– $19,999	$20,000– $29,999	$30,000– $39,999	$40,000– $49,999	$50,000– $69,999	$70,000 or more
Household furnishings and equipment	100	25	44	50	50	71	116	172
Household textiles	100	20	71	84	79	55	113	144
Furniture	100	17	44	40	49	75	96	195
Floor coverings	100	20	27	12	52	38	102	219
Major appliances	100	35	25	58	60	45	106	191
Small appliances, miscellaneous housewares	100	48	79	51	52	95	117	143
Miscellaneous household equipment	100	24	41	51	44	75	132	160
APPAREL AND RELATED SERVICES	100	67	54	65	70	88	91	154
Men and boys	100	35	64	66	69	81	109	147
Men, aged 16 or older	100	29	55	59	67	78	112	153
Boys, aged 2 to 15	100	54	93	88	77	89	102	125
Women and girls	100	74	47	62	74	96	81	156
Women, aged 16 or older	100	59	39	52	69	102	78	166
Girls, aged 2 to 15	100	127	75	98	93	73	94	121
Children under age 2	100	137	57	64	73	93	107	134
Footwear	100	78	65	81	75	101	95	132
Other apparel products and services	100	48	39	53	58	67	74	193
TRANSPORTATION	100	34	49	67	81	83	114	150
Vehicle purchases	100	24	46	66	78	67	117	160
Cars and trucks, new	100	39	17	23	58	64	97	214
Cars and trucks, used	100	30	78	104	98	69	126	117
Other vehicles	100	–	87	53	3	68	274	108
Gasoline and motor oil	100	44	63	76	87	100	114	131
Other vehicle expenses	100	39	42	61	84	97	112	147
Vehicle finance charges	100	17	32	49	63	87	124	168
Maintenance and repairs	100	34	62	65	81	95	123	136
Vehicle insurance	100	53	39	66	108	112	110	123
Vehicle rentals, leases, licenses, other charges	100	35	28	58	61	79	92	185
Public transportation	100	52	41	45	70	63	90	186
HEALTH CARE	100	26	34	51	75	103	115	158
Health insurance	100	26	29	48	73	96	130	156
Medical services	100	20	36	49	73	119	94	168
Drugs	100	39	44	63	87	89	106	151
Medical supplies	100	43	54	77	85	113	97	138
ENTERTAINMENT	100	37	42	59	65	84	102	167
Fees and admissions	100	16	33	42	59	74	91	195
Audio and visual equipment and services	100	49	62	79	76	88	97	149
Pets, toys, and playground equipment	100	38	33	51	69	88	108	161
Other entertainment products and services	100	30	21	40	45	83	118	180
PERSONAL CARE PRODUCTS AND SERVICES	100	34	64	57	73	82	101	156
READING	100	46	56	48	64	83	95	173
EDUCATION	100	128	100	75	93	85	101	113
TOBACCO PRODUCTS AND SMOKING SUPPLIES	100	122	87	115	102	115	111	79
MISCELLANEOUS	100	62	54	44	75	87	122	148
CASH CONTRIBUTIONS	100	34	48	58	78	77	103	166
PERSONAL INSURANCE AND PENSIONS	100	7	20	37	58	75	105	197
Life and other personal insurance	100	32	28	32	46	70	100	202
Pensions and Social Security	100	7	20	38	59	75	105	197
PERSONAL TAXES	100	–	–	–	21	72	116	251
Federal income taxes	100	–	–	–	9	72	115	274
State and local income taxes	100	–	–	23	40	78	116	212
Other taxes	100	8	16	35	55	41	130	199
GIFTS FOR PEOPLE IN OTHER HOUSEHOLDS	100	36	45	44	52	53	174	142

Note: "–" means sample is too small to make a reliable estimate or not applicable.
Source: Calculations by New Strategist based on the Bureau of Labor Statistics' 2006 and 2007 Consumer Expenditure Surveys

Table 12. Aged 35 to 44: Average spending by income, 2006–07

(average annual spending of consumer units (CUs) headed by people aged 35 to 44 by product and service category and before-tax income of consumer unit, 2006–07)

	total consumer units aged 35 to 44	under $10,000	$10,000– $19,999	$20,000– $29,999	$30,000– $39,999	$40,000– $49,999	$50,000– $69,999	$70,000 or more
Number of consumer units (in 000s)	23,683	1,075	1,587	2,155	2,416	2,532	4,234	9,684
Average number of persons per CU	3.2	2.2	2.7	2.9	2.8	3.0	3.3	3.6
Average before-tax income of CUs	$76,071	$3,199	$15,077	$25,119	$34,819	$44,674	$59,517	$131,228
Average annual spending of consumer units	58,447	22,538	24,669	30,831	35,356	41,536	52,337	87,296
FOOD	**7,361**	**3,681**	**4,292**	**4,629**	**5,061**	**6,142**	**7,130**	**10,010**
Food at home	**4,127**	**2,229**	**3,111**	**3,084**	**3,130**	**3,637**	**4,051**	**5,198**
Cereals and bakery products	551	277	372	392	389	482	552	712
Cereals and cereal products	181	106	136	143	140	158	172	227
Bakery products	370	172	236	249	249	323	379	485
Meats, poultry, fish, and eggs	969	617	772	805	834	912	931	1,152
Beef	278	178	194	224	248	275	266	332
Pork	186	146	174	170	176	180	185	201
Other meats	129	53	90	96	107	125	132	159
Poultry	182	122	148	154	164	152	172	220
Fish and seafood	147	88	126	119	93	139	122	191
Eggs	47	30	40	43	46	42	55	48
Dairy products	455	201	331	317	349	383	478	578
Fresh milk and cream	183	104	141	133	148	159	193	223
Other dairy products	272	97	189	184	201	223	285	355
Fruits and vegetables	674	353	521	509	514	597	618	865
Fresh fruits	223	101	173	146	164	206	199	295
Fresh vegetables	214	125	158	181	164	187	192	271
Processed fruits	128	56	96	97	95	101	122	168
Processed vegetables	110	72	94	84	91	102	105	132
Other food at home	1,477	780	1,116	1,061	1,044	1,263	1,472	1,891
Sugar and other sweets	148	87	98	98	105	122	144	196
Fats and oils	99	51	73	88	80	91	106	116
Miscellaneous foods	787	337	614	566	528	649	789	1,025
Nonalcoholic beverages	395	300	322	296	302	372	397	473
Food prepared by consumer unit on trips	48	7	9	12	29	29	36	81
Food away from home	**3,235**	**1,452**	**1,181**	**1,546**	**1,930**	**2,505**	**3,079**	**4,812**
ALCOHOLIC BEVERAGES	**483**	**141**	**163**	**239**	**331**	**343**	**467**	**722**
HOUSING	**20,691**	**9,564**	**10,065**	**11,853**	**13,186**	**15,173**	**17,585**	**30,351**
Shelter	**12,599**	**6,104**	**6,304**	**7,105**	**8,115**	**9,114**	**10,587**	**18,485**
Owned dwellings	9,097	2,196	2,039	2,899	3,792	5,107	6,968	15,697
Mortgage interest and charges	6,075	1,225	1,355	1,920	2,392	3,365	4,674	10,551
Property taxes	1,943	599	452	582	833	1,070	1,451	3,360
Maintenance, repair, insurance, other expenses	1,079	373	232	397	567	672	844	1,785
Rented dwellings	2,894	3,843	4,227	4,134	4,162	3,610	3,264	1,629
Other lodging	608	65	37	72	161	398	354	1,159
Utilities, fuels, and public services	**3,890**	**2,354**	**2,503**	**2,929**	**3,141**	**3,386**	**3,869**	**4,830**
Natural gas	547	286	311	396	423	439	499	728
Electricity	1,449	991	1,055	1,171	1,229	1,315	1,422	1,727
Fuel oil and other fuels	145	15	44	71	106	117	135	213
Telephone services	1,282	802	817	985	1,072	1,140	1,326	1,549
Water and other public services	468	259	275	306	312	375	487	613
Household services	**1,401**	**227**	**317**	**390**	**502**	**719**	**860**	**2,573**
Personal services	827	75	135	171	227	367	451	1,605
Other household services	574	153	181	219	275	351	409	968
Housekeeping supplies	**704**	**378**	**306**	**388**	**442**	**493**	**623**	**1,051**
Laundry and cleaning supplies	183	172	111	138	175	188	165	218
Other household products	378	176	149	175	187	219	355	595
Postage and stationery	142	30	46	76	80	87	103	237

	total consumer units aged 35 to 44	under $10,000	$10,000– $19,999	$20,000– $29,999	$30,000– $39,999	$40,000– $49,999	$50,000– $69,999	$70,000 or more
Household furnishings and equipment	$2,097	$501	$636	$1,041	$985	$1,461	$1,647	$3,413
Household textiles	154	39	42	46	57	111	129	260
Furniture	588	149	218	151	308	307	421	1,014
Floor coverings	45	12	18	5	18	20	29	83
Major appliances	259	76	83	103	111	180	222	415
Small appliances, miscellaneous housewares	115	20	42	53	49	112	88	182
Miscellaneous household equipment	936	211	232	683	442	731	757	1,459
APPAREL AND RELATED SERVICES	**2,362**	**1,584**	**912**	**1,323**	**1,512**	**1,574**	**2,044**	**3,526**
Men and boys	**578**	**250**	**171**	**291**	**357**	**376**	**548**	**880**
Men, aged 16 or older	405	170	67	167	244	257	416	626
Boys, aged 2 to 15	173	80	104	123	113	119	133	254
Women and girls	**899**	**640**	**338**	**524**	**664**	**574**	**763**	**1,333**
Women, aged 16 or older	638	496	213	408	489	399	568	924
Girls, aged 2 to 15	262	143	125	116	176	176	195	409
Children under age 2	**123**	**78**	**87**	**82**	**55**	**72**	**112**	**180**
Footwear	**401**	**465**	**153**	**273**	**284**	**364**	**343**	**538**
Other apparel products and services	**360**	**152**	**163**	**153**	**152**	**187**	**278**	**595**
TRANSPORTATION	**10,287**	**3,542**	**4,267**	**5,774**	**6,392**	**6,795**	**10,442**	**14,867**
Vehicle purchases	**4,119**	**1,395**	**1,336**	**2,249**	**2,309**	**2,023**	**4,375**	**6,181**
Cars and trucks, new	1,977	1,505	248	580	625	791	1,864	3,431
Cars and trucks, used	2,038	699	1,205	1,651	1,604	1,168	2,443	2,569
Other vehicles	103	–	15	19	80	63	69	181
Gasoline and motor oil	**2,751**	**1,028**	**1,460**	**1,867**	**2,012**	**2,347**	**2,932**	**3,562**
Other vehicle expenses	**2,867**	**964**	**1,286**	**1,470**	**1,804**	**2,110**	**2,763**	**4,181**
Vehicle finance charges	387	94	132	161	235	298	410	563
Maintenance and repairs	776	282	297	485	545	604	781	1,077
Vehicle insurance	1,096	312	714	667	750	896	1,065	1,516
Vehicle rentals, leases, licenses, other charges	608	277	143	158	274	312	508	1,025
Public transportation	**550**	**155**	**185**	**188**	**267**	**316**	**372**	**943**
HEALTH CARE	**2,299**	**795**	**889**	**1,147**	**1,351**	**1,941**	**2,306**	**3,284**
Health insurance	1,241	339	491	592	793	1,096	1,313	1,727
Medical services	642	216	191	305	261	509	601	987
Drugs	324	191	180	211	244	269	316	427
Medical supplies	92	49	27	39	53	67	77	143
ENTERTAINMENT	**3,406**	**934**	**1,077**	**1,327**	**1,867**	**2,319**	**2,807**	**5,497**
Fees and admissions	922	177	144	156	358	450	604	1,716
Audio and visual equipment and services	1,131	464	533	641	798	928	1,232	1,506
Pets, toys, and playground equipment	717	172	227	307	535	461	536	1,163
Other entertainment products and services	636	121	174	223	176	480	435	1,112
PERSONAL CARE PRODUCTS AND SERVICES	**675**	**203**	**330**	**315**	**413**	**492**	**649**	**995**
READING	**110**	**40**	**37**	**40**	**45**	**71**	**84**	**183**
EDUCATION	**838**	**325**	**207**	**285**	**248**	**383**	**612**	**1,490**
TOBACCO PRODUCTS AND SMOKING SUPPLIES	**366**	**437**	**490**	**416**	**422**	**398**	**398**	**291**
MISCELLANEOUS	**895**	**455**	**470**	**372**	**608**	**637**	**833**	**1,298**
CASH CONTRIBUTIONS	**1,639**	**350**	**427**	**609**	**1,019**	**1,180**	**1,329**	**2,620**
PERSONAL INSURANCE AND PENSIONS	**7,035**	**486**	**1,042**	**2,502**	**2,902**	**4,089**	**5,649**	**12,161**
Life and other personal insurance	325	67	80	89	109	159	280	564
Pensions and Social Security	6,710	420	961	2,413	2,794	3,930	5,369	11,597
PERSONAL TAXES	**2,832**	**223**	**–335**	**–339**	**311**	**960**	**1,564**	**6,020**
Federal income taxes	1,995	186	–445	–481	58	521	1,008	4,448
State and local income taxes	645	–4	37	113	187	319	440	1,225
Other taxes	192	41	72	28	66	120	116	347
GIFTS FOR PEOPLE IN OTHER HOUSEHOLDS	**811**	**347**	**302**	**434**	**401**	**585**	**861**	**1,179**

Note: Spending by category does not add to total spending because gift spending is also included in the preceding product and service categories and personal taxes are not included in the total. "–" means sample is too small to make a reliable estimate.
Source: Bureau of Labor Statistics, 2006 and 2007 Consumer Expenditure Surveys, Internet site http://www.bls.gov/cex/; calculations by New Strategist

Table 13. Aged 35 to 44: Indexed spending by income, 2006–07

(indexed average annual spending of consumer units headed by people aged 35 to 44 by product and service category and before-tax income of consumer unit, 2006–07; index definition: an index of 100 is the average for all consumer units; an index of 132 means that spending by consumer units in that group is 32 percent above the average for all consumer units; an index of 68 indicates spending that is 32 percent below the average for all consumer units)

	total consumer units aged 35 to 44	under $10,000	$10,000–$19,999	$20,000–$29,999	$30,000–$39,999	$40,000–$49,999	$50,000–$69,999	$70,000 or more
Average spending of consumer units, total	$58,447	$22,538	$24,669	$30,831	$35,356	$41,536	$52,337	$87,296
Average spending of consumer units, index	100	39	42	53	60	71	90	149
FOOD	100	50	58	63	69	83	97	136
Food at home	100	54	75	75	76	88	98	126
Cereals and bakery products	100	50	68	71	71	87	100	129
Cereals and cereal products	100	59	75	79	77	87	95	125
Bakery products	100	46	64	67	67	87	102	131
Meats, poultry, fish, and eggs	100	64	80	83	86	94	96	119
Beef	100	64	70	81	89	99	96	119
Pork	100	79	94	91	95	97	99	108
Other meats	100	41	69	74	83	97	102	123
Poultry	100	67	81	85	90	84	95	121
Fish and seafood	100	60	85	81	63	95	83	130
Eggs	100	64	86	91	98	89	117	102
Dairy products	100	44	73	70	77	84	105	127
Fresh milk and cream	100	57	77	73	81	87	105	122
Other dairy products	100	36	70	68	74	82	105	131
Fruits and vegetables	100	52	77	76	76	89	92	128
Fresh fruits	100	45	78	65	74	92	89	132
Fresh vegetables	100	59	74	85	77	87	90	127
Processed fruits	100	44	75	76	74	79	95	131
Processed vegetables	100	65	86	76	83	93	95	120
Other food at home	100	53	76	72	71	86	100	128
Sugar and other sweets	100	59	66	66	71	82	97	132
Fats and oils	100	52	74	89	81	92	107	117
Miscellaneous foods	100	43	78	72	67	82	100	130
Nonalcoholic beverages	100	76	82	75	76	94	101	120
Food prepared by consumer unit on trips	100	14	18	25	60	60	75	169
Food away from home	100	45	37	48	60	77	95	149
ALCOHOLIC BEVERAGES	100	29	34	49	69	71	97	149
HOUSING	100	46	49	57	64	73	85	147
Shelter	100	48	50	56	64	72	84	147
Owned dwellings	100	24	22	32	42	56	77	173
Mortgage interest and charges	100	20	22	32	39	55	77	174
Property taxes	100	31	23	30	43	55	75	173
Maintenance, repair, insurance, other expenses	100	35	22	37	53	62	78	165
Rented dwellings	100	133	146	143	144	125	113	56
Other lodging	100	11	6	12	26	65	58	191
Utilities, fuels, and public services	100	61	64	75	81	87	99	124
Natural gas	100	52	57	72	77	80	91	133
Electricity	100	68	73	81	85	91	98	119
Fuel oil and other fuels	100	10	30	49	73	81	93	147
Telephone services	100	63	64	77	84	89	103	121
Water and other public services	100	55	59	65	67	80	104	131
Household services	100	16	23	28	36	51	61	184
Personal services	100	9	16	21	27	44	55	194
Other household services	100	27	32	38	48	61	71	169
Housekeeping supplies	100	54	43	55	63	70	88	149
Laundry and cleaning supplies	100	94	61	75	96	103	90	119
Other household products	100	47	40	46	49	58	94	157
Postage and stationery	100	21	32	54	56	61	73	167

	total consumer units aged 35 to 44	under $10,000	$10,000– $19,999	$20,000– $29,999	$30,000– $39,999	$40,000– $49,999	$50,000– $69,999	$70,000 or more
Household furnishings and equipment	100	24	30	50	47	70	79	163
Household textiles	100	25	27	30	37	72	84	169
Furniture	100	25	37	26	52	52	72	172
Floor coverings	100	27	41	11	40	44	64	184
Major appliances	100	29	32	40	43	69	86	160
Small appliances, miscellaneous housewares	100	17	37	46	43	97	77	158
Miscellaneous household equipment	100	23	25	73	47	78	81	156
APPAREL AND RELATED SERVICES	100	67	39	56	64	67	87	149
Men and boys	100	43	30	50	62	65	95	152
Men, aged 16 or older	100	42	17	41	60	63	103	155
Boys, aged 2 to 15	100	46	60	71	65	69	77	147
Women and girls	100	71	38	58	74	64	85	148
Women, aged 16 or older	100	78	33	64	77	63	89	145
Girls, aged 2 to 15	100	55	48	44	67	67	74	156
Children under age 2	100	63	71	67	45	59	91	146
Footwear	100	116	38	68	71	91	86	134
Other apparel products and services	100	42	45	43	42	52	77	165
TRANSPORTATION	100	34	41	56	62	66	102	145
Vehicle purchases	100	34	32	55	56	49	106	150
Cars and trucks, new	100	76	13	29	32	40	94	174
Cars and trucks, used	100	34	59	81	79	57	120	126
Other vehicles	100	–	15	18	78	61	67	176
Gasoline and motor oil	100	37	53	68	73	85	107	129
Other vehicle expenses	100	34	45	51	63	74	96	146
Vehicle finance charges	100	24	34	42	61	77	106	145
Maintenance and repairs	100	36	38	63	70	78	101	139
Vehicle insurance	100	28	65	61	68	82	97	138
Vehicle rentals, leases, licenses, other charges	100	46	24	26	45	51	84	169
Public transportation	100	28	34	34	49	57	68	171
HEALTH CARE	100	35	39	50	59	84	100	143
Health insurance	100	27	40	48	64	88	106	139
Medical services	100	34	30	48	41	79	94	154
Drugs	100	59	56	65	75	83	98	132
Medical supplies	100	54	29	42	58	73	84	155
ENTERTAINMENT	100	27	32	39	55	68	82	161
Fees and admissions	100	19	16	17	39	49	66	186
Audio and visual equipment and services	100	41	47	57	71	82	109	133
Pets, toys, and playground equipment	100	24	32	43	75	64	75	162
Other entertainment products and services	100	19	27	35	28	75	68	175
PERSONAL CARE PRODUCTS AND SERVICES	100	30	49	47	61	73	96	147
READING	100	36	34	36	41	65	76	166
EDUCATION	100	39	25	34	30	46	73	178
TOBACCO PRODUCTS AND SMOKING SUPPLIES	100	119	134	114	115	109	109	80
MISCELLANEOUS	100	51	53	42	68	71	93	145
CASH CONTRIBUTIONS	100	21	26	37	62	72	81	160
PERSONAL INSURANCE AND PENSIONS	100	7	15	36	41	58	80	173
Life and other personal insurance	100	21	25	27	34	49	86	174
Pensions and Social Security	100	6	14	36	42	59	80	173
PERSONAL TAXES	100	8	–	–	11	34	55	213
Federal income taxes	100	9	–	–	3	26	51	223
State and local income taxes	100	–	6	18	29	49	68	190
Other taxes	100	21	37	15	34	63	60	181
GIFTS FOR PEOPLE IN OTHER HOUSEHOLDS	100	43	37	54	49	72	106	145

Note: "–" means sample is too small to make a reliable estimate or not applicable.
Source: Calculations by New Strategist based on the Bureau of Labor Statistics' 2006 and 2007 Consumer Expenditure Surveys

Table 14. Aged 45 to 54: Average spending by income, 2006–07

(average annual spending of consumer units (CUs) headed by people aged 45 to 54 by product and service category and before-tax income of consumer unit, 2006–07)

	total consumer units aged 45 to 54	under $10,000	$10,000–$19,999	$20,000–$29,999	$30,000–$39,999	$40,000–$49,999	$50,000–$69,999	$70,000 or more
Number of consumer units (in 000s)	24,971	1,343	1,871	2,129	2,530	2,310	4,005	10,783
Average number of persons per CU	2.7	1.6	2.1	2.2	2.3	2.4	2.7	3.1
Average before-tax income of CUs	$78,821	$1,889	$15,097	$25,060	$34,736	$44,462	$59,895	$134,803
Average annual spending of consumer units	58,369	21,214	22,839	28,554	34,756	39,502	49,991	87,610
FOOD	**7,254**	**3,399**	**3,315**	**4,158**	**4,729**	**5,571**	**6,553**	**10,176**
Food at home	**4,019**	**2,394**	**2,190**	**2,745**	**2,858**	**3,331**	**3,806**	**5,256**
Cereals and bakery products	516	314	294	372	353	418	485	675
Cereals and cereal products	162	96	102	120	124	125	145	211
Bakery products	355	218	191	252	230	293	340	464
Meats, poultry, fish, and eggs	939	610	575	713	672	834	865	1,195
Beef	275	141	178	225	204	227	258	349
Pork	183	126	115	141	140	164	194	218
Other meats	129	74	70	87	94	122	111	170
Poultry	166	129	102	122	130	142	142	213
Fish and seafood	144	110	72	100	70	143	121	195
Eggs	43	30	38	39	35	37	39	50
Dairy products	431	235	235	283	323	356	415	562
Fresh milk and cream	162	105	112	121	136	137	154	198
Other dairy products	269	130	122	161	187	220	261	364
Fruits and vegetables	684	423	319	464	475	595	629	906
Fresh fruits	229	149	96	153	153	197	204	309
Fresh vegetables	225	125	111	147	143	198	204	304
Processed fruits	120	70	51	87	83	104	116	158
Processed vegetables	109	78	60	77	97	96	105	135
Other food at home	1,449	814	768	913	1,035	1,127	1,412	1,918
Sugar and other sweets	153	79	73	92	101	114	163	203
Fats and oils	102	67	64	71	73	91	99	129
Miscellaneous foods	730	391	371	438	509	567	703	981
Nonalcoholic beverages	412	256	248	296	323	336	407	518
Food prepared by consumer unit on trips	52	21	12	17	28	18	41	86
Food away from home	**3,235**	**1,005**	**1,125**	**1,413**	**1,871**	**2,240**	**2,747**	**4,920**
ALCOHOLIC BEVERAGES	**555**	**130**	**258**	**271**	**276**	**433**	**451**	**839**
HOUSING	**18,828**	**8,577**	**9,490**	**11,139**	**12,415**	**13,916**	**16,343**	**26,701**
Shelter	**11,260**	**5,023**	**5,734**	**6,808**	**7,515**	**8,375**	**9,480**	**16,033**
Owned dwellings	8,329	2,089	2,157	3,269	4,212	5,559	7,230	13,143
Mortgage interest and charges	4,957	1,090	1,229	1,786	2,519	3,347	4,380	7,842
Property taxes	2,106	686	607	789	1,062	1,343	1,754	3,342
Maintenance, repair, insurance, other expenses	1,266	313	322	694	631	869	1,096	1,959
Rented dwellings	2,059	2,836	3,469	3,450	3,114	2,582	1,808	1,178
Other lodging	872	97	107	89	188	235	442	1,712
Utilities, fuels, and public services	**3,983**	**2,310**	**2,669**	**2,941**	**3,070**	**3,453**	**3,921**	**4,977**
Natural gas	568	320	296	392	410	474	548	746
Electricity	1,472	927	1,116	1,170	1,201	1,301	1,432	1,777
Fuel oil and other fuels	171	89	100	122	116	110	164	233
Telephone services	1,300	716	848	938	998	1,142	1,314	1,623
Water and other public services	471	257	308	319	345	427	463	598
Household services	**830**	**217**	**273**	**271**	**354**	**388**	**599**	**1,406**
Personal services	192	36	44	60	89	46	151	334
Other household services	638	181	229	211	265	341	448	1,072
Housekeeping supplies	**726**	**331**	**259**	**394**	**616**	**454**	**639**	**1,032**
Laundry and cleaning supplies	161	103	97	104	150	128	161	198
Other household products	367	154	131	194	203	241	316	549
Postage and stationery	198	74	31	97	263	85	162	285

	total consumer units aged 45 to 54	under $10,000	$10,000– $19,999	$20,000– $29,999	$30,000– $39,999	$40,000– $49,999	$50,000– $69,999	$70,000 or more
Household furnishings and equipment	**$2,028**	**$695**	**$555**	**$724**	**$860**	**$1,245**	**$1,704**	**$3,253**
Household textiles	145	48	54	74	59	101	125	223
Furniture	523	200	131	147	188	244	391	893
Floor coverings	51	5	17	6	16	13	38	93
Major appliances	272	180	98	119	124	176	244	409
Small appliances, miscellaneous housewares	140	45	27	28	86	87	153	209
Miscellaneous household equipment	897	220	228	350	387	624	753	1,426
APPAREL AND RELATED SERVICES	**2,182**	**1,319**	**778**	**960**	**1,198**	**1,580**	**1,893**	**3,224**
Men and boys	**525**	**330**	**148**	**257**	**276**	**464**	**444**	**766**
Men, aged 16 or older	434	275	117	176	194	394	363	646
Boys, aged 2 to 15	92	55	31	81	82	70	81	120
Women and girls	**935**	**471**	**351**	**305**	**501**	**626**	**817**	**1,420**
Women, aged 16 or older	802	360	315	252	425	550	720	1,213
Girls, aged 2 to 15	133	111	36	54	76	77	97	207
Children under age 2	**63**	**99**	**38**	**29**	**50**	**50**	**56**	**78**
Footwear	**363**	**318**	**132**	**252**	**232**	**241**	**332**	**497**
Other apparel products and services	**295**	**102**	**108**	**116**	**138**	**199**	**244**	**463**
TRANSPORTATION	**10,283**	**3,091**	**3,384**	**4,526**	**6,778**	**6,452**	**9,444**	**15,466**
5Vehicle purchases	3,599	657	769	948	2,044	1,700	3,527	5,779
Cars and trucks, new	1,863	296	225	346	616	767	1,597	3,269
Cars and trucks, used	1,606	310	536	539	1,312	933	1,891	2,270
Other vehicles	130	93	15	63	116	–	39	240
Gasoline and motor oil	**2,770**	**1,015**	**1,382**	**1,783**	**2,123**	**2,344**	**2,827**	**3,646**
Other vehicle expenses	**3,275**	**1,252**	**1,036**	**1,575**	**2,349**	**2,155**	**2,721**	**4,914**
Vehicle finance charges	335	70	78	116	187	246	373	495
Maintenance and repairs	904	313	417	414	577	644	829	1,318
Vehicle insurance	1,502	717	397	821	1,357	934	1,078	2,239
Vehicle rentals, leases, licenses, other charges	535	152	144	224	228	331	441	861
Public transportation	**639**	**167**	**197**	**220**	**262**	**252**	**370**	**1,127**
HEALTH CARE	**2,774**	**1,035**	**1,268**	**1,736**	**1,808**	**2,381**	**2,680**	**3,801**
Health insurance	1,348	461	541	771	941	1,197	1,363	1,835
Medical services	785	234	383	517	485	630	695	1,113
Drugs	498	204	307	382	305	467	505	639
Medical supplies	143	136	36	66	77	86	117	214
ENTERTAINMENT	**3,093**	**1,048**	**955**	**1,176**	**1,483**	**1,828**	**2,486**	**4,960**
Fees and admissions	806	161	88	177	227	345	474	1,492
Audio and visual equipment and services	1,069	582	552	559	691	850	984	1,487
Pets, toys, and playground equipment	717	265	250	302	422	487	651	1,071
Other entertainment products and services	501	41	66	138	142	147	377	910
PERSONAL CARE PRODUCTS AND SERVICES	**691**	**242**	**210**	**339**	**421**	**505**	**590**	**1,037**
READING	**135**	**42**	**30**	**52**	**57**	**88**	**112**	**218**
EDUCATION	**1,711**	**311**	**252**	**440**	**270**	**630**	**1,006**	**3,220**
TOBACCO PRODUCTS AND SMOKING SUPPLIES	**410**	**416**	**453**	**432**	**430**	**389**	**505**	**363**
MISCELLANEOUS	**990**	**479**	**881**	**464**	**916**	**596**	**796**	**1,351**
CASH CONTRIBUTIONS	**2,044**	**456**	**567**	**821**	**870**	**1,074**	**1,306**	**3,497**
PERSONAL INSURANCE AND PENSIONS	**7,418**	**667**	**998**	**2,041**	**3,106**	**4,060**	**5,825**	**12,757**
Life and other personal insurance	407	72	111	134	163	224	279	698
Pensions and Social Security	7,011	595	886	1,907	2,943	3,836	5,546	12,059
PERSONAL TAXES	**3,423**	**211**	**–57**	**187**	**912**	**990**	**1,957**	**6,721**
Federal income taxes	2,444	82	–161	9	551	561	1,307	4,940
State and local income taxes	741	40	48	119	231	272	454	1,398
Other taxes	239	89	56	58	130	157	195	384
GIFTS FOR PEOPLE IN OTHER HOUSEHOLDS	**1,839**	**714**	**262**	**420**	**697**	**828**	**1,145**	**3,271**

Note: Spending by category does not add to total spending because gift spending is also included in the preceding product and service categories and personal taxes are not included in the total. "–" means sample is too small to make a reliable estimate.
Source: Bureau of Labor Statistics, 2006 and 2007 Consumer Expenditure Surveys, Internet site http://www.bls.gov/cex/; calculations by New Strategist

Table 15. Aged 45 to 54: Indexed spending by income, 2006–07

(indexed average annual spending of consumer units headed by people aged 45 to 54 by product and service category and before-tax income of consumer unit, 2006–07; index definition: an index of 100 is the average for all consumer units; an index of 132 means that spending by consumer units in that group is 32 percent above the average for all consumer units; an index of 68 indicates spending that is 32 percent below the average for all consumer units)

	total consumer units aged 45 to 54	under $10,000	$10,000–$19,999	$20,000–$29,999	$30,000–$39,999	$40,000–$49,999	$50,000–$69,999	$70,000 or more
Average spending of consumer units, total	$58,369	$21,214	$22,839	$28,554	$34,756	$39,502	$49,991	$87,610
Average spending of consumer units, index	100	36	39	49	60	68	86	150
FOOD	100	47	46	57	65	77	90	140
Food at home	100	60	54	68	71	83	95	131
Cereals and bakery products	100	61	57	72	68	81	94	131
Cereals and cereal products	100	59	63	74	77	77	90	130
Bakery products	100	61	54	71	65	83	96	131
Meats, poultry, fish, and eggs	100	65	61	76	72	89	92	127
Beef	100	51	65	82	74	83	94	127
Pork	100	69	63	77	77	90	106	119
Other meats	100	57	54	67	73	95	86	132
Poultry	100	78	62	73	78	86	86	128
Fish and seafood	100	76	50	69	49	99	84	135
Eggs	100	70	88	91	81	86	91	116
Dairy products	100	54	54	66	75	83	96	130
Fresh milk and cream	100	65	69	75	84	85	95	122
Other dairy products	100	48	45	60	70	82	97	135
Fruits and vegetables	100	62	47	68	69	87	92	132
Fresh fruits	100	65	42	67	67	86	89	135
Fresh vegetables	100	56	49	65	64	88	91	135
Processed fruits	100	58	43	73	69	87	97	132
Processed vegetables	100	71	55	71	89	88	96	124
Other food at home	100	56	53	63	71	78	97	132
Sugar and other sweets	100	52	48	60	66	75	107	133
Fats and oils	100	66	63	70	72	89	97	126
Miscellaneous foods	100	54	51	60	70	78	96	134
Nonalcoholic beverages	100	62	60	72	78	82	99	126
Food prepared by consumer unit on trips	100	40	24	33	54	35	79	165
Food away from home	100	31	35	44	58	69	85	152
ALCOHOLIC BEVERAGES	100	23	46	49	50	78	81	151
HOUSING	100	46	50	59	66	74	87	142
Shelter	100	45	51	60	67	74	84	142
Owned dwellings	100	25	26	39	51	67	87	158
Mortgage interest and charges	100	22	25	36	51	68	88	158
Property taxes	100	33	29	37	50	64	83	159
Maintenance, repair, insurance, other expenses	100	25	25	55	50	69	87	155
Rented dwellings	100	138	168	168	151	125	88	57
Other lodging	100	11	12	10	22	27	51	196
Utilities, fuels, and public services	100	58	67	74	77	87	98	125
Natural gas	100	56	52	69	72	83	96	131
Electricity	100	63	76	79	82	88	97	121
Fuel oil and other fuels	100	52	59	71	68	64	96	136
Telephone services	100	55	65	72	77	88	101	125
Water and other public services	100	55	65	68	73	91	98	127
Household services	100	26	33	33	43	47	72	169
Personal services	100	19	23	31	46	24	79	174
Other household services	100	28	36	33	42	53	70	168
Housekeeping supplies	100	46	36	54	85	63	88	142
Laundry and cleaning supplies	100	64	60	65	93	80	100	123
Other household products	100	42	36	53	55	66	86	150
Postage and stationery	100	37	16	49	133	43	82	144

	total consumer units aged 45 to 54	under $10,000	$10,000–$19,999	$20,000–$29,999	$30,000–$39,999	$40,000–$49,999	$50,000–$69,999	$70,000 or more
Household furnishings and equipment	100	34	27	36	42	61	84	160
Household textiles	100	33	37	51	41	70	86	154
Furniture	100	38	25	28	36	47	75	171
Floor coverings	100	11	33	12	31	25	75	182
Major appliances	100	66	36	44	46	65	90	150
Small appliances, miscellaneous housewares	100	32	19	20	61	62	109	149
Miscellaneous household equipment	100	24	25	39	43	70	84	159
APPAREL AND RELATED SERVICES	100	60	36	44	55	72	87	148
Men and boys	100	63	28	49	53	88	85	146
Men, aged 16 or older	100	63	27	41	45	91	84	149
Boys, aged 2 to 15	100	59	34	88	89	76	88	130
Women and girls	100	50	38	33	54	67	87	152
Women, aged 16 or older	100	45	39	31	53	69	90	151
Girls, aged 2 to 15	100	84	27	41	57	58	73	156
Children under age 2	100	157	61	46	79	79	89	124
Footwear	100	88	36	69	64	66	91	137
Other apparel products and services	100	35	37	39	47	67	83	157
TRANSPORTATION	100	30	33	44	66	63	92	150
Vehicle purchases	100	18	21	26	57	47	98	161
Cars and trucks, new	100	16	12	19	33	41	86	175
Cars and trucks, used	100	19	33	34	82	58	118	141
Other vehicles	100	72	12	48	89	–	30	185
Gasoline and motor oil	100	37	50	64	77	85	102	132
Other vehicle expenses	100	38	32	48	72	66	83	150
Vehicle finance charges	100	21	23	35	56	73	111	148
Maintenance and repairs	100	35	46	46	64	71	92	146
Vehicle insurance	100	48	26	55	90	62	72	149
Vehicle rentals, leases, licenses, other charges	100	28	27	42	43	62	82	161
Public transportation	100	26	31	34	41	39	58	176
HEALTH CARE	100	37	46	63	65	86	97	137
Health insurance	100	34	40	57	70	89	101	136
Medical services	100	30	49	66	62	80	89	142
Drugs	100	41	62	77	61	94	101	128
Medical supplies	100	95	25	46	54	60	82	150
ENTERTAINMENT	100	34	31	38	48	59	80	160
Fees and admissions	100	20	11	22	28	43	59	185
Audio and visual equipment and services	100	54	52	52	65	80	92	139
Pets, toys, and playground equipment	100	37	35	42	59	68	91	149
Other entertainment products and services	100	8	13	28	28	29	75	182
PERSONAL CARE PRODUCTS AND SERVICES	100	35	30	49	61	73	85	150
READING	100	31	22	39	42	65	83	161
EDUCATION	100	18	15	26	16	37	59	188
TOBACCO PRODUCTS AND SMOKING SUPPLIES	100	102	110	105	105	95	123	89
MISCELLANEOUS	100	48	89	47	93	60	80	136
CASH CONTRIBUTIONS	100	22	28	40	43	53	64	171
PERSONAL INSURANCE AND PENSIONS	100	9	13	28	42	55	79	172
Life and other personal insurance	100	18	27	33	40	55	69	171
Pensions and Social Security	100	8	13	27	42	55	79	172
PERSONAL TAXES	100	6	–	5	27	29	57	196
Federal income taxes	100	3	–	0	23	23	53	202
State and local income taxes	100	5	6	16	31	37	61	189
Other taxes	100	37	23	24	54	66	82	161
GIFTS FOR PEOPLE IN OTHER HOUSEHOLDS	100	39	14	23	38	45	62	178

Note: "–" means sample is too small to make a reliable estimate or not applicable.
Source: Calculations by New Strategist based on the Bureau of Labor Statistics' 2006 and 2007 Consumer Expenditure Surveys

Table 16. Aged 55 to 64: Average spending by income, 2006–07

(average annual spending of consumer units (CUs) headed by people aged 55 to 64 by product and service category and before-tax income of consumer unit, 2006–07)

	total consumer units aged 55 to 64	under $10,000	$10,000– $19,999	$20,000– $29,999	$30,000– $39,999	$40,000– $49,999	$50,000– $69,999	$70,000 or more
Number of consumer units (in 000s)	19,207	1,485	2,087	2,057	2,015	2,010	3,031	6,521
Average number of persons per CU	2.1	1.4	1.7	1.8	1.9	2.0	2.2	2.5
Average before-tax income of CUs	$67,780	$3,762	$15,013	$24,862	$34,604	$44,896	$59,598	$133,893
Average annual spending of consumer units	52,461	21,399	25,270	31,126	34,637	39,896	49,496	84,697
FOOD	**6,186**	**3,298**	**3,371**	**4,124**	**4,219**	**5,178**	**6,002**	**8,988**
Food at home	**3,488**	**2,334**	**2,343**	**2,717**	**2,526**	**3,014**	**3,528**	**4,589**
Cereals and bakery products	454	313	317	355	345	404	440	594
Cereals and cereal products	132	113	106	108	99	119	125	164
Bakery products	322	200	211	246	245	285	314	430
Meats, poultry, fish, and eggs	779	576	547	642	587	671	792	991
Beef	212	126	150	181	158	188	231	266
Pork	152	141	127	118	128	126	169	177
Other meats	103	63	80	87	69	84	114	131
Poultry	136	124	86	116	112	112	114	181
Fish and seafood	133	91	70	104	87	116	125	185
Eggs	42	33	35	35	33	45	39	50
Dairy products	377	239	254	284	284	326	384	496
Fresh milk and cream	135	101	111	110	110	124	140	162
Other dairy products	242	138	143	174	174	202	244	334
Fruits and vegetables	648	436	400	505	441	558	640	878
Fresh fruits	224	149	134	161	160	175	215	315
Fresh vegetables	213	140	135	161	126	193	224	285
Processed fruits	110	70	65	101	76	101	100	148
Processed vegetables	101	77	66	83	79	89	102	130
Other food at home	1,229	770	825	932	870	1,054	1,273	1,630
Sugar and other sweets	120	71	78	89	84	105	113	166
Fats and oils	97	58	70	86	74	99	94	121
Miscellaneous foods	610	381	399	452	418	503	661	809
Nonalcoholic beverages	342	239	250	277	266	301	342	435
Food prepared by consumer unit on trips	59	21	29	28	28	46	62	100
Food away from home	**2,699**	**964**	**1,028**	**1,407**	**1,693**	**2,164**	**2,474**	**4,399**
ALCOHOLIC BEVERAGES	**505**	**153**	**204**	**273**	**248**	**397**	**528**	**808**
HOUSING	**16,900**	**8,744**	**9,374**	**10,918**	**11,978**	**13,329**	**16,249**	**25,785**
Shelter	**9,485**	**5,230**	**5,106**	**6,296**	**6,701**	**7,114**	**8,820**	**14,761**
Owned dwellings	6,966	2,495	2,715	3,980	4,351	5,054	6,923	11,703
Mortgage interest and charges	3,347	1,160	1,004	1,739	2,106	2,299	3,354	5,805
Property taxes	2,024	861	964	1,149	1,312	1,490	1,895	3,350
Maintenance, repair, insurance, other expenses	1,595	474	748	1,093	933	1,265	1,674	2,548
Rented dwellings	1,500	2,449	2,122	2,056	2,085	1,608	1,173	848
Other lodging	1,019	287	268	259	266	451	724	2,210
Utilities, fuels, and public services	**3,698**	**2,129**	**2,749**	**2,860**	**3,264**	**3,500**	**3,906**	**4,721**
Natural gas	560	289	407	382	496	523	591	742
Electricity	1,383	855	1,094	1,124	1,242	1,303	1,391	1,741
Fuel oil and other fuels	169	118	138	162	138	159	211	185
Telephone services	1,126	648	815	854	1,005	1,075	1,211	1,432
Water and other public services	461	220	295	338	383	439	502	619
Household services	**897**	**313**	**397**	**362**	**389**	**585**	**671**	**1,721**
Personal services	190	14	82	12	38	42	65	470
Other household services	707	299	314	350	351	543	606	1,251
Housekeeping supplies	**821**	**383**	**356**	**481**	**464**	**669**	**745**	**1,288**
Laundry and cleaning supplies	149	85	99	101	89	154	182	188
Other household products	470	196	165	240	257	330	364	807
Postage and stationery	201	101	92	141	118	185	199	293

	total consumer units aged 55 to 64	under $10,000	$10,000– $19,999	$20,000– $29,999	$30,000– $39,999	$40,000– $49,999	$50,000– $69,999	$70,000 or more
Household furnishings and equipment	**$2,000**	**$689**	**$767**	**$919**	**$1,160**	**$1,462**	**$2,107**	**$3,294**
Household textiles	186	34	66	58	107	88	292	288
Furniture	467	160	137	287	187	261	472	836
Floor coverings	64	52	36	23	16	51	21	126
Major appliances	267	127	142	155	139	242	284	412
Small appliances, miscellaneous housewares	102	51	47	44	103	59	128	143
Miscellaneous household equipment	914	264	339	352	608	761	910	1,490
APPAREL AND RELATED SERVICES	**1,898**	**918**	**826**	**960**	**1,194**	**1,255**	**1,826**	**3,058**
Men and boys	**406**	**222**	**101**	**258**	**213**	**256**	**373**	**678**
Men, aged 16 or older	366	178	81	230	191	233	329	620
Boys, aged 2 to 15	40	43	20	27	22	23	44	58
Women and girls	**815**	**358**	**372**	**392**	**520**	**523**	**827**	**1,289**
Women, aged 16 or older	748	319	345	344	479	487	761	1,184
Girls, aged 2 to 15	67	39	27	48	41	36	66	105
Children under age 2	**61**	**21**	**34**	**27**	**41**	**43**	**67**	**94**
Footwear	**320**	**191**	**156**	**158**	**300**	**192**	**297**	**479**
Other apparel products and services	**297**	**126**	**164**	**126**	**119**	**241**	**262**	**518**
TRANSPORTATION	**9,203**	**3,227**	**4,492**	**6,724**	**6,585**	**7,192**	**8,626**	**14,466**
Vehicle purchases	**3,258**	**731**	**1,341**	**2,879**	**2,337**	**1,939**	**2,690**	**5,522**
Cars and trucks, new	1,782	222	879	1,290	910	687	1,311	3,409
Cars and trucks, used	1,428	509	458	1,589	1,406	1,215	1,370	1,997
Other vehicles	47	–	7	–	20	38	9	116
Gasoline and motor oil	**2,397**	**1,092**	**1,440**	**1,754**	**1,935**	**2,160**	**2,598**	**3,327**
Other vehicle expenses	**2,873**	**1,153**	**1,343**	**1,901**	**2,099**	**2,716**	**2,804**	**4,296**
Vehicle finance charges	312	68	122	220	256	298	354	460
Maintenance and repairs	842	357	442	484	607	808	859	1,264
Vehicle insurance	1,134	496	553	937	964	1,201	1,081	1,509
Vehicle rentals, leases, licenses, other charges	584	232	226	259	272	409	512	1,063
Public transportation	**674**	**251**	**368**	**190**	**214**	**377**	**535**	**1,321**
HEALTH CARE	**3,516**	**1,462**	**2,238**	**2,683**	**3,275**	**3,226**	**3,817**	**4,666**
Health insurance	1,714	664	1,099	1,459	1,475	1,658	1,882	2,243
Medical services	930	415	536	551	1,058	769	970	1,286
Drugs	716	324	522	580	662	661	777	906
Medical supplies	156	58	82	93	80	138	188	232
ENTERTAINMENT	**2,771**	**1,087**	**1,406**	**1,363**	**1,635**	**2,294**	**2,492**	**4,589**
Fees and admissions	624	186	209	176	294	332	500	1,235
Audio and visual equipment and services	931	500	599	721	793	882	873	1,283
Pets, toys, and playground equipment	651	225	298	386	447	622	682	956
Other entertainment products and services	566	175	300	81	101	457	437	1,114
PERSONAL CARE PRODUCTS AND SERVICES	**609**	**209**	**313**	**315**	**384**	**455**	**579**	**984**
READING	**149**	**58**	**61**	**76**	**98**	**124**	**136**	**249**
EDUCATION	**797**	**288**	**182**	**127**	**240**	**364**	**514**	**1,755**
TOBACCO PRODUCTS AND SMOKING SUPPLIES	**361**	**340**	**315**	**392**	**469**	**379**	**426**	**302**
MISCELLANEOUS	**1,094**	**410**	**512**	**626**	**542**	**604**	**1,096**	**1,892**
CASH CONTRIBUTIONS	**2,509**	**690**	**1,208**	**861**	**1,253**	**1,511**	**1,848**	**4,864**
PERSONAL INSURANCE AND PENSIONS	**5,963**	**516**	**767**	**1,685**	**2,520**	**3,587**	**5,358**	**12,292**
Life and other personal insurance	460	120	184	288	242	310	417	813
Pensions and Social Security	5,503	396	584	1,397	2,278	3,277	4,941	11,479
PERSONAL TAXES	**3,304**	**363**	**130**	**586**	**787**	**1,050**	**2,375**	**7,751**
Federal income taxes	2,417	191	−61	317	437	626	1,614	5,916
State and local income taxes	603	84	37	116	181	209	445	1,382
Other taxes	284	88	154	153	169	215	316	453
GIFTS FOR PEOPLE IN OTHER HOUSEHOLDS	**1,735**	**574**	**590**	**569**	**844**	**948**	**1,324**	**3,372**

Note: Spending by category does not add to total spending because gift spending is also included in the preceding product and service categories and personal taxes are not included in the total. "−" means sample is too small to make a reliable estimate.
Source: Bureau of Labor Statistics, 2006 and 2007 Consumer Expenditure Surveys, Internet site http://www.bls.gov/cex/; calculations by New Strategist

Table 17. Aged 55 to 64: Indexed spending by income, 2006–07

(indexed average annual spending of consumer units headed by people aged 55 to 64 by product and service category and before-tax income of consumer unit, 2006–07; index definition: an index of 100 is the average for all consumer units; an index of 132 means that spending by consumer units in that group is 32 percent above the average for all consumer units; an index of 68 indicates spending that is 32 percent below the average for all consumer units)

	total consumer units aged 55 to 64	under $10,000	$10,000– $19,999	$20,000– $29,999	$30,000– $39,999	$40,000– $49,999	$50,000– $69,999	$70,000 or more
Average spending of consumer units, total	$52,461	$21,399	$25,270	$31,126	$34,637	$39,896	$49,496	$84,697
Average spending of consumer units, index	100	41	48	59	66	76	94	161
FOOD	100	53	54	67	68	84	97	145
Food at home	100	67	67	78	72	86	101	132
Cereals and bakery products	100	69	70	78	76	89	97	131
Cereals and cereal products	100	86	80	82	75	90	95	124
Bakery products	100	62	65	76	76	89	98	134
Meats, poultry, fish, and eggs	100	74	70	82	75	86	102	127
Beef	100	59	71	85	75	89	109	125
Pork	100	93	84	78	84	83	111	116
Other meats	100	61	77	84	67	82	111	127
Poultry	100	91	63	85	82	82	84	133
Fish and seafood	100	68	53	78	65	87	94	139
Eggs	100	77	84	83	79	107	93	119
Dairy products	100	63	67	75	75	86	102	132
Fresh milk and cream	100	75	82	81	81	92	104	120
Other dairy products	100	57	59	72	72	83	101	138
Fruits and vegetables	100	67	62	78	68	86	99	135
Fresh fruits	100	66	60	72	71	78	96	141
Fresh vegetables	100	66	63	76	59	91	105	134
Processed fruits	100	64	59	92	69	92	91	135
Processed vegetables	100	76	65	82	78	88	101	129
Other food at home	100	63	67	76	71	86	104	133
Sugar and other sweets	100	59	65	74	70	88	94	138
Fats and oils	100	60	72	89	76	102	97	125
Miscellaneous foods	100	62	65	74	69	82	108	133
Nonalcoholic beverages	100	70	73	81	78	88	100	127
Food prepared by consumer unit on trips	100	36	49	47	47	78	105	169
Food away from home	100	36	38	52	63	80	92	163
ALCOHOLIC BEVERAGES	100	30	40	54	49	79	105	160
HOUSING	100	52	55	65	71	79	96	153
Shelter	100	55	54	66	71	75	93	156
Owned dwellings	100	36	39	57	62	73	99	168
Mortgage interest and charges	100	35	30	52	63	69	100	173
Property taxes	100	43	48	57	65	74	94	166
Maintenance, repair, insurance, other expenses	100	30	47	69	58	79	105	160
Rented dwellings	100	163	141	137	139	107	78	57
Other lodging	100	28	26	25	26	44	71	217
Utilities, fuels, and public services	100	58	74	77	88	95	106	128
Natural gas	100	52	73	68	89	93	106	133
Electricity	100	62	79	81	90	94	101	126
Fuel oil and other fuels	100	70	82	96	82	94	125	109
Telephone services	100	58	72	76	89	95	108	127
Water and other public services	100	48	64	73	83	95	109	134
Household services	100	35	44	40	43	65	75	192
Personal services	100	8	43	6	20	22	34	247
Other household services	100	42	44	50	50	77	86	177
Housekeeping supplies	100	47	43	59	57	81	91	157
Laundry and cleaning supplies	100	57	66	68	60	103	122	126
Other household products	100	42	35	51	55	70	77	172
Postage and stationery	100	50	46	70	59	92	99	146

	total consumer units aged 55 to 64	under $10,000	$10,000– $19,999	$20,000– $29,999	$30,000– $39,999	$40,000– $49,999	$50,000– $69,999	$70,000 or more
Household furnishings and equipment	100	34	38	46	58	73	105	165
Household textiles	100	18	35	31	58	47	157	155
Furniture	100	34	29	61	40	56	101	179
Floor coverings	100	82	56	36	25	80	33	197
Major appliances	100	48	53	58	52	91	106	154
Small appliances, miscellaneous housewares	100	50	46	43	101	58	125	140
Miscellaneous household equipment	100	29	37	39	67	83	100	163
APPAREL AND RELATED SERVICES	100	48	44	51	63	66	96	161
Men and boys	100	55	25	64	52	63	92	167
Men, aged 16 or older	100	49	22	63	52	64	90	169
Boys, aged 2 to 15	100	108	50	68	55	58	110	145
Women and girls	100	44	46	48	64	64	101	158
Women, aged 16 or older	100	43	46	46	64	65	102	158
Girls, aged 2 to 15	100	59	40	72	61	54	99	157
Children under age 2	100	35	55	44	67	70	110	154
Footwear	100	60	49	49	94	60	93	150
Other apparel products and services	100	43	55	42	40	81	88	174
TRANSPORTATION	100	35	49	73	72	78	94	157
Vehicle purchases	100	22	41	88	72	60	83	169
Cars and trucks, new	100	12	49	72	51	39	74	191
Cars and trucks, used	100	36	32	111	98	85	96	140
Other vehicles	100	–	15	–	43	81	19	247
Gasoline and motor oil	100	46	60	73	81	90	108	139
Other vehicle expenses	100	40	47	66	73	95	98	150
Vehicle finance charges	100	22	39	71	82	96	113	147
Maintenance and repairs	100	42	52	57	72	96	102	150
Vehicle insurance	100	44	49	83	85	106	95	133
Vehicle rentals, leases, licenses, other charges	100	40	39	44	47	70	88	182
Public transportation	100	37	55	28	32	56	79	196
HEALTH CARE	100	42	64	76	93	92	109	133
Health insurance	100	39	64	85	86	97	110	131
Medical services	100	45	58	59	114	83	104	138
Drugs	100	45	73	81	92	92	109	127
Medical supplies	100	37	52	60	51	88	121	149
ENTERTAINMENT	100	39	51	49	59	83	90	166
Fees and admissions	100	30	33	28	47	53	80	198
Audio and visual equipment and services	100	54	64	77	85	95	94	138
Pets, toys, and playground equipment	100	35	46	59	69	96	105	147
Other entertainment products and services	100	31	53	14	18	81	77	197
PERSONAL CARE PRODUCTS AND SERVICES	100	34	51	52	63	75	95	162
READING	100	39	41	51	66	83	91	167
EDUCATION	100	36	23	16	30	46	64	220
TOBACCO PRODUCTS AND SMOKING SUPPLIES	100	94	87	109	130	105	118	84
MISCELLANEOUS	100	38	47	57	50	55	100	173
CASH CONTRIBUTIONS	100	27	48	34	50	60	74	194
PERSONAL INSURANCE AND PENSIONS	100	9	13	28	42	60	90	206
Life and other personal insurance	100	26	40	63	53	67	91	177
Pensions and Social Security	100	7	11	25	41	60	90	209
PERSONAL TAXES	100	11	4	18	24	32	72	235
Federal income taxes	100	8	–	13	18	26	67	245
State and local income taxes	100	14	6	19	30	35	74	229
Other taxes	100	31	54	54	60	76	111	160
GIFTS FOR PEOPLE IN OTHER HOUSEHOLDS	100	33	34	33	49	55	76	194

Note: "–" means sample is too small to make a reliable estimate or not applicable.
Source: Calculations by New Strategist based on the Bureau of Labor Statistics' 2006 and 2007 Consumer Expenditure Surveys

Table 18. Aged 65 or Older: Average spending by income, 2006–07

(average annual spending of consumer units (CUs) headed by people aged 65 or older by product and service category and before-tax income of consumer unit, 2006–07)

	total consumer units 65 or older	under $10,000	$10,000–$19,999	$20,000–$29,999	$30,000–$39,999	$40,000–$49,999	$50,000–$69,999	$70,000 or more
Number of consumer units (in 000s)	23,204	2,542	6,238	4,467	2,749	1,796	2,311	3,101
Average number of persons per CU	1.7	1.3	1.3	1.7	1.9	2.0	2.1	2.3
Average before-tax income of CUs	$39,153	$6,427	$14,931	$24,672	$34,895	$44,798	$58,693	$121,513
Average annual spending of consumer units	35,994	15,727	20,888	29,323	34,931	41,824	48,717	79,782
FOOD	**4,417**	**2,364**	**2,795**	**3,727**	**4,436**	**4,942**	**5,921**	**8,584**
Food at home	**2,783**	**1,725**	**1,975**	**2,496**	**2,933**	**3,037**	**3,447**	**4,724**
Cereals and bakery products	388	231	277	367	418	432	481	616
Cereals and cereal products	109	67	82	111	110	125	136	157
Bakery products	279	164	194	256	308	306	345	459
Meats, poultry, fish, and eggs	623	407	468	550	594	655	784	1,069
Beef	175	105	129	152	164	180	206	331
Pork	131	81	91	121	127	150	178	214
Other meats	82	64	59	74	69	82	119	134
Poultry	98	68	81	90	96	91	118	157
Fish and seafood	102	63	79	80	99	116	123	186
Eggs	35	26	28	33	39	37	40	47
Dairy products	313	193	220	285	353	350	376	508
Fresh milk and cream	120	91	90	118	131	132	138	167
Other dairy products	193	102	131	167	222	218	238	341
Fruits and vegetables	532	351	367	475	566	585	638	915
Fresh fruits	182	112	123	169	174	212	219	326
Fresh vegetables	168	126	112	138	181	186	206	297
Processed fruits	100	63	74	93	119	106	116	155
Processed vegetables	81	51	57	74	92	82	98	137
Other food at home	928	543	643	819	1,002	1,014	1,167	1,616
Sugar and other sweets	118	69	84	95	138	134	133	214
Fats and oils	81	51	66	74	90	85	95	122
Miscellaneous foods	460	260	312	410	524	491	589	786
Nonalcoholic beverages	235	158	170	221	221	253	299	388
Food prepared by consumer unit on trips	34	6	10	19	29	51	53	105
Food away from home	**1,634**	**639**	**820**	**1,231**	**1,503**	**1,905**	**2,474**	**3,859**
ALCOHOLIC BEVERAGES	**274**	**122**	**109**	**242**	**251**	**271**	**375**	**699**
HOUSING	**12,133**	**7,166**	**8,402**	**10,734**	**11,705**	**13,116**	**15,424**	**22,975**
Shelter	**6,470**	**3,724**	**4,689**	**5,805**	**6,162**	**6,530**	**8,050**	**12,324**
Owned dwellings	4,313	1,656	2,320	3,843	4,390	4,822	5,812	9,694
Mortgage interest and charges	1,312	506	464	824	1,258	1,323	1,873	4,003
Property taxes	1,612	679	952	1,567	1,712	1,885	1,990	3,241
Maintenance, repair, insurance, other expenses	1,389	472	904	1,451	1,420	1,613	1,949	2,450
Rented dwellings	1,634	2,004	2,260	1,752	1,275	1,205	1,327	699
Other lodging	523	64	108	210	497	503	910	1,931
Utilities, fuels, and public services	**3,063**	**2,039**	**2,381**	**2,874**	**3,211**	**3,488**	**3,694**	**4,699**
Natural gas	502	311	425	484	501	575	610	719
Electricity	1,165	853	911	1,098	1,252	1,299	1,351	1,732
Fuel oil and other fuels	192	116	156	176	205	200	188	339
Telephone services	788	509	585	724	820	921	1,029	1,234
Water and other public services	416	251	304	392	433	493	517	676
Household services	**773**	**315**	**413**	**528**	**651**	**966**	**1,053**	**2,012**
Personal services	155	104	72	78	111	243	254	392
Other household services	617	210	342	450	540	723	798	1,620
Housekeeping supplies	**558**	**377**	**329**	**504**	**544**	**634**	**823**	**967**
Laundry and cleaning supplies	114	65	80	100	125	124	149	190
Other household products	293	189	163	271	278	355	453	500
Postage and stationery	151	122	86	134	141	155	220	276

	total consumer units 65 or older	under $10,000	$10,000– $19,999	$20,000– $29,999	$30,000– $39,999	$40,000– $49,999	$50,000– $69,999	$70,000 or more
Household furnishings and equipment	**$1,269**	**$711**	**$591**	**$1,023**	**$1,137**	**$1,497**	**$1,804**	**$2,973**
Household textiles	140	55	66	127	109	211	235	276
Furniture	259	86	141	172	226	339	355	679
Floor coverings	47	6	21	27	107	24	57	115
Major appliances	191	82	87	234	185	211	228	396
Small appliances, miscellaneous housewares	86	27	41	88	83	111	103	184
Miscellaneous household equipment	546	455	234	375	427	601	826	1,323
APPAREL AND RELATED SERVICES	**987**	**451**	**518**	**707**	**797**	**954**	**1,689**	**2,376**
Men and boys	**209**	**71**	**109**	**153**	**133**	**194**	**322**	**586**
Men, aged 16 or older	188	59	100	139	112	173	289	529
Boys, aged 2 to 15	21	12	9	14	21	21	33	57
Women and girls	**454**	**238**	**229**	**334**	**411**	**441**	**860**	**950**
Women, aged 16 or older	423	225	215	315	384	388	813	875
Girls, aged 2 to 15	31	13	14	19	27	52	47	74
Children under age 2	**22**	**22**	**9**	**19**	**15**	**36**	**29**	**44**
Footwear	**147**	**63**	**110**	**119**	**127**	**118**	**222**	**307**
Other apparel products and services	**156**	**56**	**60**	**82**	**111**	**165**	**255**	**490**
TRANSPORTATION	**5,831**	**1,874**	**3,019**	**4,328**	**5,932**	**7,830**	**8,048**	**13,758**
Vehicle purchases	**2,138**	**472**	**1,230**	**1,188**	**2,226**	**2,417**	**2,597**	**6,115**
Cars and trucks, new	1,296	673	832	771	838	1,160	1,449	4,249
Cars and trucks, used	828	267	398	410	1,364	1,256	1,149	1,789
Other vehicles	15	–	–	7	25	–	–	77
Gasoline and motor oil	**1,411**	**622**	**746**	**1,273**	**1,555**	**1,817**	**2,033**	**2,766**
Other vehicle expenses	**1,866**	**708**	**883**	**1,656**	**1,771**	**3,228**	**2,655**	**3,565**
Vehicle finance charges	122	23	38	87	159	161	213	302
Maintenance and repairs	526	154	257	425	618	673	699	1,220
Vehicle insurance	942	458	476	960	770	2,045	1,235	1,310
Vehicle rentals, leases, licenses, other charges	275	72	112	184	224	349	508	732
Public transportation	**417**	**73**	**159**	**212**	**380**	**368**	**763**	**1,312**
HEALTH CARE	**4,482**	**1,824**	**3,010**	**4,599**	**5,256**	**5,445**	**6,156**	**6,936**
Health insurance	2,694	1,187	1,968	2,799	3,283	3,311	3,375	3,850
Medical services	754	208	359	750	703	737	1,282	1,664
Drugs	873	390	607	899	1,071	1,132	1,273	1,120
Medical supplies	162	40	76	150	200	265	226	301
ENTERTAINMENT	**1,821**	**606**	**864**	**1,352**	**2,004**	**1,707**	**2,714**	**4,589**
Fees and admissions	428	31	116	228	408	398	737	1,454
Audio and visual equipment and services	679	366	475	631	707	769	911	1,162
Pets, toys, and playground equipment	354	144	195	311	415	380	554	658
Other entertainment products and services	360	64	80	182	475	160	513	1,316
PERSONAL CARE PRODUCTS AND SERVICES	**502**	**194**	**276**	**440**	**531**	**571**	**719**	**1,041**
READING	**140**	**47**	**87**	**119**	**135**	**180**	**213**	**279**
EDUCATION	**256**	**45**	**63**	**118**	**160**	**270**	**305**	**1,047**
TOBACCO PRODUCTS AND SMOKING SUPPLIES	**174**	**119**	**146**	**159**	**251**	**200**	**202**	**190**
MISCELLANEOUS	**716**	**285**	**349**	**650**	**631**	**851**	**865**	**1,782**
CASH CONTRIBUTIONS	**2,429**	**433**	**999**	**1,299**	**1,807**	**3,744**	**3,408**	**7,631**
PERSONAL INSURANCE AND PENSIONS	**1,832**	**195**	**251**	**848**	**1,034**	**1,744**	**2,679**	**7,896**
Life and other personal insurance	314	113	154	342	303	325	384	713
Pensions and Social Security	1,517	82	96	506	731	1,420	2,295	7,184
PERSONAL TAXES	**1,177**	**60**	**131**	**317**	**777**	**852**	**1,239**	**5,934**
Federal income taxes	782	14	29	136	456	442	720	4,392
State and local income taxes	150	–10	5	29	59	97	209	811
Other taxes	245	56	98	152	263	313	310	731
GIFTS FOR PEOPLE IN OTHER HOUSEHOLDS	**1,070**	**420**	**507**	**607**	**508**	**807**	**2,159**	**3,243**

Note: Spending by category does not add to total spending because gift spending is also included in the preceding product and service categories and personal taxes are not included in the total. "–" means sample is too small to make a reliable estimate.
Source: Bureau of Labor Statistics, 2006 and 2007 Consumer Expenditure Surveys, Internet site http://www.bls.gov/cex/; calculations by New Strategist

Table 19. Aged 65 or Older: Indexed spending by income, 2006–07

(indexed average annual spending of consumer units headed by people aged 65 or older by product and service category and before-tax income of consumer unit, 2006–07; index definition: an index of 100 is the average for all consumer units; an index of 132 means that spending by consumer units in that group is 32 percent above the average for all consumer units; an index of 68 indicates spending that is 32 percent below the average for all consumer units)

	total consumer units 65 or older	under $10,000	$10,000–$19,999	$20,000–$29,999	$30,000–$39,999	$40,000–$49,999	$50,000–$69,999	$70,000 or more
Average spending of consumer units, total	$35,994	$15,727	$20,888	$29,323	$34,931	$41,824	$48,717	$79,782
Average spending of consumer units, index	100	44	58	81	97	116	135	222
FOOD	100	54	63	84	100	112	134	194
Food at home	100	62	71	90	105	109	124	170
Cereals and bakery products	100	59	71	95	108	111	124	159
Cereals and cereal products	100	61	75	102	101	115	125	144
Bakery products	100	59	70	92	110	110	124	165
Meats, poultry, fish, and eggs	100	65	75	88	95	105	126	172
Beef	100	60	74	87	94	103	118	189
Pork	100	62	69	92	97	115	136	163
Other meats	100	78	71	90	84	100	145	163
Poultry	100	69	83	92	98	93	120	160
Fish and seafood	100	62	78	78	97	114	121	182
Eggs	100	75	80	94	111	106	114	134
Dairy products	100	62	70	91	113	112	120	162
Fresh milk and cream	100	76	75	98	109	110	115	139
Other dairy products	100	53	68	87	115	113	123	177
Fruits and vegetables	100	66	69	89	106	110	120	172
Fresh fruits	100	61	68	93	96	116	120	179
Fresh vegetables	100	75	67	82	108	111	123	177
Processed fruits	100	63	74	93	119	106	116	155
Processed vegetables	100	63	71	91	114	101	121	169
Other food at home	100	59	69	88	108	109	126	174
Sugar and other sweets	100	59	72	81	117	114	113	181
Fats and oils	100	63	81	91	111	105	117	151
Miscellaneous foods	100	57	68	89	114	107	128	171
Nonalcoholic beverages	100	67	72	94	94	108	127	165
Food prepared by consumer unit on trips	100	16	30	56	85	150	156	309
Food away from home	100	39	50	75	92	117	151	236
ALCOHOLIC BEVERAGES	100	44	40	88	92	99	137	255
HOUSING	100	59	69	88	96	108	127	189
Shelter	100	58	72	90	95	101	124	190
Owned dwellings	100	38	54	89	102	112	135	225
Mortgage interest and charges	100	39	35	63	96	101	143	305
Property taxes	100	42	59	97	106	117	123	201
Maintenance, repair, insurance, other expenses	100	34	65	104	102	116	140	176
Rented dwellings	100	123	138	107	78	74	81	43
Other lodging	100	12	21	40	95	96	174	369
Utilities, fuels, and public services	100	67	78	94	105	114	121	153
Natural gas	100	62	85	96	100	115	122	143
Electricity	100	73	78	94	107	112	116	149
Fuel oil and other fuels	100	61	81	92	107	104	98	177
Telephone services	100	65	74	92	104	117	131	157
Water and other public services	100	60	73	94	104	119	124	163
Household services	100	41	53	68	84	125	136	260
Personal services	100	67	46	50	72	157	164	253
Other household services	100	34	55	73	88	117	129	263
Housekeeping supplies	100	68	59	90	97	114	147	173
Laundry and cleaning supplies	100	57	71	88	110	109	131	167
Other household products	100	65	56	92	95	121	155	171
Postage and stationery	100	81	57	89	93	103	146	183

	total consumer units 65 or older	under $10,000	$10,000–$19,999	$20,000–$29,999	$30,000–$39,999	$40,000–$49,999	$50,000–$69,999	$70,000 or more
Household furnishings and equipment	100	56	47	81	90	118	142	234
Household textiles	100	39	47	91	78	151	168	197
Furniture	100	33	55	66	87	131	137	262
Floor coverings	100	12	46	57	228	51	121	245
Major appliances	100	43	46	123	97	110	119	207
Small appliances, miscellaneous housewares	100	32	48	102	97	129	120	214
Miscellaneous household equipment	100	83	43	69	78	110	151	242
APPAREL AND RELATED SERVICES	100	46	52	72	81	97	171	241
Men and boys	100	34	52	73	64	93	154	280
Men, aged 16 or older	100	31	53	74	60	92	154	281
Boys, aged 2 to 15	100	58	44	67	100	100	157	271
Women and girls	100	52	50	74	91	97	189	209
Women, aged 16 or older	100	53	51	74	91	92	192	207
Girls, aged 2 to 15	100	42	46	61	87	168	152	239
Children under age 2	100	102	42	86	68	164	132	200
Footwear	100	43	75	81	86	80	151	209
Other apparel products and services	100	36	39	53	71	106	163	314
TRANSPORTATION	100	32	52	74	102	134	138	236
Vehicle purchases	100	22	58	56	104	113	121	286
Cars and trucks, new	100	52	64	59	65	90	112	328
Cars and trucks, used	100	32	48	50	165	152	139	216
Other vehicles	100	–	–	47	167	–	–	513
Gasoline and motor oil	100	44	53	90	110	129	144	196
Other vehicle expenses	100	38	47	89	95	173	142	191
Vehicle finance charges	100	19	31	71	130	132	175	248
Maintenance and repairs	100	29	49	81	117	128	133	232
Vehicle insurance	100	49	51	102	82	217	131	139
Vehicle rentals, leases, licenses, other charges	100	26	41	67	81	127	185	266
Public transportation	100	18	38	51	91	88	183	315
HEALTH CARE	100	41	67	103	117	121	137	155
Health insurance	100	44	73	104	122	123	125	143
Medical services	100	28	48	99	93	98	170	221
Drugs	100	45	70	103	123	130	146	128
Medical supplies	100	25	47	93	123	164	140	186
ENTERTAINMENT	100	33	47	74	110	94	149	252
Fees and admissions	100	7	27	53	95	93	172	340
Audio and visual equipment and services	100	54	70	93	104	113	134	171
Pets, toys, and playground equipment	100	41	55	88	117	107	156	186
Other entertainment products and services	100	18	22	51	132	44	143	366
PERSONAL CARE PRODUCTS AND SERVICES	100	39	55	88	106	114	143	207
READING	100	33	62	85	96	129	152	199
EDUCATION	100	18	25	46	63	105	119	409
TOBACCO PRODUCTS AND SMOKING SUPPLIES	100	68	84	91	144	115	116	109
MISCELLANEOUS	100	40	49	91	88	119	121	249
CASH CONTRIBUTIONS	100	18	41	53	74	154	140	314
PERSONAL INSURANCE AND PENSIONS	100	11	14	46	56	95	146	431
Life and other personal insurance	100	36	49	109	96	104	122	227
Pensions and Social Security	100	5	6	33	48	94	151	474
PERSONAL TAXES	100	5	11	27	66	72	105	504
Federal income taxes	100	2	4	17	58	57	92	562
State and local income taxes	100	–	4	19	39	65	139	541
Other taxes	100	23	40	62	107	128	127	298
GIFTS FOR PEOPLE IN OTHER HOUSEHOLDS	100	39	47	57	47	75	202	303

Note: "–" means sample is too small to make a reliable estimate or not applicable.
Source: Calculations by New Strategist based on the Bureau of Labor Statistics' 2006 and 2007 Consumer Expenditure Surveys

Spending by Household Type, 2007

Married couples spent 29 percent more than the average household in 2007. Among married couples, those with school-aged or older children at home spend the most, an average of more than $70,000 in 2007. Behind the higher spending levels of married couples are their higher incomes, due primarily to the greater number of earners in the household. Married couples with children at home average 2.0 earners per household. Those with adult children at home average 2.5 earners. The more earners, the greater the spending—particularly on products and services needed by workers such as food away from home, men's and women's clothes, and transportation.

Married couples with children under age 18 have distinct spending patterns. Couples with school-aged children spend 43 percent more than the average household overall. They spend 65 percent more than the average household on milk and 69 percent more on cereal. They spend over twice the average on fees and admissions to entertainment events and 30 percent more than average on children's clothes. The biggest spenders on household personal services (mostly day care) are married couples with preschoolers, while couples without children at home (mostly empty-nesters) spend more than other household types on health care.

Single parents spend less than the average household on most items. Some of the exceptions are rent, children's clothes, and household personal services (mostly day care).

Table 20. Average spending by household type, 2007

(average annual spending of consumer units (CUs) by product and service category and type of consumer unit, 2007)

	total married couples	married couples, no children	married couples with children				single parent, at least one child <18	single person
			total	oldest child under 6	oldest child 6 to 17	oldest child 18 or older		
Number of consumer units (in 000s)	60,747	25,923	29,984	5,865	15,265	8,854	7,139	35,740
Average number of persons per CU	3.2	2.0	3.9	3.5	4.2	3.9	2.9	1.0
Average before-tax income of CUs	$85,803	$78,434	$92,655	$83,372	$92,569	$98,952	$35,490	$31,962
Average annual spending of consumer units	64,104	58,637	69,101	62,403	70,766	70,822	38,239	29,285
FOOD	**7,900**	**6,690**	**8,876**	**7,137**	**9,151**	**9,623**	**5,614**	**3,328**
Food at home	**4,460**	**3,617**	**5,080**	**4,243**	**5,115**	**5,626**	**3,295**	**1,814**
Cereals and bakery products	596	472	693	516	730	750	456	238
Cereals and cereal products	183	134	221	163	242	221	149	72
Bakery products	414	337	472	353	488	529	307	166
Meats, poultry, fish, and eggs	986	790	1,113	784	1,122	1,337	793	390
Beef	277	214	319	254	325	353	191	104
Pork	190	162	208	151	209	249	168	69
Other meats	131	101	154	103	153	193	113	54
Poultry	182	134	213	138	213	269	146	70
Fish and seafood	152	135	159	93	159	207	132	67
Eggs	53	44	60	45	63	66	42	24
Dairy products	511	424	581	514	605	582	356	201
Fresh milk and cream	199	150	239	229	254	216	153	80
Other dairy products	312	274	342	285	351	366	203	121
Fruits and vegetables	780	676	848	735	856	914	492	322
Fresh fruits	265	233	287	264	290	297	148	111
Fresh vegetables	253	224	269	222	271	299	131	100
Processed fruits	142	118	159	141	157	177	110	62
Processed vegetables	120	101	133	107	138	142	104	49
Other food at home	1,586	1,255	1,845	1,694	1,802	2,043	1,198	662
Sugar and other sweets	160	135	181	121	192	201	115	66
Fats and oils	120	106	128	92	127	155	82	47
Miscellaneous foods	827	618	995	1,069	945	1,041	663	346
Nonalcoholic beverages	418	329	480	367	465	595	317	180
Food prepared by consumer unit on trips	62	67	61	45	73	51	21	23
Food away from home	**3,440**	**3,073**	**3,796**	**2,894**	**4,036**	**3,997**	**2,319**	**1,514**
ALCOHOLIC BEVERAGES	**506**	**559**	**470**	**513**	**405**	**566**	**212**	**428**
HOUSING	**20,922**	**18,420**	**23,078**	**24,354**	**24,032**	**20,596**	**14,354**	**11,269**
Shelter	**12,036**	**10,358**	**13,458**	**13,815**	**14,343**	**11,696**	**8,512**	**7,212**
Owned dwellings	9,350	7,707	10,819	10,757	11,627	9,466	3,931	3,628
Mortgage interest and charges	5,491	3,757	6,961	7,568	7,621	5,422	2,584	1,818
Property taxes	2,348	2,273	2,470	2,037	2,619	2,500	902	1,030
Maintenance, repair, insurance, other expenses	1,511	1,677	1,387	1,152	1,387	1,544	445	780
Rented dwellings	1,657	1,370	1,774	2,637	1,779	1,195	4,323	3,228
Other lodging	1,029	1,280	865	421	937	1,035	258	356
Utilities, fuels, and public services	**4,233**	**3,785**	**4,518**	**3,828**	**4,567**	**4,891**	**3,214**	**2,206**
Natural gas	588	537	631	526	632	697	369	325
Electricity	1,597	1,431	1,688	1,431	1,722	1,800	1,265	804
Fuel oil and other fuels	184	190	177	169	188	165	80	107
Telephone services	1,318	1,126	1,449	1,204	1,442	1,622	1,121	706
Water and other public services	546	500	573	497	583	606	380	264
Household services	**1,351**	**879**	**1,786**	**3,431**	**1,644**	**943**	**1,056**	**486**
Personal services	614	89	1,074	2,811	886	249	662	92
Other household services	737	790	712	620	758	694	395	394
Housekeeping supplies	**869**	**963**	**789**	**750**	**767**	**861**	**500**	**316**
Laundry and cleaning supplies	177	149	191	154	197	207	174	69
Other household products	501	601	418	449	379	472	237	156
Postage and stationery	192	213	180	147	191	181	90	91

	total married couples	married couples, no children	married couples with children				single parent, at least one child <18	single person
			total	oldest child under 6	oldest child 6 to 17	oldest child 18 or older		
Household furnishings and equipment	**$2,433**	**$2,436**	**$2,527**	**$2,531**	**$2,711**	**$2,206**	**$1,071**	**$1,049**
Household textiles	178	170	186	238	181	160	77	88
Furniture	622	619	657	657	763	477	359	228
Floor coverings	65	56	75	87	88	44	26	24
Major appliances	319	345	300	296	299	305	153	112
Small appliances and miscellaneous housewares	128	127	132	141	121	148	62	72
Miscellaneous household equipment	1,121	1,119	1,177	1,112	1,259	1,072	394	525
APPAREL AND RELATED SERVICES	**2,369**	**1,956**	**2,723**	**2,400**	**2,766**	**2,876**	**2,077**	**971**
Men and boys	**542**	**408**	**644**	**470**	**663**	**743**	**361**	**267**
Men, aged 16 or older	424	385	451	348	379	667	149	253
Boys, aged 2 to 15	118	23	193	122	284	76	212	14
Women and girls	**944**	**842**	**1,045**	**696**	**1,169**	**1,062**	**977**	**352**
Women, aged 16 or older	776	798	756	531	736	959	679	334
Girls, aged 2 to 15	168	44	289	165	433	104	299	18
Children under age 2	**130**	**54**	**189**	**545**	**121**	**66**	**118**	**20**
Footwear	**414**	**321**	**494**	**380**	**524**	**519**	**435**	**158**
Other apparel products and services	**339**	**332**	**350**	**309**	**289**	**485**	**186**	**175**
TRANSPORTATION	**11,600**	**10,347**	**12,609**	**10,876**	**12,688**	**13,651**	**6,359**	**4,539**
Vehicle purchases	**4,435**	**3,828**	**4,919**	**4,529**	**4,912**	**5,190**	**2,139**	**1,478**
Cars and trucks, new	2,255	2,352	2,185	1,935	2,218	2,293	635	743
Cars and trucks, used	2,022	1,307	2,575	2,565	2,475	2,753	1,498	683
Other vehicles	158	169	159	29	218	144	5	53
Gasoline and motor oil	**3,109**	**2,649**	**3,421**	**2,717**	**3,474**	**3,797**	**1,771**	**1,276**
Other vehicle expenses	**3,332**	**2,994**	**3,639**	**3,112**	**3,605**	**4,076**	**2,085**	**1,461**
Vehicle finance charges	424	349	476	476	478	472	217	122
Maintenance and repairs	939	875	1,010	760	998	1,202	504	471
Vehicle insurance	1,311	1,214	1,391	1,075	1,393	1,620	1,069	621
Vehicle rentals, leases, licenses, other charges	658	556	762	801	736	782	295	247
Public transportation	**725**	**875**	**630**	**517**	**697**	**588**	**364**	**324**
HEALTH CARE	**3,870**	**4,542**	**3,328**	**2,826**	**3,286**	**3,737**	**1,282**	**1,790**
Health insurance	2,074	2,459	1,765	1,480	1,742	1,993	640	994
Medical services	992	1,065	940	919	957	925	383	403
Drugs	639	829	472	340	434	628	202	325
Medical supplies	165	189	151	88	153	190	57	69
ENTERTAINMENT	**3,578**	**3,324**	**3,915**	**3,102**	**4,366**	**3,682**	**2,062**	**1,413**
Fees and admissions	958	857	1,100	704	1,386	863	468	323
Audio and visual equipment and services	1,207	1,072	1,334	1,118	1,398	1,376	831	642
Pets, toys, and playground equipment	731	713	756	703	767	775	487	291
Other entertainment products and services	681	683	725	576	816	669	275	157
PERSONAL CARE PRODUCTS AND SERVICES	**741**	**716**	**768**	**637**	**758**	**881**	**522**	**364**
READING	**147**	**166**	**137**	**105**	**143**	**149**	**61**	**97**
EDUCATION	**1,250**	**860**	**1,643**	**431**	**1,560**	**2,587**	**768**	**621**
TOBACCO PRODUCTS AND SMOKING SUPPLIES	**324**	**293**	**316**	**257**	**321**	**346**	**256**	**223**
MISCELLANEOUS	**979**	**1,069**	**892**	**749**	**883**	**1,011**	**746**	**533**
CASH CONTRIBUTIONS	**2,466**	**3,232**	**1,937**	**1,407**	**1,991**	**2,194**	**729**	**1,219**
PERSONAL INSURANCE AND PENSIONS	**7,452**	**6,462**	**8,408**	**7,607**	**8,416**	**8,923**	**3,197**	**2,491**
Life and other personal insurance	465	441	489	306	504	585	145	146
Pensions and Social Security	6,988	6,021	7,918	7,301	7,912	8,339	3,052	2,345
PERSONAL TAXES	**3,079**	**3,629**	**2,826**	**2,665**	**2,730**	**3,100**	**445**	**1,423**
Federal income taxes	2,161	2,656	1,906	1,806	1,812	2,135	143	1,033
State and local income taxes	642	676	658	667	654	657	179	269
Other taxes	276	297	263	193	264	307	122	121
GIFTS FOR PEOPLE IN OTHER HOUSEHOLDS	**1,587**	**2,261**	**1,103**	**618**	**1,104**	**1,426**	**695**	**837**

Note: Spending by category does not add to total spending because gift spending is also included in the preceding product and service categories and personal taxes are not included in the total.

Source: Bureau of Labor Statistics, 2007 Consumer Expenditure Survey, Internet site http://www.bls.gov/cex/; calculations by New Strategist

Table 21. Indexed spending by household type, 2007

(indexed average annual spending of consumer units by product and service category and type of consumer unit, 2007; index definition: an index of 100 is the average for all consumer units; an index of 132 means that spending by consumer units in that group is 32 percent above the average for all consumer units; an index of 68 indicates spending that is 32 percent below the average for all consumer units)

| | total married couples | married couples, no children | married couples with children | | | | single parent, at least one child <18 | single person |
			total	oldest child under 6	oldest child 6 to 17	oldest child 18 or older		
Average spending of consumer units, total	$64,104	$58,637	$69,101	$62,403	$70,766	$70,822	$38,239	$29,285
Average spending of consumer units, index	129	118	139	126	143	143	77	59
FOOD	**129**	**109**	**145**	**116**	**149**	**157**	**92**	**54**
Food at home	**129**	**104**	**147**	**122**	**148**	**162**	**95**	**52**
Cereals and bakery products	130	103	151	112	159	163	99	52
Cereals and cereal products	128	94	155	114	169	155	104	50
Bakery products	131	106	149	111	154	167	97	52
Meats, poultry, fish, and eggs	127	102	143	101	144	172	102	50
Beef	128	99	148	118	150	163	88	48
Pork	127	108	139	101	139	166	112	46
Other meats	126	97	148	99	147	186	109	52
Poultry	128	94	150	97	150	189	103	49
Fish and seafood	125	111	130	76	130	170	108	55
Eggs	123	102	140	105	147	153	98	56
Dairy products	132	110	150	133	156	150	92	52
Fresh milk and cream	129	97	155	149	165	140	99	52
Other dairy products	133	117	146	122	150	156	87	52
Fruits and vegetables	130	113	141	123	143	152	82	54
Fresh fruits	131	115	142	131	144	147	73	55
Fresh vegetables	133	118	142	117	143	157	69	53
Processed fruits	127	105	142	126	140	158	98	55
Processed vegetables	125	105	139	111	144	148	108	51
Other food at home	128	101	149	137	145	165	97	53
Sugar and other sweets	129	109	146	98	155	162	93	53
Fats and oils	132	116	141	101	140	170	90	52
Miscellaneous foods	127	95	153	164	145	160	102	53
Nonalcoholic beverages	126	99	144	110	140	179	95	54
Food prepared by consumer unit on trips	144	156	142	105	170	119	49	53
Food away from home	**129**	**115**	**142**	**108**	**151**	**150**	**87**	**57**
ALCOHOLIC BEVERAGES	**111**	**122**	**103**	**112**	**89**	**124**	**46**	**94**
HOUSING	**124**	**109**	**136**	**144**	**142**	**122**	**85**	**67**
Shelter	**120**	**103**	**134**	**138**	**143**	**117**	**85**	**72**
Owned dwellings	139	115	161	160	173	141	58	54
Mortgage interest and charges	141	97	179	195	196	139	66	47
Property taxes	137	133	145	119	153	146	53	60
Maintenance, repair, insurance, other expenses	134	148	123	102	123	137	39	69
Rented dwellings	64	53	68	101	68	46	166	124
Other lodging	149	185	125	61	136	150	37	52
Utilities, fuels, and public services	**122**	**109**	**130**	**110**	**131**	**141**	**92**	**63**
Natural gas	123	112	131	110	132	145	77	68
Electricity	123	110	130	110	132	138	97	62
Fuel oil and other fuels	122	126	117	112	125	109	53	71
Telephone services	119	101	131	108	130	146	101	64
Water and other public services	126	115	132	115	134	140	88	61
Household services	**137**	**89**	**182**	**349**	**167**	**96**	**107**	**49**
Personal services	148	21	259	677	213	60	160	22
Other household services	130	139	125	109	133	122	69	69
Housekeeping supplies	**136**	**151**	**123**	**117**	**120**	**135**	**78**	**49**
Laundry and cleaning supplies	126	106	136	110	141	148	124	49
Other household products	144	173	120	129	109	136	68	45
Postage and stationery	126	140	118	97	126	119	59	60

	total married couples	married couples, no children	married couples with children				single parent, at least one child <18	single person
			total	oldest child under 6	oldest child 6 to 17	oldest child 18 or older		
Household furnishings and equipment	**135**	**136**	**141**	**141**	**151**	**123**	**60**	**58**
Household textiles	134	128	140	179	136	120	58	66
Furniture	139	139	147	147	171	107	80	51
Floor coverings	141	122	163	189	191	96	57	52
Major appliances	138	149	130	128	129	132	66	48
Small appliances and miscellaneous housewares	127	126	131	140	120	147	61	71
Miscellaneous household equipment	133	133	140	132	150	128	47	63
APPAREL AND RELATED SERVICES	**126**	**104**	**145**	**128**	**147**	**153**	**110**	**52**
Men and boys	**125**	**94**	**148**	**108**	**152**	**171**	**83**	**61**
Men, aged 16 or older	121	110	128	99	108	190	42	72
Boys, aged 2 to 15	140	27	230	145	338	90	252	17
Women and girls	**126**	**112**	**140**	**93**	**156**	**142**	**130**	**47**
Women, aged 16 or older	124	127	121	85	117	153	108	53
Girls, aged 2 to 15	138	36	237	135	355	85	245	15
Children under age 2	**140**	**58**	**203**	**586**	**130**	**71**	**127**	**22**
Footwear	**127**	**98**	**151**	**116**	**160**	**159**	**133**	**48**
Other apparel products and services	**123**	**120**	**127**	**112**	**105**	**176**	**67**	**63**
TRANSPORTATION	**132**	**118**	**144**	**124**	**145**	**156**	**73**	**52**
Vehicle purchases	**137**	**118**	**152**	**140**	**151**	**160**	**66**	**46**
Cars and trucks, new	143	150	139	123	141	160	40	47
Cars and trucks, used	129	83	164	164	158	146	96	47
Other vehicles	150	161	151	28	208	137	5	50
Gasoline and motor oil	**130**	**111**	**143**	**114**	**146**	**159**	**74**	**54**
Other vehicle expenses	**129**	**116**	**140**	**120**	**139**	**157**	**80**	**56**
Vehicle finance charges	139	114	156	156	157	155	71	40
Maintenance and repairs	127	119	137	103	135	163	68	64
Vehicle insurance	122	113	130	100	130	151	100	58
Vehicle rentals, leases, licenses, other charges	138	116	159	168	154	164	62	52
Public transportation	**135**	**163**	**117**	**96**	**130**	**109**	**68**	**60**
HEALTH CARE	**136**	**159**	**117**	**99**	**115**	**131**	**45**	**63**
Health insurance	134	159	114	96	113	129	41	64
Medical services	140	150	133	130	135	130	54	57
Drugs	133	172	98	71	90	131	42	68
Medical supplies	140	160	128	75	130	161	48	58
ENTERTAINMENT	**133**	**123**	**145**	**115**	**162**	**136**	**76**	**52**
Fees and admissions	146	130	167	107	211	131	71	49
Audio and visual equipment and services	122	109	135	113	142	139	84	65
Pets, toys, and playground equipment	131	127	135	126	137	138	87	52
Other entertainment products and services	138	139	147	117	166	136	56	32
PERSONAL CARE PRODUCTS AND SERVICES	**126**	**122**	**131**	**108**	**129**	**150**	**89**	**62**
READING	**125**	**141**	**116**	**89**	**121**	**126**	**52**	**82**
EDUCATION	**132**	**91**	**174**	**46**	**165**	**274**	**81**	**66**
TOBACCO PRODUCTS AND SMOKING SUPPLIES	**100**	**91**	**98**	**80**	**99**	**107**	**79**	**69**
MISCELLANEOUS	**121**	**132**	**110**	**93**	**109**	**125**	**92**	**66**
CASH CONTRIBUTIONS	**135**	**177**	**106**	**77**	**109**	**120**	**40**	**67**
PERSONAL INSURANCE AND PENSIONS	**140**	**121**	**158**	**143**	**158**	**167**	**60**	**47**
Life and other personal insurance	150	143	158	99	163	189	47	47
Pensions and Social Security	139	120	158	145	157	166	61	47
PERSONAL TAXES	**138**	**163**	**127**	**119**	**122**	**139**	**20**	**64**
Federal income taxes	138	169	121	115	115	136	9	66
State and local income taxes	137	144	141	143	140	140	38	57
Other taxes	141	152	134	98	135	157	62	62
GIFTS FOR PEOPLE IN OTHER HOUSEHOLDS	**132**	**189**	**92**	**52**	**92**	**119**	**58**	**70**

Note: Spending index for total consumer units is 100.
Source: Calculations by New Strategist based on the Bureau of Labor Statistics' 2007 Consumer Expenditure Survey

Spending by Single Person Consumer Units by Age, 2006–07

The 19 million women who live alone spent an annual average of $28,060 in 2006–07, only 57 percent of the $49,279 spent by the average household during that time period. Forty-one percent of women who live alone are aged 65 or older, many of them elderly widows with low incomes.

Among women who live alone, average annual spending peaked in the 35-to-44 age group at $38,086 in 2006–07. Women under age 25 spend much more than the average household on education, with an index of 268. Women aged 25 to 44 who live alone spend two-thirds more than the average household on women's clothes. Among women who live alone, those aged 65 or older spend less than their middle-aged counterparts, an average of $22,995 in 2006–07. But they spend more than the average household on out-of-pocket health care costs, especially on drugs.

Men who live alone spent an annual average of $31,139 in 2006–07, only 63 percent of what the average household spent during the time period. Among men who live alone, those under age 25 spend well more than twice the average on education, with an index of 230. Men aged 25 to 34 who live alone spend twice the average on rent and well more than twice the average on alcoholic beverages.

Men aged 65 or older who live alone spend less than their middle-aged counterparts, an average of $27,810 in 2006–07. They spend only 52 percent of what the average household spends on food away from home, and 46 percent of the average on entertainment.

Table 22. Average spending of single-person consumer units headed by women, by age, 2006–07

(average annual spending of single-person consumer units headed by women by product and service category and age, 2006–07)

	total single-person consumer units headed by women	under 25	25 to 34	35 to 44	45 to 54	55 to 64	65 or older
Number of consumer units (in 000s)	19,340	1,815	1,945	1,552	2,680	3,448	7,899
Average before-tax income of consumer units	$27,994	$13,040	$36,572	$41,801	$37,473	$34,113	$20,718
Average annual spending of consumer units	28,060	19,014	33,553	38,086	33,347	32,798	22,955
FOOD	**3,051**	**2,479**	**3,547**	**4,158**	**3,674**	**3,498**	**2,427**
Food at home	**1,844**	**996**	**1,708**	**2,108**	**2,187**	**2,161**	**1,737**
Cereals and bakery products	246	150	198	237	289	280	248
Cereals and cereal products	71	57	65	78	75	80	68
Bakery products	175	93	132	158	214	200	180
Meats, poultry, fish, and eggs	376	167	302	457	478	438	354
Beef	105	41	72	133	139	110	105
Pork	72	34	37	84	94	90	68
Other meats	50	21	44	48	60	62	49
Poultry	66	34	79	79	79	75	58
Fish and seafood	61	28	50	91	82	76	51
Eggs	22	9	18	23	24	25	23
Dairy products	205	124	174	210	235	242	200
Fresh milk and cream	75	47	62	66	96	82	76
Other dairy products	129	77	112	144	139	160	124
Fruits and vegetables	349	160	317	380	385	421	346
Fresh fruits	122	48	110	133	137	145	122
Fresh vegetables	114	53	99	126	126	144	111
Processed fruits	63	33	64	67	59	74	65
Processed vegetables	50	27	44	54	63	57	48
Other food at home	668	395	717	824	801	780	589
Sugar and other sweets	80	62	51	76	106	75	83
Fats and oils	48	22	50	48	51	61	47
Miscellaneous foods	342	202	420	430	403	382	300
Nonalcoholic beverages	175	95	165	231	210	228	146
Food prepared by consumer unit on trips	23	14	31	39	30	34	13
Food away from home	**1,207**	**1,483**	**1,839**	**2,050**	**1,487**	**1,337**	**690**
ALCOHOLIC BEVERAGES	**241**	**327**	**545**	**446**	**280**	**230**	**112**
HOUSING	**11,353**	**6,443**	**13,668**	**15,222**	**12,997**	**12,880**	**9,918**
Shelter	**7,102**	**4,541**	**9,685**	**10,504**	**8,234**	**7,665**	**5,756**
Owned dwellings	3,800	324	3,726	5,787	4,896	5,245	3,224
Mortgage interest and charges	1,792	161	2,665	3,702	3,079	2,461	848
Property taxes	1,107	113	693	1,187	1,183	1,440	1,251
Maintenance, repair, insurance, other expenses	901	50	368	898	633	1,343	1,126
Rented dwellings	2,968	3,942	5,678	4,147	2,979	1,849	2,330
Other lodging	334	275	281	569	359	571	202
Utilities, fuels, and public services	**2,280**	**862**	**1,944**	**2,516**	**2,662**	**2,689**	**2,334**
Natural gas	372	83	226	366	440	475	408
Electricity	818	306	695	902	916	927	868
Fuel oil and other fuels	99	6	30	50	79	109	150
Telephone services	711	420	816	941	873	845	593
Water and other public services	280	48	177	258	354	333	315
Household services	**523**	**168**	**375**	**469**	**480**	**615**	**626**
Personal services	75	–	29	30	28	35	146
Other household services	448	168	346	440	452	580	479
Housekeeping supplies	**402**	**182**	**327**	**431**	**408**	**532**	**398**
Laundry and cleaning supplies	81	58	82	94	87	91	76
Other household products	192	53	124	224	199	260	196
Postage and stationery	129	72	120	113	121	181	126

	total single-person consumer units headed by women	under 25	25 to 34	35 to 44	45 to 54	55 to 64	65 or older
Household furnishings and equipment	**$1,047**	**$689**	**$1,338**	**$1,301**	**$1,213**	**$1,379**	**$804**
Household textiles	110	24	152	122	72	178	100
Furniture	259	199	381	416	361	295	157
Floor coverings	33	11	14	9	23	56	41
Major appliances	130	62	88	150	166	174	119
Small appliances, miscellaneous housewares	83	40	147	83	90	86	76
Miscellaneous household equipment	433	353	556	521	500	591	311
APPAREL AND RELATED SERVICES	**1,071**	**1,043**	**1,733**	**1,789**	**1,283**	**1,477**	**546**
Men and boys	**69**	**100**	**76**	**158**	**77**	**71**	**37**
Men, aged 16 or older	54	89	61	135	63	51	27
Boys, aged 2 to 15	14	10	15	22	15	20	10
Women and girls	**630**	**638**	**1,074**	**1,074**	**772**	**836**	**309**
Women, aged 16 or older	612	631	1,061	1,053	744	804	298
Girls, aged 2 to 15	18	7	13	21	28	32	12
Children under age 2	**29**	**25**	**44**	**21**	**30**	**52**	**19**
Footwear	**172**	**169**	**285**	**273**	**197**	**257**	**84**
Other apparel products and services	**171**	**111**	**255**	**264**	**206**	**261**	**96**
TRANSPORTATION	**3,987**	**3,128**	**5,551**	**6,381**	**4,806**	**4,583**	**2,787**
Vehicle purchases	**1,295**	**1,328**	**1,853**	**2,437**	**1,444**	**1,329**	**860**
Cars and trucks, new	724	776	876	1,766	870	562	490
Cars and trucks, used	570	552	969	671	575	767	369
Other vehicles	1	–	8	–	–	–	–
Gasoline and motor oil	**990**	**957**	**1,344**	**1,349**	**1,345**	**1,225**	**618**
Other vehicle expenses	**1,364**	**593**	**1,855**	**2,073**	**1,657**	**1,612**	**1,069**
Vehicle finance charges	98	72	147	220	124	151	35
Maintenance and repairs	373	236	480	463	517	476	267
Vehicle insurance	640	144	840	979	646	698	605
Vehicle rentals, leases, licenses, other charges	253	142	388	411	369	286	161
Public transportation	**338**	**251**	**500**	**521**	**360**	**417**	**241**
HEALTH CARE	**2,167**	**413**	**1,200**	**1,214**	**1,855**	**2,281**	**3,048**
Health insurance	1,147	153	505	622	789	965	1,837
Medical services	492	153	394	326	616	731	479
Drugs	445	80	246	211	365	457	644
Medical supplies	83	27	55	55	85	128	88
ENTERTAINMENT	**1,293**	**869**	**1,475**	**1,874**	**1,632**	**1,734**	**914**
Fees and admissions	286	243	384	427	394	340	186
Audio and visual equipment and services	552	373	663	644	622	682	469
Pets, toys, and playground equipment	368	187	286	652	513	576	223
Other entertainment products and services	86	65	141	151	103	135	36
PERSONAL CARE PRODUCTS AND SERVICES	**508**	**410**	**593**	**806**	**533**	**558**	**420**
READING	**103**	**54**	**93**	**93**	**106**	**121**	**110**
EDUCATION	**460**	**2,456**	**701**	**337**	**375**	**183**	**115**
TOBACCO PRODUCTS AND SMOKING SUPPLIES	**142**	**70**	**136**	**194**	**245**	**211**	**85**
MISCELLANEOUS	**517**	**222**	**638**	**545**	**606**	**655**	**461**
CASH CONTRIBUTIONS	**1,148**	**173**	**433**	**897**	**1,321**	**1,402**	**1,428**
PERSONAL INSURANCE AND PENSIONS	**2,019**	**927**	**3,240**	**4,130**	**3,635**	**2,985**	**585**
Life and other personal insurance	131	8	55	117	128	205	150
Pensions and Social Security	1,888	919	3,184	4,013	3,506	2,780	435
PERSONAL TAXES	**1,175**	**505**	**1,534**	**2,054**	**1,869**	**1,979**	**480**
Federal income taxes	832	386	1,169	1,570	1,398	1,337	293
State and local income taxes	226	108	323	405	355	419	65
Other taxes	117	11	42	79	116	223	122
GIFTS FOR PEOPLE IN OTHER HOUSEHOLDS	**856**	**372**	**561**	**726**	**1,177**	**1,148**	**827**

Note: Spending by category does not add to total spending because gift spending is also included in the preceding product and service categories and personal taxes are not included in the total. "–" means sample is too small to make a reliable estimate.

Source: Bureau of Labor Statistics, 2006 and 2007 Consumer Expenditure Surveys, Internet site http://www.bls.gov/cex/

Table 23. Indexed spending of single-person consumer units headed by women, by age, 2006–07

(indexed average annual spending of single-person consumer units headed by women by product and service category and age, 2006–07; index definition: an index of 100 is the average for all consumer units; an index of 132 means that spending by consumer units in that group is 32 percent above the average for all consumer units; an index of 68 indicates spending that is 32 percent below the average for all consumer units)

	total single-person consumer units headed by women	under 25	25 to 34	35 to 44	45 to 54	55 to 64	65 or older
Average spending of consumer units, total	$28,060	$19,014	$33,553	$38,086	$33,347	$32,798	$22,955
Average spending of consumer units, index	57	39	68	77	68	67	47
FOOD	**50**	**40**	**58**	**68**	**60**	**57**	**40**
Food at home	**54**	**29**	**50**	**61**	**64**	**63**	**50**
Cereals and bakery products	54	33	44	52	64	62	55
Cereals and cereal products	50	40	45	55	52	56	48
Bakery products	56	30	43	51	69	65	58
Meats, poultry, fish, and eggs	48	21	38	58	61	56	45
Beef	46	18	32	59	62	49	46
Pork	47	22	24	55	61	59	44
Other meats	48	20	42	46	57	59	47
Poultry	47	24	56	56	56	53	41
Fish and seafood	50	23	41	75	67	62	42
Eggs	55	23	45	58	60	63	58
Dairy products	54	33	46	56	62	64	53
Fresh milk and cream	51	32	42	45	65	56	52
Other dairy products	56	33	48	62	60	69	54
Fruits and vegetables	59	27	53	64	65	71	58
Fresh fruits	61	24	55	67	69	73	61
Fresh vegetables	59	28	52	66	66	75	58
Processed fruits	57	30	58	60	53	67	59
Processed vegetables	53	28	46	57	66	60	51
Other food at home	54	32	58	67	65	64	48
Sugar and other sweets	64	50	41	61	85	60	66
Fats and oils	54	25	56	54	57	69	53
Miscellaneous foods	54	32	66	67	63	60	47
Nonalcoholic beverages	53	29	50	69	63	68	44
Food prepared by consumer unit on trips	53	33	72	91	70	79	30
Food away from home	**45**	**55**	**69**	**76**	**55**	**50**	**26**
ALCOHOLIC BEVERAGES	**51**	**69**	**114**	**94**	**59**	**48**	**23**
HOUSING	**68**	**39**	**82**	**91**	**78**	**77**	**59**
Shelter	**72**	**46**	**98**	**107**	**84**	**78**	**58**
Owned dwellings	57	5	56	87	74	79	49
Mortgage interest and charges	47	4	70	97	81	64	22
Property taxes	66	7	41	71	70	86	75
Maintenance, repair, insurance, other expenses	80	4	33	80	56	120	100
Rented dwellings	114	152	219	160	115	71	90
Other lodging	53	44	45	90	57	91	32
Utilities, fuels, and public services	**66**	**25**	**57**	**73**	**77**	**78**	**68**
Natural gas	75	17	46	74	89	96	83
Electricity	64	24	54	70	71	72	68
Fuel oil and other fuels	69	4	21	35	55	76	104
Telephone services	65	38	74	86	80	77	54
Water and other public services	67	12	43	62	85	80	76
Household services	**54**	**17**	**39**	**49**	**50**	**64**	**65**
Personal services	19	–	7	7	7	9	36
Other household services	80	30	62	78	80	103	85
Housekeeping supplies	**63**	**28**	**51**	**67**	**64**	**83**	**62**
Laundry and cleaning supplies	55	40	56	64	60	62	52
Other household products	57	16	37	66	59	77	58
Postage and stationery	83	46	77	73	78	117	81

	total single-person consumer units headed by women	under 25	25 to 34	35 to 44	45 to 54	55 to 64	65 or older
Household furnishings and equipment	58	38	75	73	68	77	45
Household textiles	77	17	106	85	50	124	70
Furniture	56	43	82	90	78	64	34
Floor coverings	70	23	30	19	49	119	87
Major appliances	57	27	38	66	72	76	52
Small appliances, miscellaneous housewares	76	37	135	76	83	79	70
Miscellaneous household equipment	54	44	69	65	62	74	39
APPAREL AND RELATED SERVICES	57	55	92	95	68	78	29
Men and boys	16	23	17	36	17	16	8
Men, aged 16 or older	15	25	17	38	18	14	8
Boys, aged 2 to 15	16	11	17	25	17	23	11
Women and girls	84	85	142	142	102	111	41
Women, aged 16 or older	97	100	169	168	118	128	47
Girls, aged 2 to 15	14	6	10	17	22	25	10
Children under age 2	31	26	46	22	32	55	20
Footwear	54	53	90	86	62	81	27
Other apparel products and services	59	39	89	92	72	91	33
TRANSPORTATION	46	36	64	73	55	52	32
Vehicle purchases	39	40	56	73	43	40	26
Cars and trucks, new	43	46	52	105	52	33	29
Cars and trucks, used	36	35	62	43	37	49	24
Other vehicles	1	–	10	–	–	–	–
Gasoline and motor oil	43	42	58	58	58	53	27
Other vehicle expenses	53	23	72	80	64	63	41
Vehicle finance charges	32	24	49	73	41	50	12
Maintenance and repairs	52	33	67	65	73	67	37
Vehicle insurance	59	13	78	90	60	64	56
Vehicle rentals, leases, licenses, other charges	53	30	81	86	77	60	34
Public transportation	65	48	96	100	69	80	46
HEALTH CARE	77	15	43	43	66	81	108
Health insurance	76	10	34	41	52	64	122
Medical services	71	22	57	47	89	106	69
Drugs	90	16	49	42	73	92	130
Medical supplies	71	23	47	47	73	109	75
ENTERTAINMENT	49	33	56	71	62	66	35
Fees and admissions	45	38	60	67	61	53	29
Audio and visual equipment and services	58	39	70	68	66	72	49
Pets, toys, and playground equipment	65	33	50	114	90	101	39
Other entertainment products and services	18	14	29	32	22	28	8
PERSONAL CARE PRODUCTS AND SERVICES	87	70	101	138	91	95	72
READING	88	46	79	79	91	103	94
EDUCATION	50	268	76	37	41	20	13
TOBACCO PRODUCTS AND SMOKING SUPPLIES	44	22	42	60	75	65	26
MISCELLANEOUS	63	27	77	66	73	79	56
CASH CONTRIBUTIONS	62	9	23	49	72	76	77
PERSONAL INSURANCE AND PENSIONS	38	17	61	78	69	56	11
Life and other personal insurance	41	3	17	37	41	65	47
Pensions and Social Security	38	18	64	80	70	56	9
PERSONAL TAXES	50	22	66	88	80	85	21
Federal income taxes	51	24	71	96	85	82	18
State and local income taxes	46	22	66	82	72	85	13
Other taxes	59	6	21	40	58	112	61
GIFTS FOR PEOPLE IN OTHER HOUSEHOLDS	72	31	47	61	99	96	69

Note: Spending index for total consumer units is 100. "–" means sample is too small to make a reliable estimate.
Source: Calculations by New Strategist based on the Bureau of Labor Statistics' 2006 and 2007 Consumer Expenditure Surveys

Table 24. Average spending of single-person consumer units headed by men, by age, 2006–07

(average annual spending of single-person consumer units headed by men by product and service category and age, 2006–07)

	total single-person consumer units headed by men	under 25	25 to 34	35 to 44	45 to 54	55 to 64	65 or older
Number of consumer units (in 000s)	16,141	2,250	2,797	2,683	2,945	2,565	2,901
Average before-tax income of consumer units	$36,274	$16,328	$38,986	$47,090	$43,129	$40,215	$28,683
Average annual spending of consumer units	31,139	19,101	33,918	37,244	34,022	32,421	27,810
FOOD	**3,562**	**2,604**	**4,208**	**3,913**	**3,793**	**3,512**	**3,075**
Food at home	**1,689**	**1,057**	**1,721**	**1,874**	**1,824**	**1,797**	**1,690**
Cereals and bakery products	215	130	227	210	222	237	235
Cereals and cereal products	66	51	65	64	73	76	65
Bakery products	148	79	162	146	149	161	169
Meats, poultry, fish, and eggs	382	199	390	475	435	362	377
Beef	100	65	94	131	121	92	90
Pork	68	30	64	89	77	62	76
Other meats	55	35	53	62	63	59	53
Poultry	69	35	80	93	70	66	63
Fish and seafood	67	22	73	74	84	61	71
Eggs	22	12	26	26	20	22	23
Dairy products	183	128	181	193	208	183	186
Fresh milk and cream	74	54	64	81	81	74	81
Other dairy products	109	74	117	112	127	108	105
Fruits and vegetables	275	149	265	278	274	330	319
Fresh fruits	94	51	87	87	86	119	121
Fresh vegetables	81	45	79	88	91	89	86
Processed fruits	57	34	60	54	56	66	64
Processed vegetables	43	19	38	49	42	56	48
Other food at home	635	450	658	717	685	685	574
Sugar and other sweets	58	41	50	58	56	64	72
Fats and oils	43	27	40	47	48	42	49
Miscellaneous foods	329	244	360	356	343	359	290
Nonalcoholic beverages	181	128	186	223	206	190	144
Food prepared by consumer unit on trips	24	10	22	34	31	29	18
Food away from home	**1,873**	**1,547**	**2,487**	**2,039**	**1,969**	**1,714**	**1,385**
ALCOHOLIC BEVERAGES	**640**	**669**	**1,050**	**657**	**546**	**617**	**315**
HOUSING	**10,998**	**6,161**	**12,400**	**13,830**	**12,147**	**11,317**	**9,261**
Shelter	**7,317**	**4,441**	**8,407**	**9,732**	**8,120**	**7,323**	**5,441**
Owned dwellings	3,447	529	3,068	5,120	4,686	4,298	2,516
Mortgage interest and charges	1,925	262	2,130	3,409	2,777	2,126	601
Property taxes	902	192	636	1,135	1,105	1,074	1,137
Maintenance, repair, insurance, other expenses	620	75	302	577	804	1,097	778
Rented dwellings	3,548	3,779	5,110	4,167	3,058	2,589	2,634
Other lodging	322	133	228	444	376	436	291
Utilities, fuels, and public services	**2,059**	**917**	**1,969**	**2,324**	**2,326**	**2,272**	**2,330**
Natural gas	308	97	226	331	425	326	392
Electricity	752	365	733	827	815	840	857
Fuel oil and other fuels	100	10	56	104	99	146	170
Telephone services	677	375	768	830	713	705	618
Water and other public services	223	69	185	231	275	254	293
Household services	**381**	**107**	**325**	**448**	**310**	**449**	**598**
Personal services	57	3	17	91	9	24	184
Other household services	324	104	308	357	301	425	414
Housekeeping supplies	**233**	**129**	**180**	**260**	**241**	**304**	**261**
Laundry and cleaning supplies	53	30	47	71	57	63	46
Other household products	122	66	80	134	131	162	146
Postage and stationery	58	33	53	55	53	80	69

	total single-person consumer units headed by men	under 25	25 to 34	35 to 44	45 to 54	55 to 64	65 or older
Household furnishings and equipment	**$1,008**	**$567**	**$1,519**	**$1,066**	**$1,150**	**$969**	**$631**
Household textiles	56	11	70	56	62	111	20
Furniture	267	137	260	340	439	288	114
Floor coverings	19	12	11	25	18	32	17
Major appliances	96	61	85	140	105	126	59
Small appliances, miscellaneous housewares	58	38	96	51	99	27	27
Miscellaneous household equipment	512	309	996	455	427	385	393
APPAREL AND RELATED SERVICES	**917**	**543**	**1,608**	**1,228**	**908**	**617**	**474**
Men and boys	**433**	**331**	**664**	**530**	**467**	**345**	**237**
Men, aged 16 or older	424	329	655	511	455	338	231
Boys, aged 2 to 15	9	2	9	19	12	7	6
Women and girls	**44**	**30**	**63**	**70**	**53**	**20**	**26**
Women, aged 16 or older	32	29	43	51	29	11	24
Girls, aged 2 to 15	13	1	20	18	24	9	2
Children under age 2	**11**	**8**	**17**	**12**	**7**	**17**	**3**
Footwear	**130**	**31**	**183**	**213**	**156**	**71**	**92**
Other apparel products and services	**299**	**142**	**681**	**402**	**225**	**165**	**116**
TRANSPORTATION	**5,198**	**3,358**	**5,813**	**6,220**	**5,240**	**5,695**	**4,579**
Vehicle purchases	**1,786**	**1,167**	**1,989**	**2,363**	**1,647**	**1,875**	**1,596**
Cars and trucks, new	856	444	978	1,320	513	945	899
Cars and trucks, used	865	602	935	991	994	930	697
Other vehicles	64	121	76	53	141	–	–
Gasoline and motor oil	**1,521**	**1,102**	**1,734**	**1,809**	**1,610**	**1,654**	**1,169**
Other vehicle expenses	**1,541**	**914**	**1,648**	**1,622**	**1,628**	**1,761**	**1,543**
Vehicle finance charges	145	103	240	181	167	113	62
Maintenance and repairs	532	334	571	576	574	682	438
Vehicle insurance	588	338	492	552	643	599	809
Vehicle rentals, leases, licenses, other charges	276	138	345	313	244	368	235
Public transportation	**349**	**175**	**441**	**426**	**355**	**405**	**271**
HEALTH CARE	**1,379**	**305**	**703**	**1,192**	**1,187**	**1,785**	**2,867**
Health insurance	761	160	403	704	609	885	1,667
Medical services	319	70	219	283	312	475	512
Drugs	246	52	58	162	217	361	581
Medical supplies	53	24	23	43	49	64	107
ENTERTAINMENT	**1,669**	**1,140**	**1,795**	**1,886**	**1,843**	**2,079**	**1,204**
Fees and admissions	390	282	494	498	450	324	272
Audio and visual equipment and services	730	594	901	844	777	705	534
Pets, toys, and playground equipment	226	105	173	280	291	207	267
Other entertainment products and services	323	158	226	263	326	843	132
PERSONAL CARE PRODUCTS AND SERVICES	**192**	**149**	**217**	**231**	**221**	**181**	**148**
READING	**83**	**45**	**68**	**81**	**95**	**96**	**108**
EDUCATION	**657**	**2,105**	**806**	**211**	**343**	**454**	**301**
TOBACCO PRODUCTS AND SMOKING SUPPLIES	**324**	**195**	**336**	**373**	**377**	**451**	**202**
MISCELLANEOUS	**692**	**173**	**502**	**658**	**930**	**890**	**872**
CASH CONTRIBUTIONS	**1,732**	**377**	**727**	**2,165**	**1,793**	**1,449**	**3,542**
PERSONAL INSURANCE AND PENSIONS	**3,097**	**1,279**	**3,685**	**4,598**	**4,600**	**3,278**	**863**
Life and other personal insurance	153	11	73	130	140	200	335
Pensions and Social Security	2,943	1,267	3,612	4,469	4,460	3,079	528
PERSONAL TAXES	**1,916**	**583**	**1,975**	**2,407**	**2,569**	**2,035**	**1,670**
Federal income taxes	1,424	457	1,509	1,769	1,939	1,472	1,209
State and local income taxes	369	122	432	491	511	359	254
Other taxes	122	5	34	148	119	204	206
GIFTS FOR PEOPLE IN OTHER HOUSEHOLDS	**856**	**319**	**627**	**910**	**1,049**	**1,041**	**1,072**

Note: Spending by category does not add to total spending because gift spending is also included in the preceding product and service categories and personal taxes are not included in the total. "–" means sample is too small to make a reliable estimate.
Source: Bureau of Labor Statistics, 2006 and 2007 Consumer Expenditure Surveys, Internet site http://www.bls.gov/cex/

Table 25. Indexed spending of single-person consumer units headed by men, by age, 2006–07

(indexed average annual spending of single-person consumer units headed by men by product and service category and age, 2006–07; index definition: an index of 100 is the average for all consumer units; an index of 132 means that spending by consumer units in that group is 32 percent above the average for all consumer units; an index of 68 indicates spending that is 32 percent below the average for all consumer units)

	total single-person consumer units headed by men	under 25	25 to 34	35 to 44	45 to 54	55 to 64	65 or older
Average spending of consumer units, total	$31,139	$19,101	$33,918	$37,244	$34,022	$32,421	$27,810
Average spending of consumer units, index	63	39	69	76	69	66	56
FOOD	**58**	**43**	**69**	**64**	**62**	**57**	**50**
Food at home	**49**	**31**	**50**	**54**	**53**	**52**	**49**
Cereals and bakery products	47	29	50	46	49	52	52
Cereals and cereal products	46	36	45	45	51	53	45
Bakery products	48	25	52	47	48	52	55
Meats, poultry, fish, and eggs	49	25	50	60	55	46	48
Beef	44	29	42	58	54	41	40
Pork	44	20	42	58	50	41	50
Other meats	52	33	50	59	60	56	50
Poultry	49	25	57	66	50	47	45
Fish and seafood	55	18	60	61	69	50	58
Eggs	55	30	65	65	50	55	58
Dairy products	48	34	48	51	55	48	49
Fresh milk and cream	50	37	44	55	55	50	55
Other dairy products	47	32	51	48	55	47	45
Fruits and vegetables	46	25	44	47	46	55	54
Fresh fruits	47	26	44	44	43	60	61
Fresh vegetables	42	23	41	46	47	46	45
Processed fruits	51	31	54	49	50	59	58
Processed vegetables	45	20	40	52	44	59	51
Other food at home	52	37	54	58	56	56	47
Sugar and other sweets	46	33	40	46	45	51	58
Fats and oils	48	30	45	53	54	47	55
Miscellaneous foods	52	38	56	56	54	56	45
Nonalcoholic beverages	54	38	56	67	62	57	43
Food prepared by consumer unit on trips	56	23	51	79	72	67	42
Food away from home	**70**	**58**	**93**	**76**	**73**	**64**	**52**
ALCOHOLIC BEVERAGES	**134**	**140**	**220**	**138**	**114**	**129**	**66**
HOUSING	**66**	**37**	**74**	**83**	**73**	**68**	**56**
Shelter	**74**	**45**	**85**	**99**	**82**	**74**	**55**
Owned dwellings	52	8	46	77	71	65	38
Mortgage interest and charges	50	7	56	89	73	56	16
Property taxes	54	11	38	68	66	64	68
Maintenance, repair, insurance, other expenses	55	7	27	51	72	98	69
Rented dwellings	137	146	197	161	118	100	101
Other lodging	51	21	36	71	60	69	46
Utilities, fuels, and public services	**60**	**27**	**57**	**68**	**68**	**66**	**68**
Natural gas	62	20	46	67	86	66	79
Electricity	59	28	57	64	63	65	67
Fuel oil and other fuels	69	7	39	72	69	101	118
Telephone services	62	34	70	76	65	64	56
Water and other public services	54	17	44	56	66	61	70
Household services	**39**	**11**	**34**	**46**	**32**	**46**	**62**
Personal services	14	1	4	23	2	6	46
Other household services	58	19	55	64	54	76	74
Housekeeping supplies	**36**	**20**	**28**	**41**	**38**	**48**	**41**
Laundry and cleaning supplies	36	21	32	49	39	43	32
Other household products	36	20	24	40	39	48	43
Postage and stationery	37	21	34	35	34	52	45

	total single-person consumer units headed by men	under 25	25 to 34	35 to 44	45 to 54	55 to 64	65 or older
Household furnishings and equipment	56	32	85	59	64	54	35
Household textiles	39	8	49	39	43	78	14
Furniture	58	30	56	73	95	62	25
Floor coverings	40	26	23	53	38	68	36
Major appliances	42	27	37	61	46	55	26
Small appliances, miscellaneous housewares	53	35	88	47	91	25	25
Miscellaneous household equipment	64	39	124	57	53	48	49
APPAREL AND RELATED SERVICES	48	29	85	65	48	33	25
Men and boys	98	75	151	120	106	78	54
Men, aged 16 or older	120	93	185	144	129	95	65
Boys, aged 2 to 15	10	2	10	22	14	8	7
Women and girls	6	4	8	9	7	3	3
Women, aged 16 or older	5	5	7	8	5	2	4
Girls, aged 2 to 15	10	1	16	14	19	7	2
Children under age 2	12	8	18	13	7	18	3
Footwear	41	10	58	67	49	22	29
Other apparel products and services	104	49	236	140	78	57	40
TRANSPORTATION	59	38	67	71	60	65	52
Vehicle purchases	54	35	60	71	49	56	48
Cars and trucks, new	51	26	58	78	30	56	53
Cars and trucks, used	55	38	60	63	63	59	44
Other vehicles	80	151	95	66	176	–	–
Gasoline and motor oil	66	48	75	78	70	72	51
Other vehicle expenses	60	35	64	63	63	68	60
Vehicle finance charges	48	34	79	60	55	37	21
Maintenance and repairs	75	47	80	81	81	96	61
Vehicle insurance	54	31	45	51	59	55	75
Vehicle rentals, leases, licenses, other charges	58	29	72	65	51	77	49
Public transportation	67	34	85	82	68	78	52
HEALTH CARE	49	11	25	42	42	64	102
Health insurance	51	11	27	47	40	59	111
Medical services	46	10	32	41	45	69	74
Drugs	49	10	12	33	44	73	117
Medical supplies	45	21	20	37	42	55	91
ENTERTAINMENT	63	43	68	72	70	79	46
Fees and admissions	61	44	77	78	70	51	42
Audio and visual equipment and services	77	63	95	89	82	74	56
Pets, toys, and playground equipment	40	18	30	49	51	36	47
Other entertainment products and services	68	33	47	55	68	176	28
PERSONAL CARE PRODUCTS AND SERVICES	33	25	37	39	38	31	25
READING	71	38	58	69	81	82	92
EDUCATION	72	230	88	23	37	50	33
TOBACCO PRODUCTS AND SMOKING SUPPLIES	100	60	103	115	116	139	62
MISCELLANEOUS	84	21	61	80	112	108	105
CASH CONTRIBUTIONS	94	20	39	117	97	79	192
PERSONAL INSURANCE AND PENSIONS	58	24	69	87	87	62	16
Life and other personal insurance	48	3	23	41	44	63	106
Pensions and Social Security	59	25	72	90	89	62	11
PERSONAL TAXES	82	25	85	103	110	87	72
Federal income taxes	87	28	92	108	118	90	74
State and local income taxes	75	25	88	100	104	73	52
Other taxes	61	3	17	74	60	103	104
GIFTS FOR PEOPLE IN OTHER HOUSEHOLDS	72	27	53	76	88	87	90

Note: Spending index for total consumer units is 100. "–" means sample is too small to make a reliable estimate.
Source: Calculations by New Strategist based on the Bureau of Labor Statistics' 2006 and 2007 Consumer Expenditure Surveys

Spending by Region, 2007

Households in the West spent $56,291 in 2007, 13 percent more than the average household and $5,000 to $11,000 more than households in the other regions. Spending by households in the Northeast is 4 percent above average, at $51,624. Households in the Midwest spent $48,014, or 3 percent less than the average amount. In the South, average household spending was 8 percent below average at $45,464 in 2007.

Households in the Northeast and West spend more than the average household on most products and services, whereas those in the Midwest and the South spend less than average on most items. Households in the Northeast spend the most on property taxes, 55 percent more than average. Those in the West spend the most on mortgage interest and rent. Households in the Midwest and Northeast spend the most on tobacco. Households in the South spend 16 percent less than average on alcoholic beverages.

The biggest consumers of natural gas, households in the Midwest, spend 44 percent more than the average household on this item. Households in the South spend the most on electricity, while those in the Northeast spend the most on fuel oil. Western households spend 25 percent more than the average household on water and other public services.

Households in the West spend the most on entertainment. Spending on public transportation is highest in the Northeast. Households in the South spend 9 percent more than average on drugs.

Table 26. Average spending by region, 2007

(average annual spending of consumer units by product and service category and region of residence, 2007)

	total	Northeast	Midwest	South	West
Number of consumer units (in 000s)	120,171	22,382	27,462	43,152	27,176
Average number of persons per consumer unit	2.5	2.4	2.4	2.5	2.6
Average before-tax income of consumer units	$63,091	$69,937	$59,389	$58,224	$68,923
Average annual spending of consumer units	49,638	51,624	48,014	45,464	56,291
FOOD	**6,133**	**6,419**	**5,793**	**5,780**	**6,811**
Food at home	**3,465**	**3,595**	**3,252**	**3,311**	**3,822**
Cereals and bakery products	460	495	444	438	480
Cereals and cereal products	143	157	131	134	157
Bakery products	317	339	313	304	323
Meats, poultry, fish, and eggs	777	832	691	770	830
Beef	216	207	201	219	235
Pork	150	149	140	160	144
Other meats	104	121	109	97	98
Poultry	142	151	112	148	154
Fish and seafood	122	159	96	103	148
Eggs	43	45	33	42	51
Dairy products	387	400	375	366	422
Fresh milk and cream	154	151	145	156	161
Other dairy products	234	249	230	211	261
Fruits and vegetables	600	647	546	552	693
Fresh fruits	202	216	191	177	241
Fresh vegetables	190	205	161	175	233
Processed fruits	112	133	105	102	119
Processed vegetables	96	93	89	98	100
Other food at home	1,241	1,221	1,196	1,185	1,396
Sugar and other sweets	124	125	125	117	136
Fats and oils	91	93	87	90	97
Miscellaneous foods	650	626	630	622	734
Nonalcoholic beverages	333	333	313	325	366
Food prepared by consumer unit on trips	43	44	42	31	63
Food away from home	**2,668**	**2,824**	**2,541**	**2,470**	**2,988**
ALCOHOLIC BEVERAGES	**457**	**508**	**501**	**382**	**488**
HOUSING	**16,920**	**19,085**	**15,380**	**14,911**	**19,885**
Shelter	**10,023**	**11,640**	**8,839**	**8,233**	**12,729**
Owned dwellings	6,730	7,616	6,238	5,723	8,097
Mortgage interest and charges	3,890	3,715	3,310	3,420	5,366
Property taxes	1,709	2,649	1,801	1,259	1,555
Maintenance, repair, insurance, other expenses	1,131	1,252	1,126	1,044	1,176
Rented dwellings	2,602	3,036	1,883	2,072	3,811
Other lodging	691	988	717	437	821
Utilities, fuels, and public services	**3,477**	**3,832**	**3,323**	**3,547**	**3,229**
Natural gas	480	653	689	285	437
Electricity	1,303	1,276	1,116	1,568	1,093
Fuel oil and other fuels	151	455	116	71	62
Telephone services	1,110	1,120	1,025	1,167	1,095
Water and other public services	434	330	377	456	541
Household services	**984**	**1,011**	**855**	**933**	**1,174**
Personal services	415	434	394	400	447
Other household services	569	577	462	533	727
Housekeeping supplies	**639**	**576**	**620**	**595**	**782**
Laundry and cleaning supplies	140	121	145	152	132
Other household products	347	303	320	309	471
Postage and stationery	152	152	155	134	179

	total consumer units	Northeast	Midwest	South	West
Household furnishings and equipment	**$1,797**	**$2,026**	**$1,742**	**$1,604**	**$1,970**
Household textiles	133	148	107	129	155
Furniture	446	589	401	382	472
Floor coverings	46	69	44	36	47
Major appliances	231	240	233	222	237
Small appliances and miscellaneous housewares	101	104	91	92	123
Miscellaneous household equipment	840	877	866	741	936
APPAREL AND RELATED SERVICES	**1,881**	**2,068**	**1,866**	**1,692**	**2,042**
Men and boys	**435**	**450**	**379**	**425**	**498**
Men, aged 16 or older	351	354	292	346	417
Boys, aged 2 to 15	84	97	87	79	81
Women and girls	**749**	**812**	**821**	**638**	**800**
Women, aged 16 or older	627	690	703	515	677
Girls, aged 2 to 15	122	121	117	124	123
Children under age 2	**93**	**83**	**89**	**86**	**119**
Footwear	**327**	**350**	**334**	**297**	**350**
Other apparel products and services	**276**	**374**	**244**	**246**	**275**
TRANSPORTATION	**8,758**	**8,014**	**8,684**	**8,485**	**9,882**
Vehicle purchases	**3,244**	**2,508**	**3,407**	**3,216**	**3,729**
Cars and trucks, new	1,572	1,373	1,532	1,524	1,852
Cars and trucks, used	1,567	1,095	1,698	1,597	1,776
Other vehicles	105	40	178	96	101
Gasoline and motor oil	**2,384**	**2,080**	**2,408**	**2,522**	**2,389**
Other vehicle expenses	**2,592**	**2,678**	**2,418**	**2,378**	**3,042**
Vehicle finance charges	305	250	281	342	318
Maintenance and repairs	738	716	694	689	876
Vehicle insurance	1,071	1,069	908	1,041	1,290
Vehicle rentals, leases, licenses, other charges	478	642	536	306	558
Public transportation	**538**	**749**	**451**	**368**	**721**
HEALTH CARE	**2,853**	**2,645**	**3,097**	**2,800**	**2,860**
Health insurance	1,545	1,535	1,632	1,539	1,475
Medical services	709	576	811	639	829
Drugs	481	421	514	526	425
Medical supplies	118	114	141	96	131
ENTERTAINMENT	**2,698**	**2,811**	**2,585**	**2,320**	**3,319**
Fees and admissions	658	803	630	476	857
Audio and visual equipment and services	987	1,010	913	971	1,068
Pets, toys, and playground equipment	560	581	523	517	650
Other entertainment products and services	493	417	519	357	744
PERSONAL CARE PRODUCTS AND SERVICES	**588**	**609**	**544**	**565**	**650**
READING	**118**	**135**	**126**	**89**	**140**
EDUCATION	**945**	**1,163**	**1,187**	**744**	**842**
TOBACCO PRODUCTS AND SMOKING SUPPLIES	**323**	**361**	**365**	**332**	**234**
MISCELLANEOUS	**808**	**826**	**778**	**652**	**1,071**
CASH CONTRIBUTIONS	**1,821**	**1,421**	**1,792**	**1,762**	**2,275**
PERSONAL INSURANCE AND PENSIONS	**5,336**	**5,558**	**5,315**	**4,948**	**5,791**
Life and other personal insurance	309	342	347	298	262
Pensions and Social Security	5,027	5,216	4,968	4,650	5,529
PERSONAL TAXES	**2,233**	**2,497**	**1,875**	**2,048**	**2,674**
Federal income taxes	1,569	1,596	1,164	1,582	1,935
State and local income taxes	468	599	467	325	589
Other taxes	196	301	245	140	150
GIFTS FOR PEOPLE IN OTHER HOUSEHOLDS	**1,198**	**1,284**	**1,310**	**1,073**	**1,213**

Note: Spending by category does not add to total spending because gift spending is also included in the preceding product and service categories and personal taxes are not included in the total.

Source: Bureau of Labor Statistics, 2007 Consumer Expenditure Survey, Internet site http://www.bls.gov/cex/

Table 27. Indexed spending by region, 2007

(indexed average annual spending of consumer units by product and service category and region of residence, 2007; index definition: an index of 100 is the average for all consumer units; an index of 132 means that spending by consumer units in that group is 32 percent above the average for all consumer units; an index of 68 indicates spending that is 32 percent below the average for all consumer units)

	total	Northeast	Midwest	South	West
Average spending of consumer units, total	$49,638	$51,624	$48,014	$45,464	$56,291
Average spending of consumer units, index	100	104	97	92	113
FOOD	100	105	94	94	111
Food at home	100	104	94	96	110
Cereals and bakery products	100	108	97	95	104
Cereals and cereal products	100	110	92	94	110
Bakery products	100	107	99	96	102
Meats, poultry, fish, and eggs	100	107	89	99	107
Beef	100	96	93	101	109
Pork	100	99	93	107	96
Other meats	100	116	105	93	94
Poultry	100	106	79	104	108
Fish and seafood	100	130	79	84	121
Eggs	100	105	77	98	119
Dairy products	100	103	97	95	109
Fresh milk and cream	100	98	94	101	105
Other dairy products	100	106	98	90	112
Fruits and vegetables	100	108	91	92	116
Fresh fruits	100	107	95	88	119
Fresh vegetables	100	108	85	92	123
Processed fruits	100	119	94	91	106
Processed vegetables	100	97	93	102	104
Other food at home	100	98	96	95	112
Sugar and other sweets	100	101	101	94	110
Fats and oils	100	102	96	99	107
Miscellaneous foods	100	96	97	96	113
Nonalcoholic beverages	100	100	94	98	110
Food prepared by consumer unit on trips	100	102	98	72	147
Food away from home	100	106	95	93	112
ALCOHOLIC BEVERAGES	100	111	110	84	107
HOUSING	100	113	91	88	118
Shelter	100	116	88	82	127
Owned dwellings	100	113	93	85	120
Mortgage interest and charges	100	96	85	88	138
Property taxes	100	155	105	74	91
Maintenance, repair, insurance, other expenses	100	111	100	92	104
Rented dwellings	100	117	72	80	146
Other lodging	100	143	104	63	119
Utilities, fuels, and public services	100	110	96	102	93
Natural gas	100	136	144	59	91
Electricity	100	98	86	120	84
Fuel oil and other fuels	100	301	77	47	41
Telephone services	100	101	92	105	99
Water and other public services	100	76	87	105	125
Household services	100	103	87	95	119
Personal services	100	105	95	96	108
Other household services	100	101	81	94	128
Housekeeping supplies	100	90	97	93	122
Laundry and cleaning supplies	100	86	104	109	94
Other household products	100	87	92	89	136
Postage and stationery	100	100	102	88	118

	total consumer units	Northeast	Midwest	South	West
Household furnishings and equipment	100	113	97	89	110
Household textiles	100	111	80	97	117
Furniture	100	132	90	86	106
Floor coverings	100	150	96	78	102
Major appliances	100	104	101	96	103
Small appliances and miscellaneous housewares	100	103	90	91	122
Miscellaneous household equipment	100	104	103	88	111
APPAREL AND RELATED SERVICES	100	110	99	90	109
Men and boys	100	103	87	98	114
Men, aged 16 or older	100	101	83	99	119
Boys, aged 2 to 15	100	115	104	94	96
Women and girls	100	108	110	85	107
Women, aged 16 or older	100	110	112	82	108
Girls, aged 2 to 15	100	99	96	102	101
Children under age 2	100	89	96	92	128
Footwear	100	107	102	91	107
Other apparel products and services	100	136	88	89	100
TRANSPORTATION	100	92	99	97	113
Vehicle purchases	100	77	105	99	115
Cars and trucks, new	100	87	97	97	118
Cars and trucks, used	100	70	108	102	113
Other vehicles	100	38	170	91	96
Gasoline and motor oil	100	87	101	106	100
Other vehicle expenses	100	103	93	92	117
Vehicle finance charges	100	82	92	112	104
Maintenance and repairs	100	97	94	93	119
Vehicle insurance	100	100	85	97	120
Vehicle rentals, leases, licenses, other charges	100	134	112	64	117
Public transportation	100	139	84	68	134
HEALTH CARE	100	93	109	98	100
Health insurance	100	99	106	100	95
Medical services	100	81	114	90	117
Drugs	100	88	107	109	88
Medical supplies	100	97	119	81	111
ENTERTAINMENT	100	104	96	86	123
Fees and admissions	100	122	96	72	130
Audio and visual equipment and services	100	102	93	98	108
Pets, toys, and playground equipment	100	104	93	92	116
Other entertainment products and services	100	85	105	72	151
PERSONAL CARE PRODUCTS AND SERVICES	100	104	93	96	111
READING	100	114	107	75	119
EDUCATION	100	123	126	79	89
TOBACCO PRODUCTS AND SMOKING SUPPLIES	100	112	113	103	72
MISCELLANEOUS	100	102	96	81	133
CASH CONTRIBUTIONS	100	78	98	97	125
PERSONAL INSURANCE AND PENSIONS	100	104	100	93	109
Life and other personal insurance	100	111	112	96	85
Pensions and Social Security	100	104	99	93	110
PERSONAL TAXES	100	112	84	92	120
Federal income taxes	100	102	74	101	123
State and local income taxes	100	128	100	69	126
Other taxes	100	154	125	71	77
GIFTS FOR PEOPLE IN OTHER HOUSEHOLDS	100	107	109	90	101

Source: Calculations by New Strategist based on the Bureau of Labor Statistics' 2007 Consumer Expenditure Survey

Spending by Region and Income, 2006–07

Households with incomes of $70,000 or more are most commonly found in the West and Northeast, where they account for 34 and 33 percent of households, respectively. In the Midwest, 30 percent of households have incomes of $70,000 or more, while in the South the proportion is a smaller 27 percent.

In every region, spending rises with income. The most affluent households in the Northeast spend 68 percent more than the average Northeastern household, $85,201 on average versus $50,703 in 2006–07. The spending gap is greatest for items such as mortgage interest, other lodging (a category that includes vacation homes and hotels and motels on out-of-town trips), household personal services (mostly day care), furniture, new cars and trucks, fees and admissions to entertainment events, and education.

In the Midwest, the most affluent households spent an average of $80,606 in 2006–07, or 72 percent more than the $46,812 spent by the average Midwestern household. Households with incomes of $70,000 or more in the Midwest spend more than twice as much as the average Midwestern household on items such as mortgage interest, other lodging, household personal services, floor coverings, new cars and trucks, public transportation, fees and admissions to entertainment events, and gifts for people in other households.

The most-affluent households in the South spend 75 percent more than the average Southern household, $79,027 versus $45,225 in 2006–07. The richest households in the South spend more than two times as much as the average Southern household on owned dwellings, mortgage interest, other lodging, and household personal services, among others. They spend 2 percent less than the average household in the South on tobacco and 47 percent less on rent.

The most-affluent households in the West spend 60 percent more than the average Western household, $91,151 versus $57,124 in 2006–07. The gap is greatest for items such as other lodging, household personal services, and fees and admissions to entertainment events.

Table 28. Average spending in the Northeast by income, 2006–07

(average annual spending of consumer units (CUs) in the Northeast by product and service category and before-tax income of consumer unit, 2006–07)

	total consumer units in Northeast	under $10,000	$10,000 to $19,999	$20,000 to $29,999	$30,000 to $39,999	$40,000 to $49,999	$50,000 to $69,999	$70,000 or more
Number of consumer units (in 000s)	22,570	2,000	2,845	2,572	2,314	2,071	3,238	7,530
Average number of persons per CU	2.4	1.6	1.6	2.0	2.2	2.3	2.6	3.1
Average before-tax income of CUs	$67,060	$4,786	$14,959	$24,862	$34,813	$44,823	$59,463	$136,988
Average annual spending of consumer units	50,703	17,716	21,827	29,355	35,078	40,322	50,240	85,201
FOOD	**6,320**	**2,573**	**3,143**	**3,993**	**4,806**	**5,367**	**6,755**	**9,694**
Food at home	**3,529**	**1,714**	**2,054**	**2,581**	**2,853**	**3,109**	**3,852**	**4,991**
Cereals and bakery products	486	243	287	362	385	418	531	688
Cereals and cereal products	156	96	101	121	121	142	162	212
Bakery products	331	147	186	241	264	276	369	476
Meats, poultry, fish, and eggs	825	445	517	637	652	738	883	1,141
Beef	212	87	124	185	154	211	208	301
Pork	145	90	102	107	137	134	183	176
Other meats	120	48	66	86	110	109	132	170
Poultry	159	96	103	113	121	135	151	232
Fish and seafood	147	93	87	109	95	115	164	211
Eggs	41	30	34	35	34	35	45	51
Dairy products	390	173	236	295	322	335	420	552
Fresh milk and cream	146	88	105	122	130	128	164	184
Other dairy products	244	85	130	173	192	207	256	367
Fruits and vegetables	641	324	383	493	543	551	672	897
Fresh fruits	212	101	132	158	163	192	228	298
Fresh vegetables	208	118	118	156	177	172	213	296
Processed fruits	128	57	79	108	117	101	132	178
Processed vegetables	93	48	54	70	86	86	99	126
Other food at home	1,187	529	631	794	952	1,067	1,346	1,714
Sugar and other sweets	125	76	63	95	97	106	143	174
Fats and oils	90	44	54	69	69	71	106	125
Miscellaneous foods	604	228	324	371	474	560	689	886
Nonalcoholic beverages	326	170	177	238	288	298	368	448
Food prepared by consumer unit on trips	43	11	14	21	24	31	40	80
Food away from home	**2,791**	**858**	**1,088**	**1,412**	**1,954**	**2,258**	**2,903**	**4,703**
ALCOHOLIC BEVERAGES	**513**	**130**	**173**	**244**	**325**	**398**	**531**	**905**
HOUSING	**18,408**	**7,983**	**9,668**	**11,445**	**13,621**	**15,651**	**17,725**	**29,332**
Shelter	**11,335**	**5,464**	**6,201**	**7,094**	**8,436**	**9,517**	**10,606**	**17,986**
Owned dwellings	7,452	1,584	2,046	2,973	4,271	5,283	6,943	14,376
Mortgage interest and charges	3,662	528	483	831	1,893	2,430	3,535	7,598
Property taxes	2,584	727	1,021	1,424	1,687	1,862	2,290	4,664
Maintenance, repair, insurance, other expenses	1,207	329	542	718	691	990	1,119	2,114
Rented dwellings	3,039	3,701	4,014	3,917	3,779	3,868	2,998	1,758
Other lodging	843	180	141	203	385	365	664	1,852
Utilities, fuels, and public services	**3,707**	**1,558**	**2,365**	**2,844**	**3,166**	**3,396**	**3,970**	**5,219**
Natural gas	656	259	469	510	535	647	732	888
Electricity	1,225	481	770	924	1,096	1,144	1,264	1,742
Fuel oil and other fuels	429	169	312	354	352	310	418	630
Telephone services	1,085	554	644	826	932	998	1,214	1,496
Water and other public services	312	95	170	230	251	298	341	463
Household services	**971**	**223**	**378**	**396**	**465**	**682**	**738**	**1,926**
Personal services	420	38	126	124	141	362	297	889
Other household services	551	184	253	272	324	320	441	1,037
Housekeeping supplies	**579**	**256**	**257**	**368**	**446**	**480**	**630**	**893**
Laundry and cleaning supplies	123	61	62	88	111	107	132	175
Other household products	303	130	122	164	230	275	332	477
Postage and stationery	153	65	74	116	105	97	166	241

	total consumer units in Northeast	under $10,000	$10,000 to $19,999	$20,000 to $29,999	$30,000 to $39,999	$40,000 to $49,999	$50,000 to $69,999	$70,000 or more
Household furnishings and equipment	**$1,815**	**$483**	**$466**	**$743**	**$1,108**	**$1,576**	**$1,781**	**$3,308**
Household textiles	135	36	45	90	103	148	194	189
Furniture	467	143	110	137	207	221	335	1,004
Floor coverings	70	22	28	10	106	46	46	126
Major appliances	237	82	52	161	151	201	235	411
Small appliances, miscellaneous housewares	109	32	57	36	54	118	184	154
Miscellaneous household equipment	796	168	175	308	488	842	788	1,422
APPAREL AND RELATED SERVICES	**2,069**	**1,119**	**744**	**1,237**	**1,541**	**1,665**	**2,264**	**3,287**
Men and boys	**467**	**142**	**152**	**248**	**306**	**323**	**537**	**796**
Men, aged 16 or older	373	92	127	178	236	260	459	634
Boys, aged 2 to 15	94	50	25	70	70	63	78	162
Women and girls	**817**	**487**	**287**	**522**	**642**	**718**	**877**	**1,256**
Women, aged 16 or older	685	443	252	456	539	654	767	1,008
Girls, aged 2 to 15	132	44	35	66	104	64	110	248
Children under age 2	**87**	**93**	**41**	**53**	**69**	**78**	**112**	**115**
Footwear	**354**	**268**	**108**	**256**	**327**	**270**	**434**	**504**
Other apparel products and services	**344**	**129**	**157**	**159**	**197**	**276**	**303**	**616**
TRANSPORTATION	**8,107**	**1,893**	**2,641**	**4,722**	**5,503**	**5,979**	**8,735**	**14,040**
Vehicle purchases	**2,703**	**415**	**639**	**1,516**	**1,709**	**1,302**	**3,032**	**5,044**
Cars and trucks, new	1,496	355	237	627	454	672	1,337	3,187
Cars and trucks, used	1,167	60	402	888	1,255	629	1,593	1,784
Other vehicles	39	–	–	–	–	2	101	73
Gasoline and motor oil	**1,994**	**623**	**747**	**1,274**	**1,661**	**1,858**	**2,327**	**3,073**
Other vehicle expenses	**2,722**	**602**	**970**	**1,600**	**1,755**	**2,375**	**2,853**	**4,612**
Vehicle finance charges	243	41	53	126	177	202	302	414
Maintenance and repairs	684	233	294	364	561	605	718	1,105
Vehicle insurance	1,154	193	442	824	681	1,112	1,255	1,854
Vehicle rentals, leases, licenses, other charges	640	135	180	286	336	456	578	1,239
Public transportation	**688**	**252**	**285**	**331**	**378**	**444**	**523**	**1,311**
HEALTH CARE	**2,618**	**801**	**1,949**	**2,302**	**2,354**	**2,438**	**2,664**	**3,565**
Health insurance	1,498	501	1,226	1,440	1,489	1,450	1,513	1,895
Medical services	586	131	326	363	364	461	588	981
Drugs	416	134	351	426	411	416	451	495
Medical supplies	118	34	47	74	91	111	113	195
ENTERTAINMENT	**2,666**	**797**	**951**	**1,239**	**1,754**	**2,096**	**2,499**	**4,787**
Fees and admissions	755	177	132	199	377	329	608	1,629
Audio and visual equipment and services	960	434	591	700	789	850	999	1,392
Pets, toys, and playground equipment	547	91	175	237	413	468	566	954
Other entertainment products and services	404	95	54	103	176	449	326	812
PERSONAL CARE PRODUCTS AND SERVICES	**583**	**211**	**256**	**326**	**436**	**498**	**607**	**945**
READING	**134**	**52**	**69**	**95**	**98**	**110**	**122**	**215**
EDUCATION	**1,121**	**830**	**251**	**492**	**421**	**429**	**679**	**2,337**
TOBACCO PRODUCTS AND SMOKING SUPPLIES	**346**	**274**	**253**	**368**	**434**	**395**	**466**	**300**
MISCELLANEOUS	**855**	**507**	**357**	**540**	**587**	**800**	**856**	**1,334**
CASH CONTRIBUTIONS	**1,445**	**266**	**879**	**742**	**757**	**831**	**1,037**	**2,769**
PERSONAL INSURANCE AND PENSIONS	**5,517**	**281**	**493**	**1,611**	**2,442**	**3,665**	**5,300**	**11,689**
Life and other personal insurance	338	44	97	323	134	172	282	645
Pensions and Social Security	5,179	236	396	1,288	2,308	3,493	5,018	11,044
PERSONAL TAXES	**2,481**	**−14**	**53**	**268**	**598**	**1,070**	**2,004**	**5,989**
Federal income taxes	1,608	−38	−51	36	241	544	1,211	4,093
State and local income taxes	605	−5	21	94	119	307	590	1,400
Other taxes	268	29	83	138	238	219	204	497
GIFTS FOR PEOPLE IN OTHER HOUSEHOLDS	**1,204**	**480**	**360**	**564**	**692**	**702**	**1,267**	**2,200**

Note: Spending by category does not add to total spending because gift spending is also included in the preceding product and service categories and personal taxes are not included in the total. "−" means sample is too small to make a reliable estimate.
Source: Bureau of Labor Statistics, 2006 and 2007 Consumer Expenditure Surveys, Internet site http://www.bls.gov/cex/; calculations by New Strategist

Table 29. Indexed spending in the Northeast by income, 2006–07

(indexed average annual spending of consumer units in the Northeast by product and service category and before-tax income of consumer unit, 2006–07; index definition: an index of 100 is the average for all consumer units; an index of 132 means that spending by consumer units in that group is 32 percent above the average for all consumer units; an index of 68 indicates spending that is 32 percent below the average for all consumer units)

	total consumer units in Northeast	under $10,000	$10,000 to $19,999	$20,000 to $29,999	$30,000 to $39,999	$40,000 to $49,999	$50,000 to $69,999	$70,000 or more
Average spending of consumer units, total	$50,703	$17,716	$21,827	$29,355	$35,078	$40,322	$50,240	$85,201
Average spending of consumer units, index	100	35	43	58	69	80	99	168
FOOD	100	41	50	63	76	85	107	153
Food at home	100	49	58	73	81	88	109	141
Cereals and bakery products	100	50	59	74	79	86	109	142
Cereals and cereal products	100	62	64	78	78	91	104	136
Bakery products	100	44	56	73	80	83	111	144
Meats, poultry, fish, and eggs	100	54	63	77	79	89	107	138
Beef	100	41	59	87	73	100	98	142
Pork	100	62	71	74	94	92	126	121
Other meats	100	40	55	72	92	91	110	142
Poultry	100	61	65	71	76	85	95	146
Fish and seafood	100	63	59	74	65	78	112	144
Eggs	100	72	82	85	83	85	110	124
Dairy products	100	44	60	76	83	86	108	142
Fresh milk and cream	100	61	72	84	89	88	112	126
Other dairy products	100	35	53	71	79	85	105	150
Fruits and vegetables	100	51	60	77	85	86	105	140
Fresh fruits	100	48	62	75	77	91	108	141
Fresh vegetables	100	57	57	75	85	83	102	142
Processed fruits	100	44	62	84	91	79	103	139
Processed vegetables	100	52	58	75	92	92	106	135
Other food at home	100	45	53	67	80	90	113	144
Sugar and other sweets	100	61	50	76	78	85	114	139
Fats and oils	100	49	59	77	77	79	118	139
Miscellaneous foods	100	38	54	61	78	93	114	147
Nonalcoholic beverages	100	52	54	73	88	91	113	137
Food prepared by consumer unit on trips	100	25	34	49	56	72	93	186
Food away from home	100	31	39	51	70	81	104	169
ALCOHOLIC BEVERAGES	100	25	34	48	63	78	104	176
HOUSING	100	43	53	62	74	85	96	159
Shelter	100	48	55	63	74	84	94	159
Owned dwellings	100	21	27	40	57	71	93	193
Mortgage interest and charges	100	14	13	23	52	66	97	207
Property taxes	100	28	40	55	65	72	89	180
Maintenance, repair, insurance, other expenses	100	27	45	59	57	82	93	175
Rented dwellings	100	122	132	129	124	127	99	58
Other lodging	100	21	17	24	46	43	79	220
Utilities, fuels, and public services	100	42	64	77	85	92	107	141
Natural gas	100	39	72	78	82	99	112	135
Electricity	100	39	63	75	89	93	103	142
Fuel oil and other fuels	100	39	73	83	82	72	97	147
Telephone services	100	51	59	76	86	92	112	138
Water and other public services	100	31	54	74	80	96	109	148
Household services	100	23	39	41	48	70	76	198
Personal services	100	9	30	30	34	86	71	212
Other household services	100	33	46	49	59	58	80	188
Housekeeping supplies	100	44	44	64	77	83	109	154
Laundry and cleaning supplies	100	50	50	72	90	87	107	142
Other household products	100	43	40	54	76	91	110	157
Postage and stationery	100	42	48	76	69	63	108	158

	total consumer units in Northeast	under $10,000	$10,000 to $19,999	$20,000 to $29,999	$30,000 to $39,999	$40,000 to $49,999	$50,000 to $69,999	$70,000 or more
Household furnishings and equipment	100	27	26	41	61	87	98	182
Household textiles	100	27	33	67	76	110	144	140
Furniture	100	31	24	29	44	47	72	215
Floor coverings	100	31	39	14	151	66	66	180
Major appliances	100	35	22	68	64	85	99	173
Small appliances, miscellaneous housewares	100	29	52	33	50	108	169	141
Miscellaneous household equipment	100	21	22	39	61	106	99	179
APPAREL AND RELATED SERVICES	100	54	36	60	74	80	109	159
Men and boys	100	30	32	53	66	69	115	170
Men, aged 16 or older	100	25	34	48	63	70	123	170
Boys, aged 2 to 15	100	53	27	74	74	67	83	172
Women and girls	100	60	35	64	79	88	107	154
Women, aged 16 or older	100	65	37	67	79	95	112	147
Girls, aged 2 to 15	100	33	27	50	79	48	83	188
Children under age 2	100	106	47	61	79	90	129	132
Footwear	100	76	31	72	92	76	123	142
Other apparel products and services	100	38	46	46	57	80	88	179
TRANSPORTATION	100	23	33	58	68	74	108	173
Vehicle purchases	100	15	24	56	63	48	112	187
Cars and trucks, new	100	24	16	42	30	45	89	213
Cars and trucks, used	100	5	34	76	108	54	137	153
Other vehicles	100	–	–	–	–	5	259	187
Gasoline and motor oil	100	31	37	64	83	93	117	154
Other vehicle expenses	100	22	36	59	64	87	105	169
Vehicle finance charges	100	17	22	52	73	83	124	170
Maintenance and repairs	100	34	43	53	82	88	105	162
Vehicle insurance	100	17	38	71	59	96	109	161
Vehicle rentals, leases, licenses, other charges	100	21	28	45	53	71	90	194
Public transportation	100	37	41	48	55	65	76	191
HEALTH CARE	100	31	74	88	90	93	102	136
Health insurance	100	33	82	96	99	97	101	127
Medical services	100	22	56	62	62	79	100	167
Drugs	100	32	84	102	99	100	108	119
Medical supplies	100	29	40	63	77	94	96	165
ENTERTAINMENT	100	30	36	46	66	79	94	180
Fees and admissions	100	23	17	26	50	44	81	216
Audio and visual equipment and services	100	45	62	73	82	89	104	145
Pets, toys, and playground equipment	100	17	32	43	76	86	103	174
Other entertainment products and services	100	24	13	25	44	111	81	201
PERSONAL CARE PRODUCTS AND SERVICES	100	36	44	56	75	85	104	162
READING	100	39	52	71	73	82	91	160
EDUCATION	100	74	22	44	38	38	61	208
TOBACCO PRODUCTS AND SMOKING SUPPLIES	100	79	73	106	125	114	135	87
MISCELLANEOUS	100	59	42	63	69	94	100	156
CASH CONTRIBUTIONS	100	18	61	51	52	58	72	192
PERSONAL INSURANCE AND PENSIONS	100	5	9	29	44	66	96	212
Life and other personal insurance	100	13	29	96	40	51	83	191
Pensions and Social Security	100	5	8	25	45	67	97	213
PERSONAL TAXES	100	–	2	11	24	43	81	241
Federal income taxes	100	–	–	2	15	34	75	255
State and local income taxes	100	–	3	16	20	51	98	231
Other taxes	100	11	31	51	89	82	76	185
GIFTS FOR PEOPLE IN OTHER HOUSEHOLDS	100	40	30	47	57	58	105	183

Note: "–" means sample is too small to make a reliable estimate or not applicable.
Source: Calculations by New Strategist based on the Bureau of Labor Statistics' 2006 and 2007 Consumer Expenditure Surveys

Table 30. Average spending in the Midwest by income, 2006–07

(average annual spending of consumer units (CUs) in the Midwest by product and service category and before-tax income of consumer unit, 2006–07)

	total consumer units in Midwest	under $10,000	$10,000 to $19,999	$20,000 to $29,999	$30,000 to $39,999	$40,000 to $49,999	$50,000 to $69,999	$70,000 or more
Number of consumer units (in 000s)	27,334	2,726	3,256	3,227	3,106	2,608	4,239	8,173
Average number of persons per CU	2.4	1.4	1.6	2.1	2.2	2.3	2.7	3.1
Average before-tax income of CUs	$58,688	$4,867	$14,956	$24,971	$34,509	$44,723	$59,631	$120,525
Average annual spending of consumer units	46,812	16,313	21,344	28,461	32,883	38,423	49,151	80,606
FOOD	**5,778**	**2,548**	**3,063**	**4,038**	**4,102**	**5,188**	**6,160**	**9,010**
Food at home	**3,256**	**1,519**	**1,984**	**2,615**	**2,517**	**3,116**	**3,445**	**4,686**
Cereals and bakery products	438	191	262	359	332	417	483	626
Cereals and cereal products	133	62	81	111	99	129	148	185
Bakery products	306	128	182	248	233	288	335	441
Meats, poultry, fish, and eggs	715	340	491	612	557	660	741	1,004
Beef	212	86	166	172	168	184	229	295
Pork	148	85	98	141	121	142	163	191
Other meats	112	62	63	82	91	106	128	157
Poultry	113	58	68	106	80	106	103	170
Fish and seafood	99	31	76	84	68	92	85	151
Eggs	31	18	21	27	29	29	34	40
Dairy products	370	167	210	271	298	370	410	532
Fresh milk and cream	139	68	84	112	117	140	151	192
Other dairy products	231	98	126	158	181	230	258	340
Fruits and vegetables	538	250	309	445	408	502	549	795
Fresh fruits	186	83	104	153	138	164	182	285
Fresh vegetables	162	67	90	131	120	158	157	247
Processed fruits	103	55	58	93	80	101	114	141
Processed vegetables	87	45	57	68	70	79	96	123
Other food at home	1,195	572	712	928	922	1,168	1,262	1,729
Sugar and other sweets	129	55	87	90	95	122	120	197
Fats and oils	84	35	52	75	70	81	88	117
Miscellaneous foods	627	303	365	481	465	623	646	924
Nonalcoholic beverages	315	168	195	269	270	308	368	410
Food prepared by consumer unit on trips	40	12	12	13	23	34	39	80
Food away from home	**2,522**	**1,028**	**1,080**	**1,423**	**1,585**	**2,072**	**2,716**	**4,324**
ALCOHOLIC BEVERAGES	**512**	**242**	**220**	**284**	**399**	**420**	**493**	**873**
HOUSING	**15,067**	**5,948**	**8,046**	**10,164**	**11,215**	**12,985**	**15,765**	**24,518**
Shelter	**8,531**	**3,653**	**4,534**	**5,771**	**6,482**	**7,149**	**8,572**	**14,037**
Owned dwellings	6,054	1,028	1,761	2,990	3,824	4,552	6,617	11,685
Mortgage interest and charges	3,210	393	510	1,143	1,706	2,455	3,632	6,635
Property taxes	1,756	454	755	1,068	1,191	1,332	1,765	3,204
Maintenance, repair, insurance, other expenses	1,088	181	495	779	926	765	1,220	1,846
Rented dwellings	1,848	2,435	2,619	2,634	2,452	2,249	1,495	860
Other lodging	629	190	155	148	206	349	460	1,492
Utilities, fuels, and public services	**3,303**	**1,378**	**2,349**	**2,806**	**2,958**	**3,204**	**3,692**	**4,483**
Natural gas	732	294	525	660	691	681	784	993
Electricity	1,087	528	841	955	951	1,056	1,166	1,443
Fuel oil and other fuels	112	28	90	84	106	143	141	136
Telephone services	1,012	431	663	814	898	986	1,176	1,388
Water and other public services	361	96	229	293	312	339	425	523
Household services	**891**	**159**	**291**	**401**	**419**	**563**	**759**	**1,918**
Personal services	431	36	83	124	141	230	349	1,040
Other household services	459	123	209	277	278	334	410	878
Housekeeping supplies	**613**	**219**	**298**	**419**	**482**	**557**	**583**	**999**
Laundry and cleaning supplies	138	52	71	107	150	130	155	190
Other household products	321	111	141	203	204	317	296	551
Postage and stationery	153	57	85	109	128	109	132	258

	total consumer units in Midwest	under $10,000	$10,000 to $19,999	$20,000 to $29,999	$30,000 to $39,999	$40,000 to $49,999	$50,000 to $69,999	$70,000 or more
Household furnishings and equipment	**$1,730**	**$537**	**$573**	**$767**	**$874**	**$1,511**	**$2,159**	**$3,081**
Household textiles	128	34	44	73	56	121	174	215
Furniture	424	85	153	158	189	450	466	804
Floor coverings	44	8	10	17	17	26	40	97
Major appliances	212	62	68	124	134	195	244	374
Small appliances, miscellaneous housewares	93	29	39	62	65	67	82	170
Miscellaneous household equipment	828	320	260	334	414	653	1,152	1,421
APPAREL AND RELATED SERVICES	**1,828**	**734**	**728**	**954**	**1,048**	**1,341**	**1,811**	**3,371**
Men and boys	**387**	**141**	**168**	**187**	**240**	**267**	**448**	**682**
Men, aged 16 or older	305	114	125	132	185	207	353	545
Boys, aged 2 to 15	83	27	44	55	54	60	95	137
Women and girls	**777**	**306**	**292**	**349**	**455**	**527**	**713**	**1,496**
Women, aged 16 or older	657	280	247	289	386	442	594	1,267
Girls, aged 2 to 15	119	26	46	60	69	85	119	228
Children under age 2	**93**	**55**	**48**	**51**	**60**	**97**	**101**	**145**
Footwear	**295**	**135**	**117**	**268**	**135**	**246**	**332**	**478**
Other apparel products and services	**277**	**97**	**103**	**99**	**159**	**204**	**217**	**570**
TRANSPORTATION	**8,159**	**2,243**	**3,281**	**5,104**	**6,146**	**6,227**	**9,007**	**14,191**
Vehicle purchases	**3,070**	**514**	**1,193**	**1,723**	**2,167**	**1,609**	**3,309**	**5,888**
Cars and trucks, new	1,425	192	315	274	696	388	1,437	3,369
Cars and trucks, used	1,534	429	817	1,401	1,396	1,131	1,767	2,302
Other vehicles	111	–	61	48	75	89	104	217
Gasoline and motor oil	**2,275**	**885**	**1,094**	**1,585**	**1,827**	**2,207**	**2,682**	**3,464**
Other vehicle expenses	**2,386**	**733**	**798**	**1,653**	**1,956**	**2,211**	**2,655**	**3,905**
Vehicle finance charges	265	31	58	110	174	249	362	477
Maintenance and repairs	660	217	275	455	533	622	757	1,047
Vehicle insurance	930	313	274	815	959	876	948	1,411
Vehicle rentals, leases, licenses, other charges	531	172	191	274	290	464	588	969
Public transportation	**428**	**111**	**194**	**143**	**196**	**201**	**360**	**935**
HEALTH CARE	**2,957**	**900**	**2,044**	**2,557**	**2,596**	**3,141**	**3,369**	**4,023**
Health insurance	1,569	446	1,208	1,440	1,518	1,644	1,862	1,980
Medical services	754	226	356	506	521	828	789	1,234
Drugs	507	176	421	529	470	514	563	620
Medical supplies	128	51	59	82	87	154	156	189
ENTERTAINMENT	**2,525**	**738**	**1,097**	**1,291**	**1,557**	**1,922**	**2,552**	**4,680**
Fees and admissions	636	138	183	186	266	387	517	1,436
Audio and visual equipment and services	875	380	481	631	675	804	902	1,378
Pets, toys, and playground equipment	527	125	221	297	440	424	535	912
Other entertainment products and services	487	96	212	177	176	307	597	954
PERSONAL CARE PRODUCTS AND SERVICES	**541**	**176**	**270**	**287**	**371**	**480**	**597**	**908**
READING	**127**	**41**	**74**	**82**	**88**	**101**	**127**	**219**
EDUCATION	**1,069**	**1,465**	**496**	**268**	**290**	**521**	**824**	**2,079**
TOBACCO PRODUCTS AND SMOKING SUPPLIES	**360**	**238**	**322**	**385**	**403**	**439**	**426**	**331**
MISCELLANEOUS	**792**	**179**	**305**	**563**	**592**	**554**	**902**	**1,370**
CASH CONTRIBUTIONS	**1,847**	**391**	**678**	**878**	**1,501**	**1,430**	**1,713**	**3,516**
PERSONAL INSURANCE AND PENSIONS	**5,247**	**471**	**721**	**1,605**	**2,575**	**3,676**	**5,405**	**11,517**
Life and other personal insurance	346	54	135	184	199	240	342	683
Pensions and Social Security	4,902	417	586	1,421	2,376	3,435	5,063	10,835
PERSONAL TAXES	**1,976**	**86**	**–5**	**102**	**631**	**1,004**	**1,592**	**5,156**
Federal income taxes	1,241	19	–123	–58	261	465	881	3,511
State and local income taxes	483	18	7	64	217	346	438	1,162
Other taxes	252	49	111	96	153	193	274	483
GIFTS FOR PEOPLE IN OTHER HOUSEHOLDS	**1,301**	**418**	**629**	**563**	**570**	**775**	**1,058**	**2,710**

Note: Spending by category does not add to total spending because gift spending is also included in the preceding product and service categories and personal taxes are not included in the total. "–" means sample is too small to make a reliable estimate.
Source: Bureau of Labor Statistics, 2006 and 2007 Consumer Expenditure Surveys, Internet site http://www.bls.gov/cex/; calculations by New Strategist

Table 31. Indexed spending in the Midwest by income, 2006–07

(indexed average annual spending of consumer units in the Midwest by product and service category and before-tax income of consumer unit, 2006–07; index definition: an index of 100 is the average for all consumer units; an index of 132 means that spending by consumer units in that group is 32 percent above the average for all consumer units; an index of 68 indicates spending that is 32 percent below the average for all consumer units)

	total consumer units in Midwest	under $10,000	$10,000 to $19,999	$20,000 to $29,999	$30,000 to $39,999	$40,000 to $49,999	$50,000 to $69,999	$70,000 or more
Average spending of consumer units, total	$46,812	$16,313	$21,344	$28,461	$32,883	$38,423	$49,151	$80,606
Average spending of consumer units, index	100	35	46	61	70	82	105	172
FOOD	100	44	53	70	71	90	107	156
Food at home	100	47	61	80	77	96	106	144
Cereals and bakery products	100	44	60	82	76	95	110	143
Cereals and cereal products	100	47	61	83	74	97	111	139
Bakery products	100	42	59	81	76	94	109	144
Meats, poultry, fish, and eggs	100	48	69	86	78	92	104	140
Beef	100	41	78	81	79	87	108	139
Pork	100	58	66	95	82	96	110	129
Other meats	100	55	56	73	81	95	114	140
Poultry	100	52	60	94	71	94	91	150
Fish and seafood	100	31	77	85	69	93	86	153
Eggs	100	57	68	87	94	94	110	129
Dairy products	100	45	57	73	81	100	111	144
Fresh milk and cream	100	49	60	81	84	101	109	138
Other dairy products	100	43	55	68	78	100	112	147
Fruits and vegetables	100	46	57	83	76	93	102	148
Fresh fruits	100	45	56	82	74	88	98	153
Fresh vegetables	100	41	56	81	74	98	97	152
Processed fruits	100	53	56	90	78	98	111	137
Processed vegetables	100	52	65	78	80	91	110	141
Other food at home	100	48	60	78	77	98	106	145
Sugar and other sweets	100	43	67	70	74	95	93	153
Fats and oils	100	41	62	89	83	96	105	139
Miscellaneous foods	100	48	58	77	74	99	103	147
Nonalcoholic beverages	100	53	62	85	86	98	117	130
Food prepared by consumer unit on trips	100	29	31	33	58	85	98	200
Food away from home	100	41	43	56	63	82	108	171
ALCOHOLIC BEVERAGES	100	47	43	55	78	82	96	171
HOUSING	100	39	53	67	74	86	105	163
Shelter	100	43	53	68	76	84	100	165
Owned dwellings	100	17	29	49	63	75	109	193
Mortgage interest and charges	100	12	16	36	53	76	113	207
Property taxes	100	26	43	61	68	76	101	182
Maintenance, repair, insurance, other expenses	100	17	46	72	85	70	112	170
Rented dwellings	100	132	142	143	133	122	81	47
Other lodging	100	30	25	24	33	55	73	237
Utilities, fuels, and public services	100	42	71	85	90	97	112	136
Natural gas	100	40	72	90	94	93	107	136
Electricity	100	49	77	88	87	97	107	133
Fuel oil and other fuels	100	25	81	75	95	128	126	121
Telephone services	100	43	65	80	89	97	116	137
Water and other public services	100	27	64	81	86	94	118	145
Household services	100	18	33	45	47	63	85	215
Personal services	100	8	19	29	33	53	81	241
Other household services	100	27	46	60	61	73	89	191
Housekeeping supplies	100	36	49	68	79	91	95	163
Laundry and cleaning supplies	100	38	52	78	109	94	112	138
Other household products	100	34	44	63	64	99	92	172
Postage and stationery	100	37	55	71	84	71	86	169

	total consumer units in Midwest	under $10,000	$10,000 to $19,999	$20,000 to $29,999	$30,000 to $39,999	$40,000 to $49,999	$50,000 to $69,999	$70,000 or more
Household furnishings and equipment	100	31	33	44	51	87	125	178
Household textiles	100	26	34	57	44	95	136	168
Furniture	100	20	36	37	45	106	110	190
Floor coverings	100	19	23	39	39	59	91	220
Major appliances	100	29	32	58	63	92	115	176
Small appliances, miscellaneous housewares	100	32	42	67	70	72	88	183
Miscellaneous household equipment	100	39	31	40	50	79	139	172
APPAREL AND RELATED SERVICES	100	40	40	52	57	73	99	184
Men and boys	100	36	43	48	62	69	116	176
Men, aged 16 or older	100	37	41	43	61	68	116	179
Boys, aged 2 to 15	100	32	53	66	65	72	114	165
Women and girls	100	39	38	45	59	68	92	193
Women, aged 16 or older	100	43	38	44	59	67	90	193
Girls, aged 2 to 15	100	22	38	50	58	71	100	192
Children under age 2	100	60	51	55	65	104	109	156
Footwear	100	46	40	91	46	83	113	162
Other apparel products and services	100	35	37	36	57	74	78	206
TRANSPORTATION	100	27	40	63	75	76	110	174
Vehicle purchases	100	17	39	56	71	52	108	192
Cars and trucks, new	100	13	22	19	49	27	101	236
Cars and trucks, used	100	28	53	91	91	74	115	150
Other vehicles	100	–	55	43	68	80	94	195
Gasoline and motor oil	100	39	48	70	80	97	118	152
Other vehicle expenses	100	31	33	69	82	93	111	164
Vehicle finance charges	100	12	22	42	66	94	137	180
Maintenance and repairs	100	33	42	69	81	94	115	159
Vehicle insurance	100	34	29	88	103	94	102	152
Vehicle rentals, leases, licenses, other charges	100	32	36	52	55	87	111	182
Public transportation	100	26	45	33	46	47	84	218
HEALTH CARE	100	30	69	86	88	106	114	136
Health insurance	100	28	77	92	97	105	119	126
Medical services	100	30	47	67	69	110	105	164
Drugs	100	35	83	104	93	101	111	122
Medical supplies	100	40	46	64	68	120	122	148
ENTERTAINMENT	100	29	43	51	62	76	101	185
Fees and admissions	100	22	29	29	42	61	81	226
Audio and visual equipment and services	100	43	55	72	77	92	103	157
Pets, toys, and playground equipment	100	24	42	56	83	80	102	173
Other entertainment products and services	100	20	44	36	36	63	123	196
PERSONAL CARE PRODUCTS AND SERVICES	100	32	50	53	69	89	110	168
READING	100	32	59	65	69	80	100	172
EDUCATION	100	137	46	25	27	49	77	194
TOBACCO PRODUCTS AND SMOKING SUPPLIES	100	66	89	107	112	122	118	92
MISCELLANEOUS	100	23	38	71	75	70	114	173
CASH CONTRIBUTIONS	100	21	37	48	81	77	93	190
PERSONAL INSURANCE AND PENSIONS	100	9	14	31	49	70	103	219
Life and other personal insurance	100	16	39	53	58	69	99	197
Pensions and Social Security	100	9	12	29	48	70	103	221
PERSONAL TAXES	100	4	0	5	32	51	81	261
Federal income taxes	100	2	–	–	21	37	71	283
State and local income taxes	100	4	1	13	45	72	91	241
Other taxes	100	19	44	38	61	77	109	192
GIFTS FOR PEOPLE IN OTHER HOUSEHOLDS	100	32	48	43	44	60	81	208

Note: "–" means sample is too small to make a reliable estimate or not applicable.
Source: Calculations by New Strategist based on the Bureau of Labor Statistics' 2006 and 2007 Consumer Expenditure Surveys

Table 32. Average spending in the South by income, 2006–07

(average annual spending of consumer units (CUs) in the South by product and service category and before-tax income of consumer unit, 2006–07)

	total consumer units in South	under $10,000	$10,000 to $19,999	$20,000 to $29,999	$30,000 to $39,999	$40,000 to $49,999	$50,000 to $69,999	$70,000 or more
Number of consumer units (in 000s)	42,804	3,713	5,971	5,653	5,030	4,409	6,273	11,754
Average number of persons per CU	2.5	1.7	2.0	2.3	2.5	2.5	2.8	3.0
Average before-tax income of CUs	$57,216	$4,728	$15,037	$24,787	$34,784	$44,404	$59,206	$124,160
Average annual spending of consumer units	45,225	17,996	22,252	28,135	33,792	38,847	47,641	79,027
FOOD	**5,715**	**2,802**	**3,243**	**3,910**	**4,487**	**5,340**	**6,066**	**8,937**
Food at home	**3,223**	**1,890**	**2,281**	**2,523**	**2,726**	**3,098**	**3,323**	**4,530**
Cereals and bakery products	423	247	295	334	358	415	440	589
Cereals and cereal products	132	81	99	111	124	129	129	178
Bakery products	291	166	196	224	235	287	311	411
Meats, poultry, fish, and eggs	767	485	580	643	664	769	777	1,022
Beef	225	134	158	189	196	220	228	310
Pork	162	108	129	143	152	172	171	195
Other meats	94	53	74	83	77	93	93	127
Poultry	143	93	112	119	123	135	145	190
Fish and seafood	106	73	69	76	77	110	103	157
Eggs	38	25	38	33	38	39	36	43
Dairy products	347	194	237	262	304	320	387	483
Fresh milk and cream	146	96	111	115	137	139	161	186
Other dairy products	202	98	126	147	167	181	226	297
Fruits and vegetables	532	299	367	411	430	504	536	774
Fresh fruits	167	91	109	117	131	163	167	252
Fresh vegetables	174	94	124	134	133	156	177	257
Processed fruits	96	53	67	77	80	92	96	137
Processed vegetables	96	60	68	83	87	93	96	128
Other food at home	1,154	666	801	872	970	1,089	1,183	1,661
Sugar and other sweets	115	67	77	85	99	103	116	170
Fats and oils	85	56	70	72	80	93	81	107
Miscellaneous foods	596	332	404	459	498	556	617	862
Nonalcoholic beverages	326	201	234	243	270	312	333	461
Food prepared by consumer unit on trips	32	9	15	14	24	25	35	60
Food away from home	**2,492**	**912**	**962**	**1,387**	**1,761**	**2,242**	**2,742**	**4,407**
ALCOHOLIC BEVERAGES	**374**	**124**	**134**	**212**	**274**	**380**	**433**	**634**
HOUSING	**14,719**	**7,373**	**8,408**	**10,017**	**11,418**	**12,832**	**15,312**	**24,203**
Shelter	**8,056**	**3,836**	**4,367**	**5,432**	**6,260**	**7,138**	**8,096**	**13,617**
Owned dwellings	5,536	1,506	1,889	2,720	3,215	4,226	5,607	11,464
Mortgage interest and charges	3,256	708	793	1,238	1,719	2,420	3,437	7,156
Property taxes	1,224	473	541	691	754	938	1,183	2,396
Maintenance, repair, insurance, other expenses	1,057	325	554	791	742	869	987	1,913
Rented dwellings	2,107	2,261	2,393	2,601	2,871	2,686	2,149	1,110
Other lodging	412	69	84	111	173	225	340	1,043
Utilities, fuels, and public services	**3,550**	**2,283**	**2,592**	**2,923**	**3,233**	**3,435**	**3,846**	**4,760**
Natural gas	298	206	217	230	230	260	282	454
Electricity	1,578	1,072	1,213	1,363	1,485	1,523	1,685	2,029
Fuel oil and other fuels	63	43	54	63	51	58	63	82
Telephone services	1,167	673	784	910	1,072	1,172	1,333	1,593
Water and other public services	444	289	324	358	394	423	483	602
Household services	**898**	**222**	**405**	**431**	**542**	**629**	**881**	**1,848**
Personal services	369	74	132	133	224	195	382	817
Other household services	529	149	273	299	318	434	499	1,032
Housekeeping supplies	**627**	**360**	**329**	**428**	**429**	**525**	**657**	**1,026**
Laundry and cleaning supplies	160	113	111	130	128	170	162	218
Other household products	333	173	153	211	214	243	355	581
Postage and stationery	134	73	66	87	87	112	140	227

	total consumer units in South	under $10,000	$10,000 to $19,999	$20,000 to $29,999	$30,000 to $39,999	$40,000 to $49,999	$50,000 to $69,999	$70,000 or more
Household furnishings and equipment	**$1,588**	**$673**	**$714**	**$801**	**$955**	**$1,105**	**$1,832**	**$2,952**
Household textiles	131	48	65	82	67	82	147	243
Furniture	408	137	171	193	248	285	457	803
Floor coverings	38	15	27	9	23	16	26	85
Major appliances	215	94	130	147	121	161	249	369
Small appliances, miscellaneous housewares	103	38	46	53	87	111	127	162
Miscellaneous household equipment	694	339	275	318	408	450	826	1,291
APPAREL AND RELATED SERVICES	**1,720**	**922**	**724**	**1,014**	**1,168**	**1,668**	**1,685**	**3,005**
Men and boys	**429**	**216**	**145**	**276**	**270**	**398**	**421**	**771**
Men, aged 16 or older	340	177	100	212	199	316	324	628
Boys, aged 2 to 15	89	39	44	64	72	82	96	143
Women and girls	**668**	**348**	**277**	**366**	**487**	**652**	**675**	**1,153**
Women, aged 16 or older	540	235	226	290	397	541	562	928
Girls, aged 2 to 15	128	113	50	75	90	111	112	226
Children under age 2	**87**	**67**	**48**	**67**	**72**	**78**	**96**	**126**
Footwear	**288**	**190**	**171**	**181**	**201**	**323**	**249**	**461**
Other apparel products and services	**248**	**100**	**84**	**124**	**138**	**218**	**244**	**493**
TRANSPORTATION	**8,578**	**2,765**	**4,002**	**5,388**	**7,167**	**7,389**	**9,760**	**14,626**
Vehicle purchases	**3,428**	**900**	**1,439**	**1,900**	**2,892**	**2,484**	**3,835**	**6,337**
Cars and trucks, new	1,705	342	594	767	1,028	1,164	1,702	3,646
Cars and trucks, used	1,656	540	830	1,098	1,788	1,289	2,072	2,554
Other vehicles	67	31	14	36	76	31	61	137
Gasoline and motor oil	**2,440**	**983**	**1,357**	**1,849**	**2,186**	**2,432**	**2,933**	**3,583**
Other vehicle expenses	**2,368**	**794**	**1,108**	**1,498**	**1,889**	**2,324**	**2,672**	**3,917**
Vehicle finance charges	340	68	94	176	255	343	445	608
Maintenance and repairs	670	235	324	426	561	616	727	1,133
Vehicle insurance	1,046	409	597	743	902	1,133	1,175	1,520
Vehicle rentals, leases, licenses, other charges	313	83	92	154	170	232	326	657
Public transportation	**342**	**89**	**99**	**140**	**200**	**149**	**320**	**789**
HEALTH CARE	**2,788**	**1,142**	**1,907**	**2,455**	**2,458**	**2,542**	**2,953**	**4,052**
Health insurance	1,499	587	1,134	1,359	1,336	1,451	1,626	2,059
Medical services	627	207	276	502	518	483	651	1,084
Drugs	560	289	447	504	510	528	582	743
Medical supplies	103	59	49	89	94	80	93	166
ENTERTAINMENT	**2,322**	**889**	**968**	**1,386**	**1,671**	**1,932**	**2,352**	**4,267**
Fees and admissions	458	83	98	169	266	296	434	1,050
Audio and visual equipment and services	934	492	546	684	754	918	1,024	1,423
Pets, toys, and playground equipment	561	212	210	328	437	466	618	987
Other entertainment products and services	368	102	114	204	213	251	276	807
PERSONAL CARE PRODUCTS AND SERVICES	**568**	**213**	**297**	**383**	**437**	**478**	**600**	**961**
READING	**87**	**31**	**49**	**53**	**53**	**77**	**84**	**160**
EDUCATION	**726**	**460**	**251**	**197**	**252**	**359**	**526**	**1,747**
TOBACCO PRODUCTS AND SMOKING SUPPLIES	**334**	**287**	**269**	**326**	**398**	**326**	**401**	**327**
MISCELLANEOUS	**689**	**315**	**459**	**331**	**496**	**494**	**686**	**1,249**
CASH CONTRIBUTIONS	**1,762**	**376**	**840**	**881**	**1,021**	**1,476**	**1,737**	**3,529**
PERSONAL INSURANCE AND PENSIONS	**4,843**	**299**	**702**	**1,583**	**2,491**	**3,553**	**5,047**	**11,331**
Life and other personal insurance	305	94	133	172	199	231	285	608
Pensions and Social Security	4,537	203	568	1,411	2,291	3,321	4,763	10,723
PERSONAL TAXES	**2,049**	**36**	**−121**	**71**	**549**	**959**	**1,713**	**5,969**
Federal income taxes	1,561	−10	−205	−103	287	635	1,230	4,823
State and local income taxes	334	2	21	90	142	186	317	862
Other taxes	155	46	64	84	120	138	166	284
GIFTS FOR PEOPLE IN OTHER HOUSEHOLDS	**1,003**	**368**	**360**	**346**	**465**	**616**	**944**	**2,218**

Note: Spending by category does not add to total spending because gift spending is also included in the preceding product and service categories and personal taxes are not included in the total.

Source: Bureau of Labor Statistics, 2006 and 2007 Consumer Expenditure Surveys, Internet site http://www.bls.gov/cex/; calculations by New Strategist

Table 33. Indexed spending in the South by income, 2006–07

(indexed average annual spending of consumer units in the South by product and service category and before-tax income of consumer unit, 2006–07; index definition: an index of 100 is the average for all consumer units; an index of 132 means that spending by consumer units in that group is 32 percent above the average for all consumer units; an index of 68 indicates spending that is 32 percent below the average for all consumer units)

	total consumer units in South	under $10,000	$10,000 to $19,999	$20,000 to $29,999	$30,000 to $39,999	$40,000 to $49,999	$50,000 to $69,999	$70,000 or more
Average spending of consumer units, total	$45,225	$17,996	$22,252	$28,135	$33,792	$38,847	$47,641	$79,027
Average spending of consumer units, index	100	40	49	62	75	86	105	175
FOOD	100	49	57	68	79	93	106	156
Food at home	100	59	71	78	85	96	103	141
Cereals and bakery products	100	58	70	79	85	98	104	139
Cereals and cereal products	100	61	75	84	94	98	98	135
Bakery products	100	57	67	77	81	99	107	141
Meats, poultry, fish, and eggs	100	63	76	84	87	100	101	133
Beef	100	60	70	84	87	98	101	138
Pork	100	67	80	88	94	106	106	120
Other meats	100	57	79	88	82	99	99	135
Poultry	100	65	78	83	86	94	101	133
Fish and seafood	100	69	65	72	73	104	97	148
Eggs	100	66	100	87	100	103	95	113
Dairy products	100	56	68	76	88	92	112	139
Fresh milk and cream	100	66	76	79	94	95	110	127
Other dairy products	100	48	62	73	83	90	112	147
Fruits and vegetables	100	56	69	77	81	95	101	145
Fresh fruits	100	54	66	70	78	98	100	151
Fresh vegetables	100	54	71	77	76	90	102	148
Processed fruits	100	55	70	80	83	96	100	143
Processed vegetables	100	63	70	86	91	97	100	133
Other food at home	100	58	69	76	84	94	103	144
Sugar and other sweets	100	58	67	74	86	90	101	148
Fats and oils	100	66	82	85	94	109	95	126
Miscellaneous foods	100	56	68	77	84	93	104	145
Nonalcoholic beverages	100	62	72	75	83	96	102	141
Food prepared by consumer unit on trips	100	28	47	44	75	78	109	188
Food away from home	100	37	39	56	71	90	110	177
ALCOHOLIC BEVERAGES	100	33	36	57	73	102	116	170
HOUSING	100	50	57	68	78	87	104	164
Shelter	100	48	54	67	78	89	100	169
Owned dwellings	100	27	34	49	58	76	101	207
Mortgage interest and charges	100	22	24	38	53	74	106	220
Property taxes	100	39	44	56	62	77	97	196
Maintenance, repair, insurance, other expenses	100	31	52	75	70	82	93	181
Rented dwellings	100	107	114	123	136	127	102	53
Other lodging	100	17	20	27	42	55	83	253
Utilities, fuels, and public services	100	64	73	82	91	97	108	134
Natural gas	100	69	73	77	77	87	95	152
Electricity	100	68	77	86	94	97	107	129
Fuel oil and other fuels	100	68	86	100	81	92	100	130
Telephone services	100	58	67	78	92	100	114	137
Water and other public services	100	65	73	81	89	95	109	136
Household services	100	25	45	48	60	70	98	206
Personal services	100	20	36	36	61	53	104	221
Other household services	100	28	52	57	60	82	94	195
Housekeeping supplies	100	57	52	68	68	84	105	164
Laundry and cleaning supplies	100	71	69	81	80	106	101	136
Other household products	100	52	46	63	64	73	107	174
Postage and stationery	100	55	49	65	65	84	104	169

	total consumer units in South	under $10,000	$10,000 to $19,999	$20,000 to $29,999	$30,000 to $39,999	$40,000 to $49,999	$50,000 to $69,999	$70,000 or more
Household furnishings and equipment	100	42	45	50	60	70	115	186
Household textiles	100	37	49	63	51	63	112	185
Furniture	100	34	42	47	61	70	112	197
Floor coverings	100	40	70	24	61	42	68	224
Major appliances	100	44	61	68	56	75	116	172
Small appliances, miscellaneous housewares	100	37	45	51	84	108	123	157
Miscellaneous household equipment	100	49	40	46	59	65	119	186
APPAREL AND RELATED SERVICES	100	54	42	59	68	97	98	175
Men and boys	100	50	34	64	63	93	98	180
Men, aged 16 or older	100	52	30	62	59	93	95	185
Boys, aged 2 to 15	100	43	50	72	81	92	108	161
Women and girls	100	52	41	55	73	98	101	173
Women, aged 16 or older	100	44	42	54	74	100	104	172
Girls, aged 2 to 15	100	88	39	59	70	87	88	177
Children under age 2	100	77	56	77	83	90	110	145
Footwear	100	66	59	63	70	112	86	160
Other apparel products and services	100	40	34	50	56	88	98	199
TRANSPORTATION	100	32	47	63	84	86	114	171
Vehicle purchases	100	26	42	55	84	72	112	185
Cars and trucks, new	100	20	35	45	60	68	100	214
Cars and trucks, used	100	33	50	66	108	78	125	154
Other vehicles	100	46	21	54	113	46	91	204
Gasoline and motor oil	100	40	56	76	90	100	120	147
Other vehicle expenses	100	34	47	63	80	98	113	165
Vehicle finance charges	100	20	28	52	75	101	131	179
Maintenance and repairs	100	35	48	64	84	92	109	169
Vehicle insurance	100	39	57	71	86	108	112	145
Vehicle rentals, leases, licenses, other charges	100	26	29	49	54	74	104	210
Public transportation	100	26	29	41	58	44	94	231
HEALTH CARE	100	41	68	88	88	91	106	145
Health insurance	100	39	76	91	89	97	108	137
Medical services	100	33	44	80	83	77	104	173
Drugs	100	52	80	90	91	94	104	133
Medical supplies	100	57	48	86	91	78	90	161
ENTERTAINMENT	100	38	42	60	72	83	101	184
Fees and admissions	100	18	21	37	58	65	95	229
Audio and visual equipment and services	100	53	58	73	81	98	110	152
Pets, toys, and playground equipment	100	38	38	58	78	83	110	176
Other entertainment products and services	100	28	31	55	58	68	75	219
PERSONAL CARE PRODUCTS AND SERVICES	100	37	52	67	77	84	106	169
READING	100	36	57	61	61	89	97	184
EDUCATION	100	63	35	27	35	49	72	241
TOBACCO PRODUCTS AND SMOKING SUPPLIES	100	86	80	98	119	98	120	98
MISCELLANEOUS	100	46	67	48	72	72	100	181
CASH CONTRIBUTIONS	100	21	48	50	58	84	99	200
PERSONAL INSURANCE AND PENSIONS	100	6	14	33	51	73	104	234
Life and other personal insurance	100	31	44	56	65	76	93	199
Pensions and Social Security	100	4	13	31	50	73	105	236
PERSONAL TAXES	100	2	–	3	27	47	84	291
Federal income taxes	100	–	–	–	18	41	79	309
State and local income taxes	100	1	6	27	43	56	95	258
Other taxes	100	30	41	54	77	89	107	183
GIFTS FOR PEOPLE IN OTHER HOUSEHOLDS	100	37	36	34	46	61	94	221

Note: "–" means not applicable.
Source: Calculations by New Strategist based on the Bureau of Labor Statistics' 2006 and 2007 Consumer Expenditure Surveys

Table 34. Average spending in the West by income, 2006–07

(average annual spending of consumer units (CUs) in the West by product and service category and before-tax income of consumer unit, 2006–07)

	total consumer units in South	under $10,000	$10,000 to $19,999	$20,000 to $29,999	$30,000 to $39,999	$40,000 to $49,999	$50,000 to $69,999	$70,000 or more
Number of consumer units (in 000s)	26,800	1,766	3,112	3,025	2,808	2,546	4,282	9,260
Average number of persons per CU	2.6	1.6	1.8	2.2	2.4	2.5	2.8	3.1
Average before-tax income of CUs	$67,953	$2,972	$15,045	$25,064	$34,752	$44,573	$59,375	$132,602
Average annual spending of consumer units	57,124	22,356	24,691	33,401	39,982	45,944	55,945	91,151
FOOD	**6,981**	**3,586**	**3,702**	**4,603**	**5,521**	**6,267**	**7,064**	**10,072**
Food at home	**3,918**	**2,160**	**2,538**	**2,862**	**3,304**	**3,611**	**4,091**	**5,220**
Cereals and bakery products	489	291	330	368	399	449	498	651
Cereals and cereal products	160	100	117	131	122	142	155	212
Bakery products	330	191	214	237	277	307	344	439
Meats, poultry, fish, and eggs	864	486	522	644	728	829	917	1,141
Beef	254	142	142	176	229	249	295	328
Pork	153	83	106	115	116	147	160	203
Other meats	102	56	65	72	74	92	113	138
Poultry	152	103	88	119	146	127	155	202
Fish and seafood	151	68	85	116	118	160	135	213
Eggs	51	35	36	46	46	54	59	57
Dairy products	425	239	288	313	383	399	436	556
Fresh milk and cream	158	90	117	126	147	148	159	199
Other dairy products	267	149	172	187	237	251	276	356
Fruits and vegetables	725	448	492	541	619	713	729	945
Fresh fruits	253	145	178	196	210	254	241	333
Fresh vegetables	239	170	162	178	189	241	253	305
Processed fruits	129	71	85	92	122	117	129	171
Processed vegetables	104	63	68	75	97	101	106	136
Other food at home	1,414	696	904	996	1,176	1,220	1,510	1,927
Sugar and other sweets	135	63	94	92	119	112	149	180
Fats and oils	98	58	73	79	85	91	112	119
Miscellaneous foods	748	352	482	518	619	659	812	1,014
Nonalcoholic beverages	369	199	240	280	312	313	378	500
Food prepared by consumer unit on trips	64	23	15	28	41	45	60	113
Food away from home	**3,063**	**1,426**	**1,164**	**1,741**	**2,217**	**2,657**	**2,973**	**4,852**
ALCOHOLIC BEVERAGES	**576**	**253**	**300**	**317**	**422**	**526**	**577**	**869**
HOUSING	**20,024**	**9,024**	**9,837**	**12,961**	**14,338**	**15,664**	**19,742**	**30,886**
Shelter	**12,806**	**6,107**	**6,447**	**8,184**	**9,313**	**9,677**	**12,941**	**19,588**
Owned dwellings	8,244	1,973	2,125	3,430	4,288	5,209	7,835	15,293
Mortgage interest and charges	5,485	1,110	880	1,727	2,758	3,228	5,241	10,654
Property taxes	1,565	549	570	744	889	1,039	1,368	2,803
Maintenance, repair, insurance, other expenses	1,194	313	675	958	641	941	1,226	1,837
Rented dwellings	3,766	3,949	4,195	4,587	4,714	4,056	4,512	2,605
Other lodging	796	186	127	166	311	412	594	1,689
Utilities, fuels, and public services	**3,166**	**1,627**	**1,856**	**2,314**	**2,596**	**2,988**	**3,380**	**4,301**
Natural gas	430	196	246	301	354	385	437	612
Electricity	1,068	605	680	808	914	1,025	1,130	1,401
Fuel oil and other fuels	67	41	31	53	42	57	86	89
Telephone services	1,088	543	628	820	921	1,067	1,182	1,447
Water and other public services	513	242	271	332	366	454	545	751
Household services	**1,148**	**408**	**444**	**444**	**563**	**826**	**957**	**2,106**
Personal services	419	106	118	86	158	250	356	843
Other household services	729	301	326	357	405	576	601	1,263
Housekeeping supplies	**738**	**315**	**340**	**445**	**585**	**588**	**723**	**1,137**
Laundry and cleaning supplies	149	60	114	83	121	139	201	184
Other household products	395	142	165	251	227	324	359	651
Postage and stationery	194	113	62	111	237	125	163	302

	total consumer units in West	under $10,000	$10,000 to $19,999	$20,000 to $29,999	$30,000 to $39,999	$40,000 to $49,999	$50,000 to $69,999	$70,000 or more
Household furnishings and equipment	$2,167	$567	$749	$1,574	$1,280	$1,584	$1,741	$3,754
Household textiles	182	26	84	105	153	127	184	291
Furniture	587	114	194	345	293	362	489	1,084
Floor coverings	46	8	8	26	27	19	42	87
Major appliances	263	137	72	184	164	158	220	457
Small appliances, miscellaneous housewares	135	36	56	90	94	86	108	232
Miscellaneous household equipment	955	246	336	824	550	832	699	1,603
APPAREL AND RELATED SERVICES	2,091	1,081	882	1,164	1,532	1,525	2,191	3,278
Men and boys	494	137	147	307	336	391	530	795
Men, aged 16 or older	414	107	116	264	274	319	452	666
Boys, aged 2 to 15	81	30	31	43	62	72	79	128
Women and girls	816	489	378	465	583	560	870	1,259
Women, aged 16 or older	693	458	339	407	483	456	741	1,062
Girls, aged 2 to 15	123	30	40	58	100	105	129	197
Children under age 2	114	102	63	62	101	98	102	168
Footwear	350	225	163	161	357	263	381	509
Other apparel products and services	317	129	131	169	155	213	308	547
TRANSPORTATION	10,116	3,793	4,107	5,786	7,590	8,905	10,612	15,630
Vehicle purchases	3,976	1,046	1,536	2,306	2,857	2,993	4,482	6,276
Cars and trucks, new	2,074	491	906	897	1,200	1,217	1,944	3,715
Cars and trucks, used	1,798	556	621	1,401	1,617	1,757	2,443	2,328
Other vehicles	104	–	20	7	40	20	96	233
Gasoline and motor oil	2,386	979	1,136	1,612	1,892	2,264	2,640	3,393
Other vehicle expenses	2,992	1,511	1,117	1,606	2,358	3,051	2,793	4,632
Vehicle finance charges	327	64	99	147	237	276	393	522
Maintenance and repairs	862	272	397	505	616	785	922	1,313
Vehicle insurance	1,242	853	477	763	1,173	1,607	951	1,794
Vehicle rentals, leases, licenses, other charges	561	322	145	191	331	383	526	1,002
Public transportation	762	257	317	263	484	598	696	1,330
HEALTH CARE	2,857	1,043	1,706	2,434	2,569	2,779	3,115	3,714
Health insurance	1,456	613	951	1,292	1,274	1,402	1,519	1,882
Medical services	814	202	374	624	730	787	952	1,109
Drugs	456	185	311	422	466	456	512	536
Medical supplies	130	43	70	96	99	134	131	187
ENTERTAINMENT	3,234	1,002	1,035	1,425	2,034	2,311	3,043	5,690
Fees and admissions	842	190	216	272	443	546	657	1,649
Audio and visual equipment and services	1,035	465	497	629	819	893	1,133	1,517
Pets, toys, and playground equipment	651	195	228	381	416	502	638	1,080
Other entertainment products and services	707	152	95	142	357	371	615	1,445
PERSONAL CARE PRODUCTS AND SERVICES	665	236	306	389	485	525	602	1,077
READING	142	61	67	73	81	120	134	233
EDUCATION	894	722	465	529	492	589	662	1,502
TOBACCO PRODUCTS AND SMOKING SUPPLIES	256	183	232	222	283	319	295	246
MISCELLANEOUS	1,061	344	621	625	956	739	1,057	1,605
CASH CONTRIBUTIONS	2,312	563	709	978	1,161	2,214	1,723	4,269
PERSONAL INSURANCE AND PENSIONS	5,915	466	723	1,895	2,517	3,460	5,128	12,081
Life and other personal insurance	283	70	92	128	109	169	226	549
Pensions and Social Security	5,632	396	631	1,767	2,408	3,292	4,902	11,532
PERSONAL TAXES	3,022	155	26	361	651	945	1,942	7,235
Federal income taxes	2,199	61	–77	191	429	605	1,365	5,390
State and local income taxes	664	44	37	125	191	263	440	1,528
Other taxes	158	51	66	46	32	77	136	317
GIFTS FOR PEOPLE IN OTHER HOUSEHOLDS	1,363	457	393	567	630	666	1,905	2,287

Note: Spending by category does not add to total spending because gift spending is also included in the preceding product and service categories and personal taxes are not included in the total. "–" means sample is too small to make a reliable estimate.

Source: Bureau of Labor Statistics, 2006 and 2007 Consumer Expenditure Surveys, Internet site http://www.bls.gov/cex/; calculations by New Strategist

Table 35. Indexed spending in the West by income, 2006–07

(indexed average annual spending of consumer units in the West by product and service category and before-tax income of consumer unit, 2006–07; index definition: an index of 100 is the average for all consumer units; an index of 132 means that spending by consumer units in that group is 32 percent above the average for all consumer units; an index of 68 indicates spending that is 32 percent below the average for all consumer units)

	total consumer units in South	under $10,000	$10,000 to $19,999	$20,000 to $29,999	$30,000 to $39,999	$40,000 to $49,999	$50,000 to $69,999	$70,000 or more
Average spending of consumer units, total	$57,124	$22,356	$24,691	$33,401	$39,982	$45,944	$55,945	$91,151
Average spending of consumer units, index	100	39	43	58	70	80	98	160
FOOD	100	51	53	66	79	90	101	144
Food at home	100	55	65	73	84	92	104	133
Cereals and bakery products	100	59	68	75	82	92	102	133
Cereals and cereal products	100	62	73	82	76	89	97	133
Bakery products	100	58	65	72	84	93	104	133
Meats, poultry, fish, and eggs	100	56	60	75	84	96	106	132
Beef	100	56	56	69	90	98	116	129
Pork	100	54	70	75	76	96	105	133
Other meats	100	55	64	71	73	90	111	135
Poultry	100	68	58	78	96	84	102	133
Fish and seafood	100	45	56	77	78	106	89	141
Eggs	100	69	70	90	90	106	116	112
Dairy products	100	56	68	74	90	94	103	131
Fresh milk and cream	100	57	74	80	93	94	101	126
Other dairy products	100	56	64	70	89	94	103	133
Fruits and vegetables	100	62	68	75	85	98	101	130
Fresh fruits	100	57	70	77	83	100	95	132
Fresh vegetables	100	71	68	74	79	101	106	128
Processed fruits	100	55	66	71	95	91	100	133
Processed vegetables	100	60	65	72	93	97	102	131
Other food at home	100	49	64	70	83	86	107	136
Sugar and other sweets	100	47	70	68	88	83	110	133
Fats and oils	100	59	75	81	87	93	114	121
Miscellaneous foods	100	47	64	69	83	88	109	136
Nonalcoholic beverages	100	54	65	76	85	85	102	136
Food prepared by consumer unit on trips	100	36	23	44	64	70	94	177
Food away from home	100	47	38	57	72	87	97	158
ALCOHOLIC BEVERAGES	100	44	52	55	73	91	100	151
HOUSING	100	45	49	65	72	78	99	154
Shelter	100	48	50	64	73	76	101	153
Owned dwellings	100	24	26	42	52	63	95	186
Mortgage interest and charges	100	20	16	31	50	59	96	194
Property taxes	100	35	36	48	57	66	87	179
Maintenance, repair, insurance, other expenses	100	26	57	80	54	79	103	154
Rented dwellings	100	105	111	122	125	108	120	69
Other lodging	100	23	16	21	39	52	75	212
Utilities, fuels, and public services	100	51	59	73	82	94	107	136
Natural gas	100	46	57	70	82	90	102	142
Electricity	100	57	64	76	86	96	106	131
Fuel oil and other fuels	100	61	46	79	63	85	128	133
Telephone services	100	50	58	75	85	98	109	133
Water and other public services	100	47	53	65	71	88	106	146
Household services	100	36	39	39	49	72	83	183
Personal services	100	25	28	21	38	60	85	201
Other household services	100	41	45	49	56	79	82	173
Housekeeping supplies	100	43	46	60	79	80	98	154
Laundry and cleaning supplies	100	40	76	56	81	93	135	123
Other household products	100	36	42	64	57	82	91	165
Postage and stationery	100	58	32	57	122	64	84	156

	total consumer units in West	under $10,000	$10,000 to $19,999	$20,000 to $29,999	$30,000 to $39,999	$40,000 to $49,999	$50,000 to $69,999	$70,000 or more
Household furnishings and equipment	100	26	35	73	59	73	80	173
Household textiles	100	14	46	58	84	70	101	160
Furniture	100	19	33	59	50	62	83	185
Floor coverings	100	17	18	57	59	41	91	189
Major appliances	100	52	27	70	62	60	84	174
Small appliances, miscellaneous housewares	100	26	41	67	70	64	80	172
Miscellaneous household equipment	100	26	35	86	58	87	73	168
APPAREL AND RELATED SERVICES	100	52	42	56	73	73	105	157
Men and boys	100	28	30	62	68	79	107	161
Men, aged 16 or older	100	26	28	64	66	77	109	161
Boys, aged 2 to 15	100	37	38	53	77	89	98	158
Women and girls	100	60	46	57	71	69	107	154
Women, aged 16 or older	100	66	49	59	70	66	107	153
Girls, aged 2 to 15	100	25	32	47	81	85	105	160
Children under age 2	100	89	55	54	89	86	89	147
Footwear	100	64	47	46	102	75	109	145
Other apparel products and services	100	41	41	53	49	67	97	173
TRANSPORTATION	100	37	41	57	75	88	105	155
Vehicle purchases	100	26	39	58	72	75	113	158
Cars and trucks, new	100	24	44	43	58	59	94	179
Cars and trucks, used	100	31	35	78	90	98	136	129
Other vehicles	100	–	19	7	38	19	92	224
Gasoline and motor oil	100	41	48	68	79	95	111	142
Other vehicle expenses	100	51	37	54	79	102	93	155
Vehicle finance charges	100	19	30	45	72	84	120	160
Maintenance and repairs	100	32	46	59	71	91	107	152
Vehicle insurance	100	69	38	61	94	129	77	144
Vehicle rentals, leases, licenses, other charges	100	57	26	34	59	68	94	179
Public transportation	100	34	42	35	64	78	91	175
HEALTH CARE	100	37	60	85	90	97	109	130
Health insurance	100	42	65	89	88	96	104	129
Medical services	100	25	46	77	90	97	117	136
Drugs	100	41	68	93	102	100	112	118
Medical supplies	100	33	54	74	76	103	101	144
ENTERTAINMENT	100	31	32	44	63	71	94	176
Fees and admissions	100	23	26	32	53	65	78	196
Audio and visual equipment and services	100	45	48	61	79	86	109	147
Pets, toys, and playground equipment	100	30	35	59	64	77	98	166
Other entertainment products and services	100	22	13	20	50	52	87	204
PERSONAL CARE PRODUCTS AND SERVICES	100	35	46	58	73	79	91	162
READING	100	43	47	51	57	85	94	164
EDUCATION	100	81	52	59	55	66	74	168
TOBACCO PRODUCTS AND SMOKING SUPPLIES	100	72	90	87	111	125	115	96
MISCELLANEOUS	100	32	58	59	90	70	100	151
CASH CONTRIBUTIONS	100	24	31	42	50	96	75	185
PERSONAL INSURANCE AND PENSIONS	100	8	12	32	43	58	87	204
Life and other personal insurance	100	25	33	45	39	60	80	194
Pensions and Social Security	100	7	11	31	43	58	87	205
PERSONAL TAXES	100	5	1	12	22	31	64	239
Federal income taxes	100	3	–	9	20	28	62	245
State and local income taxes	100	7	6	19	29	40	66	230
Other taxes	100	32	42	29	20	49	86	201
GIFTS FOR PEOPLE IN OTHER HOUSEHOLDS	100	33	29	42	46	49	140	168

Note: "–" means sample is too small to make a reliable estimate or not applicable.
Source: Calculations by New Strategist based on the Bureau of Labor Statistics' 2006 and 2007 Consumer Expenditure Surveys

Spending by Metropolitan Area, 2006–07

Within regions, spending levels vary considerably by metropolitan area. Among the three Northeastern metropolitan areas examined by the Consumer Expenditure Survey, average annual household spending ranged from $48,649 in Philadelphia to $56,683 in New York in 2006–07. In the Midwest, where the survey examines four cities, average annual household spending ranged from $47,890 in Cleveland to $60,059 in Minneapolis–St. Paul. Among the six selected metropolitan areas in the South, average spending was greatest in Washington, D.C. ($65,894) and lowest in Miami ($46,201). In the West, San Francisco had the highest average household spending ($69,559)—not only for the region, but among all the metropolitan areas included in the survey. Among the five Western metropolitan areas examined by the survey, household spending was lowest in San Diego, at $54,648.

Spending in metropolitan areas varies significantly by product and service category. Households in Boston spend more on alcoholic beverages (with an index of 110) than households in Philadelphia (with an index of 88). Households in Philadelphia spend more on tobacco (with an index of 117) than those in the other two Northeastern metropolitan areas.

Households in Minneapolis–St. Paul spend 81 percent more than the average Midwestern household on alcoholic beverages, while those in Cleveland spend 22 percent less than average. Households in Detroit spend 24 percent more than the average Midwestern household on tobacco, while those in Chicago spend 19 percent less.

In the South, households in Miami spend much less than those in other southern metropolitan areas on reading material. Households in Washington, D.C., spend more than households in other southern metropolitan areas on alcoholic beverages.

In San Diego, spending on tobacco is 63 percent lower than the Western average. Tobacco spending is 42 percent below the Western average in San Francisco and 22 percent lower in Los Angeles. But spending on tobacco is 36 percent above the Western average in Phoenix. Spending on food away from home is 30 percent above the Western average in San Francisco.

Table 36. Average spending in selected Northeastern metros, 2006–07

(average annual spending of consumer units in selected Northeastern metropolitan areas by product and service category, 2006–07)

	total consumer units in the Northeast	Boston	New York	Philadelphia
Number of consumer units (in 000s)	22,570	2,890	8,716	2,722
Average number of persons per consumer unit	2.4	2.3	2.5	2.4
Average income before taxes	$67,060	$80,966	$76,022	$65,637
Average annual spending	50,703	55,189	56,683	48,649
FOOD	6,320	6,700	7,023	5,600
Food at home	3,529	3,893	3,822	3,028
Cereals and bakery products	486	553	528	408
Meats, poultry, fish, and eggs	825	887	955	734
Dairy products	390	423	396	343
Fruits and vegetables	641	657	743	559
Other food at home	1,187	1,374	1,199	984
Food away from home	2,791	2,807	3,202	2,571
ALCOHOLIC BEVERAGES	513	565	533	451
HOUSING	18,408	20,174	22,295	18,411
Shelter	11,335	13,068	14,848	10,755
Owned dwellings	7,452	8,822	9,327	7,410
Rented dwellings	3,039	3,175	4,438	2,613
Other lodging	843	1,071	1,084	732
Utilities, fuels, and public services	3,707	3,850	3,879	3,981
Household services	971	1,036	1,171	1,054
Housekeeping supplies	579	542	572	602
Household furnishings and equipment	1,815	1,678	1,824	2,020
APPAREL AND RELATED SERVICES	2,069	2,093	2,619	2,041
TRANSPORTATION	8,107	8,707	8,048	7,345
Vehicle purchases	2,703	3,420	2,349	2,244
Gasoline and motor oil	1,994	2,026	1,892	2,106
Other vehicle expenses	2,722	2,642	2,721	2,447
Public transportation	688	618	1,085	548
HEALTH CARE	2,618	2,809	2,674	2,175
ENTERTAINMENT	2,666	3,352	2,600	2,327
PERSONAL CARE PRODUCTS AND SERVICES	583	546	685	602
READING	134	177	118	109
EDUCATION	1,121	1,381	1,420	1,228
TOBACCO PRODUCTS AND SMOKING SUPPLIES	346	350	221	406
MISCELLANEOUS	855	736	1,006	689
CASH CONTRIBUTIONS	1,445	1,235	1,517	1,486
PERSONAL INSURANCE AND PENSIONS	5,517	6,365	5,924	5,778
Life and other personal insurance	338	254	338	289
Pensions and Social Security	5,179	6,111	5,586	5,488

Source: Bureau of Labor Statistics, 2006 and 2007 Consumer Expenditure Surveys, Internet site http://www.bls.gov/cex/

Table 37. Indexed spending in selected Northeastern metros, 2006–07

(indexed average annual spending of consumer units in selected Northeastern metropolitan areas by product and service category, 2006–07; index definition: an index of 100 is the average for all consumer units; an index of 132 means that spending by consumer units in that group is 32 percent above the average for all consumer units; an index of 68 indicates spending that is 32 percent below the average for all consumer units)

	total consumer units in the Northeast	Boston	New York	Philadelphia
Average spending of consumer unit, total	$50,703	$55,189	$56,683	$48,649
Average spending of consumer unit, index	100	109	112	96
FOOD	100	106	111	89
Food at home	100	110	108	86
Cereals and bakery products	100	114	109	84
Meats, poultry, fish, and eggs	100	108	116	89
Dairy products	100	108	102	88
Fruits and vegetables	100	102	116	87
Other food at home	100	116	101	83
Food away from home	100	101	115	92
ALCOHOLIC BEVERAGES	100	110	104	88
HOUSING	100	110	121	100
Shelter	100	115	131	95
Owned dwellings	100	118	125	99
Rented dwellings	100	104	146	86
Other lodging	100	127	129	87
Utilities, fuels, and public services	100	104	105	107
Household services	100	107	121	109
Housekeeping supplies	100	94	99	104
Household furnishings and equipment	100	92	100	111
APPAREL AND RELATED SERVICES	100	101	127	99
TRANSPORTATION	100	107	99	91
Vehicle purchases	100	127	87	83
Gasoline and motor oil	100	102	95	106
Other vehicle expenses	100	97	100	90
Public transportation	100	90	158	80
HEALTH CARE	100	107	102	83
ENTERTAINMENT	100	126	98	87
PERSONAL CARE PRODUCTS AND SERVICES	100	94	117	103
READING	100	132	88	81
EDUCATION	100	123	127	110
TOBACCO PRODUCTS AND SMOKING SUPPLIES	100	101	64	117
MISCELLANEOUS	100	86	118	81
CASH CONTRIBUTIONS	100	85	105	103
PERSONAL INSURANCE AND PENSIONS	100	115	107	105
Life and other personal insurance	100	75	100	86
Pensions and Social Security	100	118	108	106

Source: Calculations by New Strategist based on the Bureau of Labor Statistics' 2006 and 2007 Consumer Expenditure Surveys

Table 38. Average spending in selected Midwestern metros, 2006–07

(average annual spending of consumer units in selected Midwestern metropolitan areas by product and service category, 2006–07)

	total consumer units in the Midwest	Chicago	Cleveland	Detroit	Minneapolis– St. Paul
Number of consumer units (in 000s)	27,334	3,224	1,155	2,251	1,467
Average number of persons per consumer unit	2.4	2.6	2.5	2.4	2.3
Average income before taxes	$58,688	$75,463	$62,104	$58,414	$76,772
Average annual spending	46,812	57,304	47,890	48,348	60,059
FOOD	**5,778**	**7,202**	**5,514**	**6,550**	**6,848**
Food at home	**3,256**	**4,046**	**3,331**	**3,886**	**3,845**
Cereals and bakery products	438	537	422	579	517
Meats, poultry, fish, and eggs	715	932	934	871	703
Dairy products	370	406	320	420	475
Fruits and vegetables	538	713	531	635	731
Other food at home	1,195	1,457	1,125	1,381	1,419
Food away from home	**2,522**	**3,156**	**2,183**	**2,663**	**3,003**
ALCOHOLIC BEVERAGES	**512**	**801**	**401**	**495**	**928**
HOUSING	**15,067**	**20,238**	**16,602**	**15,995**	**20,819**
Shelter	**8,531**	**12,612**	**9,719**	**9,568**	**11,559**
Owned dwellings	6,054	9,043	6,269	7,077	8,592
Rented dwellings	1,848	2,680	2,773	1,841	2,222
Other lodging	629	889	678	650	745
Utilities, fuels, and public services	**3,303**	**3,761**	**3,768**	**3,637**	**3,294**
Household services	**891**	**1,063**	**775**	**602**	**2,871**
Housekeeping supplies	**613**	**654**	**561**	**642**	**562**
Household furnishings and equipment	**1,730**	**2,146**	**1,778**	**1,545**	**2,533**
APPAREL AND RELATED SERVICES	**1,828**	**3,019**	**2,241**	**1,848**	**2,193**
TRANSPORTATION	**8,159**	**8,846**	**8,371**	**8,743**	**8,694**
Vehicle purchases	3,070	3,084	3,296	2,201	3,689
Gasoline and motor oil	2,275	2,322	2,177	2,602	2,151
Other vehicle expenses	2,386	2,635	2,644	3,506	2,204
Public transportation	428	806	253	433	649
HEALTH CARE	**2,957**	**3,020**	**3,293**	**2,307**	**3,705**
ENTERTAINMENT	**2,525**	**2,740**	**2,250**	**2,441**	**3,952**
PERSONAL CARE PRODUCTS AND SERVICES	**541**	**662**	**571**	**570**	**647**
READING	**127**	**130**	**154**	**113**	**156**
EDUCATION	**1,069**	**1,644**	**1,010**	**1,325**	**1,079**
TOBACCO PRODUCTS AND SMOKING SUPPLIES	**360**	**291**	**398**	**445**	**320**
MISCELLANEOUS	**792**	**837**	**815**	**985**	**1,149**
CASH CONTRIBUTIONS	**1,847**	**1,633**	**1,557**	**1,500**	**2,953**
PERSONAL INSURANCE AND PENSIONS	**5,247**	**6,241**	**4,713**	**5,031**	**6,615**
Life and other personal insurance	346	352	429	318	283
Pensions and Social Security	4,902	5,889	4,285	4,713	6,332

Source: Bureau of Labor Statistics, 2006 and 2007 Consumer Expenditure Surveys, Internet site http://www.bls.gov/cex/

Table 39. Indexed spending in selected Midwestern metros, 2006–07

(indexed average annual spending of consumer units in selected Midwestern metropolitan areas by product and service category, 2006–07; index definition: an index of 100 is the average for all consumer units; an index of 132 means that spending by consumer units in that group is 32 percent above the average for all consumer units; an index of 68 indicates spending that is 32 percent below the average for all consumer units)

	total consumer units in the Midwest	Chicago	Cleveland	Detroit	Minneapolis–St. Paul
Average spending of consumer units, total	$46,812	$57,304	$47,890	$48,348	$60,059
Average spending of consumer units, index	100	122	102	103	128
FOOD	100	125	95	113	119
Food at home	100	124	102	119	118
Cereals and bakery products	100	123	96	132	118
Meats, poultry, fish, and eggs	100	130	131	122	98
Dairy products	100	110	86	114	128
Fruits and vegetables	100	133	99	118	136
Other food at home	100	122	94	116	119
Food away from home	100	125	87	106	119
ALCOHOLIC BEVERAGES	100	156	78	97	181
HOUSING	100	134	110	106	138
Shelter	100	148	114	112	135
Owned dwellings	100	149	104	117	142
Rented dwellings	100	145	150	100	120
Other lodging	100	141	108	103	118
Utilities, fuels, and public services	100	114	114	110	100
Household services	100	119	87	68	322
Housekeeping supplies	100	107	92	105	92
Household furnishings and equipment	100	124	103	89	146
APPAREL AND RELATED SERVICES	100	165	123	101	120
TRANSPORTATION	100	108	103	107	107
Vehicle purchases	100	100	107	72	120
Gasoline and motor oil	100	102	96	114	95
Other vehicle expenses	100	110	111	147	92
Public transportation	100	188	59	101	152
HEALTH CARE	100	102	111	78	125
ENTERTAINMENT	100	109	89	97	157
PERSONAL CARE PRODUCTS AND SERVICES	100	122	106	105	120
READING	100	102	121	89	123
EDUCATION	100	154	94	124	101
TOBACCO PRODUCTS AND SMOKING SUPPLIES	100	81	111	124	89
MISCELLANEOUS	100	106	103	124	145
CASH CONTRIBUTIONS	100	88	84	81	160
PERSONAL INSURANCE AND PENSIONS	100	119	90	96	126
Life and other personal insurance	100	102	124	92	82
Pensions and Social Security	100	120	87	96	129

Source: Calculations by New Strategist based on the Bureau of Labor Statistics' 2006 and 2007 Consumer Expenditure Surveys

Table 40. Average spending in selected Southern metros, 2006–07

(average annual spending of consumer units in selected Southern metropolitan areas by product and service category, 2006–07)

	total consumer units in the South	Atlanta	Baltimore	Dallas–Fort Worth	Houston	Miami	Washington, D.C.
Number of consumer units (in 000s)	42,804	2,204	1,006	2,171	1,837	1,646	2,175
Average number of persons per consumer unit	2.5	2.5	2.5	2.8	2.7	2.4	2.6
Average income before taxes	$57,216	$67,859	$78,930	$67,145	$71,124	$54,990	$100,486
Average annual spending	45,225	46,705	53,244	54,334	55,381	46,201	65,894
FOOD	**5,715**	**5,646**	**6,222**	**6,160**	**6,547**	**5,728**	**7,533**
Food at home	**3,223**	**2,871**	**3,386**	**3,498**	**3,447**	**3,830**	**3,747**
Cereals and bakery products	423	368	438	434	419	476	451
Meats, poultry, fish, and eggs	767	662	820	774	802	949	864
Dairy products	347	281	338	381	355	443	407
Fruits and vegetables	532	518	573	605	607	854	780
Other food at home	1,154	1,042	1,217	1,304	1,264	1,107	1,244
Food away from home	**2,492**	**2,775**	**2,836**	**2,662**	**3,099**	**1,898**	**3,786**
ALCOHOLIC BEVERAGES	**374**	**345**	**479**	**381**	**603**	**276**	**650**
HOUSING	**14,719**	**17,716**	**19,123**	**18,169**	**17,752**	**18,708**	**25,525**
Shelter	**8,056**	**10,860**	**11,930**	**9,843**	**9,965**	**12,190**	**17,040**
Owned dwellings	5,536	7,353	8,921	6,446	6,872	8,100	12,380
Rented dwellings	2,107	2,831	2,504	2,892	2,533	3,809	3,947
Other lodging	412	676	505	505	560	281	713
Utilities, fuels, and public services	**3,550**	**3,874**	**3,951**	**4,551**	**4,297**	**3,611**	**4,037**
Household services	**898**	**1,035**	**960**	**1,192**	**1,080**	**1,197**	**1,592**
Housekeeping supplies	**627**	**515**	**650**	**728**	**746**	**569**	**703**
Household furnishings and equipment	**1,588**	**1,433**	**1,632**	**1,856**	**1,664**	**1,140**	**2,153**
APPAREL AND RELATED SERVICES	**1,720**	**1,792**	**1,755**	**1,907**	**2,345**	**1,269**	**2,440**
TRANSPORTATION	**8,578**	**8,053**	**8,673**	**10,764**	**11,119**	**7,938**	**9,531**
Vehicle purchases	3,428	2,957	3,562	4,866	4,544	2,859	3,319
Gasoline and motor oil	2,440	2,407	2,508	2,559	2,936	2,457	2,272
Other vehicle expenses	2,368	2,119	2,049	2,902	3,149	2,092	3,163
Public transportation	342	570	554	439	490	530	778
HEALTH CARE	**2,788**	**2,355**	**2,431**	**2,967**	**3,293**	**2,167**	**2,641**
ENTERTAINMENT	**2,322**	**2,130**	**2,726**	**2,515**	**2,789**	**1,583**	**2,995**
PERSONAL CARE PRODUCTS AND SERVICES	**568**	**513**	**565**	**747**	**782**	**641**	**682**
READING	**87**	**75**	**84**	**101**	**89**	**42**	**130**
EDUCATION	**726**	**420**	**1,771**	**739**	**918**	**1,054**	**1,664**
TOBACCO PRODUCTS AND SMOKING SUPPLIES	**334**	**202**	**229**	**265**	**299**	**197**	**237**
MISCELLANEOUS	**689**	**635**	**908**	**765**	**761**	**770**	**1,234**
CASH CONTRIBUTIONS	**1,762**	**1,281**	**1,891**	**2,223**	**1,821**	**1,421**	**2,168**
PERSONAL INSURANCE AND PENSIONS	**4,843**	**5,542**	**6,387**	**6,632**	**6,264**	**4,407**	**8,463**
Life and other personal insurance	305	242	546	346	417	192	341
Pensions and Social Security	4,537	5,300	5,841	6,286	5,847	4,215	8,123

Source: Bureau of Labor Statistics, 2006 and 2007 Consumer Expenditure Surveys, Internet site http://www.bls.gov/cex/

Table 41. Indexed spending in selected Southern metros, 2006–07

(indexed average annual spending of consumer units in selected Southern metropolitan areas by product and service category, 2006–07; index definition: an index of 100 is the average for all consumer units; an index of 132 means that spending by consumer units in that group is 32 percent above the average for all consumer units; an index of 68 indicates spending that is 32 percent below the average for all consumer units)

	total consumer units in the South	Atlanta	Baltimore	Dallas–Fort Worth	Houston	Miami	Washington, D.C.
Average spending of consumer units, total	$45,225	$46,705	$53,244	$54,334	$55,381	$46,201	$65,894
Average spending of consumer units, index	100	103	118	120	122	102	146
FOOD	100	99	109	108	115	100	132
Food at home	100	89	105	109	107	119	116
Cereals and bakery products	100	87	104	103	99	113	107
Meats, poultry, fish, and eggs	100	86	107	101	105	124	113
Dairy products	100	81	97	110	102	128	117
Fruits and vegetables	100	97	108	114	114	161	147
Other food at home	100	90	105	113	110	96	108
Food away from home	100	111	114	107	124	76	152
ALCOHOLIC BEVERAGES	100	92	128	102	161	74	174
HOUSING	100	120	130	123	121	127	173
Shelter	100	135	148	122	124	151	212
Owned dwellings	100	133	161	116	124	146	224
Rented dwellings	100	134	119	137	120	181	187
Other lodging	100	164	123	123	136	68	173
Utilities, fuels, and public services	100	109	111	128	121	102	114
Household services	100	115	107	133	120	133	177
Housekeeping supplies	100	82	104	116	119	91	112
Household furnishings and equipment	100	90	103	117	105	72	136
APPAREL AND RELATED SERVICES	100	104	102	111	136	74	142
TRANSPORTATION	100	94	101	125	130	93	111
Vehicle purchases	100	86	104	142	133	83	97
Gasoline and motor oil	100	99	103	105	120	101	93
Other vehicle expenses	100	89	87	123	133	88	134
Public transportation	100	167	162	128	143	155	227
HEALTH CARE	100	84	87	106	118	78	95
ENTERTAINMENT	100	92	117	108	120	68	129
PERSONAL CARE PRODUCTS AND SERVICES	100	90	99	132	138	113	120
READING	100	86	97	116	102	48	149
EDUCATION	100	58	244	102	126	145	229
TOBACCO PRODUCTS AND SMOKING SUPPLIES	100	60	69	79	90	59	71
MISCELLANEOUS	100	92	132	111	110	112	179
CASH CONTRIBUTIONS	100	73	107	126	103	81	123
PERSONAL INSURANCE AND PENSIONS	100	114	132	137	129	91	175
Life and other personal insurance	100	79	179	113	137	63	112
Pensions and Social Security	100	117	129	139	129	93	179

Source: Calculations by New Strategist based on the Bureau of Labor Statistics' 2006 and 2007 Consumer Expenditure Surveys

Table 42. Average spending in selected Western metros, 2006–07

(average annual spending of consumer units in selected Western metropolitan areas by product and service category, 2006–07)

	total consumer units in the West	Los Angeles	Phoenix	San Diego	San Francisco	Seattle
Number of consumer units (in 000s)	26,800	5,049	1,556	1,009	2,956	1,954
Average number of persons per consumer unit	2.6	2.8	2.7	2.6	2.4	2.3
Average income before taxes	$67,953	$76,384	$68,070	$73,604	$86,112	$67,923
Average annual spending	57,124	60,932	57,657	54,648	69,559	59,384
FOOD	**6,981**	**7,785**	**7,156**	**5,312**	**8,369**	**6,486**
Food at home	**3,918**	**4,257**	**4,045**	**2,819**	**4,375**	**3,615**
Cereals and bakery products	489	494	508	332	558	447
Meats, poultry, fish, and eggs	864	1,026	873	630	1,009	761
Dairy products	425	416	445	286	466	390
Fruits and vegetables	725	879	676	510	888	619
Other food at home	1,414	1,442	1,542	1,061	1,454	1,398
Food away from home	**3,063**	**3,528**	**3,112**	**2,493**	**3,994**	**2,871**
ALCOHOLIC BEVERAGES	**576**	**543**	**645**	**520**	**888**	**570**
HOUSING	**20,024**	**22,336**	**18,591**	**22,670**	**27,310**	**20,671**
Shelter	**12,806**	**15,271**	**10,615**	**16,174**	**19,519**	**13,530**
Owned dwellings	8,244	9,260	6,736	9,278	12,526	9,213
Rented dwellings	3,766	5,394	3,135	6,276	5,539	3,261
Other lodging	796	616	744	620	1,454	1,056
Utilities, fuels, and public services	**3,166**	**3,125**	**3,628**	**2,837**	**3,199**	**3,322**
Household services	**1,148**	**1,321**	**1,075**	**1,637**	**1,808**	**860**
Housekeeping supplies	**738**	**628**	**808**	**427**	**609**	**510**
Household furnishings and equipment	**2,167**	**1,990**	**2,464**	**1,596**	**2,176**	**2,449**
APPAREL AND RELATED SERVICES	**2,091**	**2,383**	**2,442**	**2,292**	**2,587**	**2,080**
TRANSPORTATION	**10,116**	**10,141**	**12,424**	**7,258**	**10,792**	**10,047**
Vehicle purchases	3,976	3,338	6,383	2,090	3,564	3,917
Gasoline and motor oil	2,386	2,712	2,594	2,504	2,489	2,288
Other vehicle expenses	2,992	3,364	2,846	1,962	3,502	2,747
Public transportation	762	727	601	702	1,238	1,094
HEALTH CARE	**2,857**	**2,324**	**3,058**	**2,613**	**3,224**	**3,127**
ENTERTAINMENT	**3,234**	**2,790**	**3,068**	**2,938**	**3,397**	**3,542**
PERSONAL CARE PRODUCTS AND SERVICES	**665**	**776**	**708**	**691**	**827**	**663**
READING	**142**	**126**	**119**	**103**	**201**	**196**
EDUCATION	**894**	**1,298**	**628**	**677**	**1,080**	**944**
TOBACCO PRODUCTS AND SMOKING SUPPLIES	**256**	**199**	**349**	**95**	**148**	**309**
MISCELLANEOUS	**1,061**	**1,141**	**897**	**890**	**1,190**	**1,101**
CASH CONTRIBUTIONS	**2,312**	**2,652**	**1,886**	**1,941**	**1,768**	**3,147**
PERSONAL INSURANCE AND PENSIONS	**5,915**	**6,439**	**5,687**	**6,648**	**7,779**	**6,501**
Life and other personal insurance	283	254	300	307	352	395
Pensions and Social Security	5,632	6,185	5,387	6,340	7,427	6,107

Source: Bureau of Labor Statistics, 2006 and 2007 Consumer Expenditure Surveys, Internet site http://www.bls.gov/cex/

Table 43. Indexed spending in selected Western metros, 2006–07

(indexed average annual spending of consumer units in selected Western metropolitan areas by product and service category, 2006–07; index definition: an index of 100 is the average for all consumer units; an index of 132 means that spending by consumer units in that group is 32 percent above the average for all consumer units; an index of 68 indicates spending that is 32 percent below the average for all consumer units)

	total consumer units in the West	Los Angeles	Phoenix	San Diego	San Francisco	Seattle
Average spending of consumer units, total	$57,124	$60,932	$57,657	$54,648	$69,559	$59,384
Average spending of consumer units, index	100	107	101	96	122	104
FOOD	100	112	103	76	120	93
Food at home	100	109	103	72	112	92
Cereals and bakery products	100	101	104	68	114	91
Meats, poultry, fish, and eggs	100	119	101	73	117	88
Dairy products	100	98	105	67	110	92
Fruits and vegetables	100	121	93	70	122	85
Other food at home	100	102	109	75	103	99
Food away from home	100	115	102	81	130	94
ALCOHOLIC BEVERAGES	100	94	112	90	154	99
HOUSING	100	112	93	113	136	103
Shelter	100	119	83	126	152	106
Owned dwellings	100	112	82	113	152	112
Rented dwellings	100	143	83	167	147	87
Other lodging	100	77	93	78	183	133
Utilities, fuels, and public services	100	99	115	90	101	105
Household services	100	115	94	143	157	75
Housekeeping supplies	100	85	109	58	83	69
Household furnishings and equipment	100	92	114	74	100	113
APPAREL AND RELATED SERVICES	100	114	117	110	124	99
TRANSPORTATION	100	100	123	72	107	99
Vehicle purchases	100	84	161	53	90	99
Gasoline and motor oil	100	114	109	105	104	96
Other vehicle expenses	100	112	95	66	117	92
Public transportation	100	95	79	92	162	144
HEALTH CARE	100	81	107	91	113	109
ENTERTAINMENT	100	86	95	91	105	110
PERSONAL CARE PRODUCTS AND SERVICES	100	117	106	104	124	100
READING	100	89	84	73	142	138
EDUCATION	100	145	70	76	121	106
TOBACCO PRODUCTS AND SMOKING SUPPLIES	100	78	136	37	58	121
MISCELLANEOUS	100	108	85	84	112	104
CASH CONTRIBUTIONS	100	115	82	84	76	136
PERSONAL INSURANCE AND PENSIONS	100	109	96	112	132	110
Life and other personal insurance	100	90	106	108	124	140
Pensions and Social Security	100	110	96	113	132	108

Source: Calculations by New Strategist based on the Bureau of Labor Statistics' 2006 and 2007 Consumer Expenditure Surveys

Spending by Race and Hispanic Origin, 2007

Asians spend more than the average household, while Hispanics and blacks spend less. The $60,402 spent by the average Asian household in 2007 was 22 percent above the overall average and surpassed the spending of every other racial or ethnic group. Black households spent $36,067 in 2007, or 27 percent less than average. Hispanic spending, at $41,501, was 16 percent below average.

Asian spending reflects their above-average incomes, a consequence of their high educational attainment. Asian households spend 72 percent more than average on education and almost three times the average on public transportation (mostly airline fares). They also spend more than two-and-one-half times the average on fish and seafood.

Hispanic and black spending exceeds that of the average household in many categories. Because of their larger families, Hispanic households spend more than the average household on many food items. They spend 59 percent more than the average household on rented dwellings and 51 percent more on clothes for infants.

Blacks spend more than the average household on a number of foods, including pork, poultry, and fish and seafood. They spend 41 percent more than the average household on rent, 29 percent more on clothes for boys, and 18 percent more on shoes.

Table 44. Average spending by race and Hispanic origin of householder, 2007

(average annual spending of consumer units by product and service category and by race and Hispanic origin of consumer unit reference person, 2007)

	total consumer units	Asian	black	Hispanic	non-Hispanic white and other
Number of consumer units (in 000s)	120,171	4,240	14,422	14,185	91,734
Average number of persons per consumer unit	2.5	2.8	2.6	3.2	2.3
Average before-tax income of consumer units	$63,091	$80,487	$44,381	$48,330	$68,285
Average annual spending of consumer units	49,638	60,402	36,067	41,501	53,003
FOOD	6,133	7,139	4,601	5,933	6,399
Food at home	3,465	3,890	2,831	3,424	3,568
Cereals and bakery products	460	469	365	410	481
Cereals and cereal products	143	195	127	154	143
Bakery products	317	275	237	255	338
Meats, poultry, fish, and eggs	777	1,026	834	890	752
Beef	216	221	185	255	215
Pork	150	160	185	162	142
Other meats	104	106	95	101	107
Poultry	142	158	189	193	127
Fish and seafood	122	321	138	119	120
Eggs	43	60	41	60	40
Dairy products	387	349	259	368	410
Fresh milk and cream	154	154	111	168	158
Other dairy products	234	196	147	200	252
Fruits and vegetables	600	887	455	652	615
Fresh fruits	202	309	131	227	209
Fresh vegetables	190	369	133	229	194
Processed fruits	112	116	107	106	114
Processed vegetables	96	93	83	91	98
Other food at home	1,241	1,159	919	1,104	1,310
Sugar and other sweets	124	133	88	97	134
Fats and oils	91	93	81	90	93
Miscellaneous foods	650	549	456	546	694
Nonalcoholic beverages	333	343	279	345	340
Food prepared by consumer unit on trips	43	40	15	27	50
Food away from home	2,668	3,249	1,771	2,508	2,831
ALCOHOLIC BEVERAGES	457	290	198	262	525
HOUSING	16,920	22,554	13,494	15,573	17,662
Shelter	10,023	15,383	8,084	9,794	10,367
Owned dwellings	6,730	10,387	4,110	5,419	7,346
Mortgage interest and charges	3,890	6,383	2,723	3,609	4,118
Property taxes	1,709	2,754	893	1,218	1,912
Maintenance, repair, insurance, other expenses	1,131	1,249	494	592	1,317
Rented dwellings	2,602	4,073	3,669	4,135	2,200
Other lodging	691	923	305	239	820
Utilities, fuels, and public services	3,477	3,436	3,500	3,274	3,505
Natural gas	480	577	475	378	497
Electricity	1,303	1,169	1,355	1,258	1,301
Fuel oil and other fuels	151	44	56	62	179
Telephone services	1,110	1,172	1,196	1,167	1,088
Water and other public services	434	475	418	409	440
Household services	984	1,157	616	681	1,088
Personal services	415	529	297	348	444
Other household services	569	627	319	333	644
Housekeeping supplies	639	496	383	571	688
Laundry and cleaning supplies	140	103	142	170	136
Other household products	347	238	184	245	386
Postage and stationery	152	155	58	157	166

	total consumer units	Asian	black	Hispanic	non-Hispanic white and other
Household furnishings and equipment	**$1,797**	**$2,081**	**$910**	**$1,253**	**$2,014**
Household textiles	133	125	51	112	149
Furniture	446	858	313	364	478
Floor coverings	46	35	32	15	54
Major appliances	231	196	119	136	263
Small appliances and miscellaneous housewares	101	103	58	98	108
Miscellaneous household equipment	840	765	336	528	962
APPAREL AND RELATED SERVICES	**1,881**	**2,709**	**1,743**	**1,994**	**1,886**
Men and boys	**435**	**602**	**344**	**539**	**435**
Men, aged 16 or older	351	512	236	425	358
Boys, aged 2 to 15	84	91	108	113	77
Women and girls	**749**	**1,234**	**671**	**636**	**777**
Women, aged 16 or older	627	1,080	513	505	663
Girls, aged 2 to 15	122	155	158	131	115
Children under age 2	**93**	**107**	**103**	**140**	**85**
Footwear	**327**	**514**	**387**	**408**	**306**
Other apparel products and services	**276**	**252**	**238**	**272**	**283**
TRANSPORTATION	**8,758**	**10,921**	**6,458**	**8,035**	**9,234**
Vehicle purchases	**3,244**	**4,007**	**2,223**	**2,876**	**3,463**
Cars and trucks, new	1,572	2,797	729	1,271	1,752
Cars and trucks, used	1,567	1,210	1,460	1,541	1,588
Other vehicles	105	–	34	63	123
Gasoline and motor oil	**2,384**	**2,391**	**1,935**	**2,304**	**2,466**
Other vehicle expenses	**2,592**	**2,978**	**2,001**	**2,525**	**2,697**
Vehicle finance charges	305	236	252	314	312
Maintenance and repairs	738	729	505	557	802
Vehicle insurance	1,071	1,550	872	1,280	1,073
Vehicle rentals, leases, licenses, other charges	478	463	371	375	510
Public transportation	**538**	**1,545**	**299**	**330**	**608**
HEALTH CARE	**2,853**	**2,170**	**1,689**	**1,486**	**3,244**
Health insurance	1,545	1,378	1,001	744	1,752
Medical services	709	487	370	468	799
Drugs	481	220	262	213	556
Medical supplies	118	86	57	62	136
ENTERTAINMENT	**2,698**	**2,454**	**1,288**	**1,674**	**3,072**
Fees and admissions	658	895	212	316	779
Audio and visual equipment and services	987	973	753	815	1,050
Pets, toys, and playground equipment	560	316	173	315	657
Other entertainment products and services	493	270	149	229	586
PERSONAL CARE PRODUCTS AND SERVICES	**588**	**564**	**485**	**526**	**614**
READING	**118**	**98**	**46**	**38**	**141**
EDUCATION	**945**	**1,627**	**700**	**415**	**1,065**
TOBACCO PRODUCTS AND SMOKING SUPPLIES	**323**	**135**	**219**	**165**	**363**
MISCELLANEOUS	**808**	**719**	**453**	**478**	**913**
CASH CONTRIBUTIONS	**1,821**	**2,153**	**1,178**	**1,083**	**2,035**
PERSONAL INSURANCE AND PENSIONS	**5,336**	**6,868**	**3,515**	**3,837**	**5,851**
Life and other personal insurance	309	353	245	109	350
Pensions and Social Security	5,027	6,515	3,271	3,729	5,501
PERSONAL TAXES	**2,233**	**2,295**	**771**	**703**	**2,697**
Federal income taxes	1,569	1,489	511	463	1,905
State and local income taxes	468	628	175	172	559
Other taxes	196	179	85	68	233
GIFTS FOR PEOPLE IN OTHER HOUSEHOLDS	**1,198**	**1,455**	**698**	**679**	**1,355**

Note: "Asian" and "black" include Hispanics and non-Hispanics who identify themselves as being of the respective race alone. "Hispanic" includes people of any race who identify themselves as Hispanic. "Other" includes people who identify themselves as non-Hispanic and as Alaska Native, American Indian, Asian (who are also included in the "Asian" column), Native Hawaiian or other Pacific Islander, as well as non-Hispanics reporting more than one race. Spending by category does not add to total spending because gift spending is also included in the preceding product and service categories and personal taxes are not included in the total. "–" means sample is too small to make a reliable estimate.
Source: Bureau of Labor Statistics, 2007 Consumer Expenditure Survey, Internet site http://www.bls.gov/cex/

Table 45. Indexed spending by race and Hispanic origin of householder, 2007

(indexed average annual spending of consumer units by product and service category and by race and Hispanic origin of consumer unit reference person, 2007; index definition: an index of 100 is the average for all consumer units; an index of 132 means that spending by consumer units in that group is 32 percent above the average for all consumer units; an index of 68 indicates spending that is 32 percent below the average for all consumer units)

	total consumer units	Asian	black	Hispanic	non-Hispanic white and other
Average spending of consumer units, total	$49,638	$60,402	$36,067	$41,501	$53,003
Average spending of consumer units, index	100	122	73	84	107
FOOD	100	116	75	97	104
Food at home	100	112	82	99	103
Cereals and bakery products	100	102	79	89	105
Cereals and cereal products	100	136	89	108	100
Bakery products	100	87	75	80	107
Meats, poultry, fish, and eggs	100	132	107	115	97
Beef	100	102	86	118	100
Pork	100	107	123	108	95
Other meats	100	102	91	97	103
Poultry	100	111	133	136	89
Fish and seafood	100	263	113	98	98
Eggs	100	140	95	140	93
Dairy products	100	90	67	95	106
Fresh milk and cream	100	100	72	109	103
Other dairy products	100	84	63	85	108
Fruits and vegetables	100	148	76	109	103
Fresh fruits	100	153	65	112	103
Fresh vegetables	100	194	70	121	102
Processed fruits	100	104	96	95	102
Processed vegetables	100	97	86	95	102
Other food at home	100	93	74	89	106
Sugar and other sweets	100	107	71	78	108
Fats and oils	100	102	89	99	102
Miscellaneous foods	100	84	70	84	107
Nonalcoholic beverages	100	103	84	104	102
Food prepared by consumer unit on trips	100	93	35	63	116
Food away from home	100	122	66	94	106
ALCOHOLIC BEVERAGES	100	63	43	57	115
HOUSING	100	133	80	92	104
Shelter	100	153	81	98	103
Owned dwellings	100	154	61	81	109
Mortgage interest and charges	100	164	70	93	106
Property taxes	100	161	52	71	112
Maintenance, repair, insurance, other expenses	100	110	44	52	116
Rented dwellings	100	157	141	159	85
Other lodging	100	134	44	35	119
Utilities, fuels, and public services	100	99	101	94	101
Natural gas	100	120	99	79	104
Electricity	100	90	104	97	100
Fuel oil and other fuels	100	29	37	41	119
Telephone services	100	106	108	105	98
Water and other public services	100	109	96	94	101
Household services	100	118	63	69	111
Personal services	100	127	72	84	107
Other household services	100	110	56	59	113
Housekeeping supplies	100	78	60	89	108
Laundry and cleaning supplies	100	74	101	121	97
Other household products	100	69	53	71	111
Postage and stationery	100	102	38	103	109

	total consumer units	Asian	black	Hispanic	non-Hispanic white and other
Household furnishings and equipment	100	116	51	70	112
Household textiles	100	94	38	84	112
Furniture	100	192	70	82	107
Floor coverings	100	76	70	33	117
Major appliances	100	85	52	59	114
Small appliances and miscellaneous housewares	100	102	57	97	107
Miscellaneous household equipment	100	91	40	63	115
APPAREL AND RELATED SERVICES	100	144	93	106	100
Men and boys	100	138	79	124	100
Men, aged 16 or older	100	146	67	121	102
Boys, aged 2 to 15	100	108	129	135	92
Women and girls	100	165	90	85	104
Women, aged 16 or older	100	172	82	81	106
Girls, aged 2 to 15	100	127	130	107	94
Children under age 2	100	115	111	151	91
Footwear	100	157	118	125	94
Other apparel products and services	100	91	86	99	103
TRANSPORTATION	100	125	74	92	105
Vehicle purchases	100	124	69	89	107
Cars and trucks, new	100	178	46	81	111
Cars and trucks, used	100	77	93	98	101
Other vehicles	100	–	32	60	117
Gasoline and motor oil	100	100	81	97	103
Other vehicle expenses	100	115	77	97	104
Vehicle finance charges	100	77	83	103	102
Maintenance and repairs	100	99	68	75	109
Vehicle insurance	100	145	81	120	100
Vehicle rentals, leases, licenses, other charges	100	97	78	78	107
Public transportation	100	287	56	61	113
HEALTH CARE	100	76	59	52	114
Health insurance	100	89	65	48	113
Medical services	100	69	52	66	113
Drugs	100	46	54	44	116
Medical supplies	100	73	48	53	115
ENTERTAINMENT	100	91	48	62	114
Fees and admissions	100	136	32	48	118
Audio and visual equipment and services	100	99	76	83	106
Pets, toys, and playground equipment	100	56	31	56	117
Other entertainment products and services	100	55	30	46	119
PERSONAL CARE PRODUCTS AND SERVICES	100	96	82	89	104
READING	100	83	39	32	119
EDUCATION	100	172	74	44	113
TOBACCO PRODUCTS AND SMOKING SUPPLIES	100	42	68	51	112
MISCELLANEOUS	100	89	56	59	113
CASH CONTRIBUTIONS	100	118	65	59	112
PERSONAL INSURANCE AND PENSIONS	100	129	66	72	110
Life and other personal insurance	100	114	79	35	113
Pensions and Social Security	100	130	65	74	109
PERSONAL TAXES	100	103	35	31	121
Federal income taxes	100	95	33	30	121
State and local income taxes	100	134	37	37	119
Other taxes	100	91	43	35	119
GIFTS FOR PEOPLE IN OTHER HOUSEHOLDS	100	121	58	57	113

Note: "Asian" and "black" include Hispanics and non-Hispanics who identify themselves as being of the respective race alone. "Hispanic" includes people of any race who identify themselves as Hispanic. "Other" includes people who identify themselves as non-Hispanic and as Alaska Native, American Indian, Asian (who are also included in the "Asian" column), Native Hawaiian or other Pacific Islander, as well as non-Hispanics reporting more than one race. "–" means sample is too small to make a reliable estimate.
Source: Calculations by New Strategist based on the Bureau of Labor Statistics' 2007 Consumer Expenditure Survey

Spending by Education, 2007

Because college graduates have the highest incomes, their spending is well above average. Households headed by college graduates spent $70,605 in 2007, or 42 percent more than the average household. In contrast, households headed by people who did not graduate from high school spent only $30,201, 39 percent less than the average household.

Households headed by the least educated—those without a high school diploma—spend substantially more than average on only two items. These are rent and tobacco.

High school graduates spent $39,164 in 2007, or 21 percent less than the average household. Their spending is below average in most categories, with a few exceptions such as tobacco.

Householders with some college experience or an associate's degree make up the largest share of households (31 percent). Their spending is close to the average on most items.

College graduates, who account for 29 percent of householders, far outspend the average household on most items—particularly those favored by the affluent. These include food away from home (43 percent above average) and alcoholic beverages (60 percent). They spend more than twice the average on other lodging (which includes college dorms, vacation homes, and hotels and motels), public transportation (which includes airfares) and fees and admissions to entertainment events, and nearly twice the average on education.

Table 46. Average spending by education of householder, 2007

(average annual spending of consumer units by product and service category and educational attainment of consumer unit reference person, 2007)

	total consumer units	not a high school graduate	high school graduate	some college or associate's degree	college degree or more
Number of consumer units (in 000s)	120,171	18,227	30,313	36,849	34,783
Average number of persons per consumer unit	2.5	2.6	2.5	2.5	2.4
Average before-tax income of consumer units	$63,091	$33,913	$46,938	$57,680	$98,193
Average annual spending of consumer units	49,638	30,201	39,164	47,860	70,605
FOOD	**6,133**	**4,491**	**5,231**	**5,959**	**7,878**
Food at home	**3,465**	**3,027**	**3,196**	**3,317**	**4,055**
Cereals and bakery products	460	396	427	442	535
Cereals and cereal products	143	135	128	137	165
Bakery products	317	261	299	305	370
Meats, poultry, fish, and eggs	777	772	779	743	812
Beef	216	224	226	206	215
Pork	150	162	168	142	136
Other meats	104	90	108	103	109
Poultry	142	144	135	139	150
Fish and seafood	122	107	101	112	157
Eggs	43	45	42	41	44
Dairy products	387	311	348	377	467
Fresh milk and cream	154	146	147	152	164
Other dairy products	234	165	201	225	303
Fruits and vegetables	600	515	504	542	781
Fresh fruits	202	168	158	176	282
Fresh vegetables	190	170	158	168	250
Processed fruits	112	92	98	105	142
Processed vegetables	96	85	89	94	107
Other food at home	1,241	1,033	1,138	1,212	1,460
Sugar and other sweets	124	99	114	120	150
Fats and oils	91	81	85	92	101
Miscellaneous foods	650	530	584	638	774
Nonalcoholic beverages	333	308	327	322	362
Food prepared by consumer unit on trips	43	15	28	40	74
Food away from home	**2,668**	**1,464**	**2,035**	**2,642**	**3,823**
ALCOHOLIC BEVERAGES	**457**	**174**	**329**	**429**	**729**
HOUSING	**16,920**	**10,947**	**13,026**	**16,159**	**24,214**
Shelter	**10,023**	**6,311**	**7,532**	**9,479**	**14,715**
Owned dwellings	6,730	3,195	4,747	6,255	10,813
Mortgage interest and charges	3,890	1,827	2,621	3,689	6,290
Property taxes	1,709	783	1,246	1,510	2,808
Maintenance, repair, insurance, other expenses	1,131	586	879	1,057	1,716
Rented dwellings	2,602	2,995	2,463	2,721	2,391
Other lodging	691	120	321	502	1,511
Utilities, fuels, and public services	**3,477**	**2,930**	**3,312**	**3,392**	**3,998**
Natural gas	480	374	439	430	625
Electricity	1,303	1,184	1,285	1,280	1,405
Fuel oil and other fuels	151	125	157	142	169
Telephone services	1,110	909	1,043	1,123	1,258
Water and other public services	434	337	388	418	541
Household services	**984**	**340**	**581**	**906**	**1,756**
Personal services	415	137	230	390	750
Other household services	569	203	351	516	1,005
Housekeeping supplies	**639**	**420**	**500**	**576**	**924**
Laundry and cleaning supplies	140	128	128	147	149
Other household products	347	183	267	290	549
Postage and stationery	152	110	104	139	227

	total consumer units	not a high school graduate	high school graduate	some college or associate's degree	college degree or more
Household furnishings and equipment	**$1,797**	**$947**	**$1,101**	**$1,806**	**$2,821**
Household textiles	133	51	83	140	208
Furniture	446	202	275	430	737
Floor coverings	46	21	28	40	83
Major appliances	231	135	177	247	312
Small appliances and miscellaneous housewares	101	66	54	114	146
Miscellaneous household equipment	840	471	484	834	1,335
APPAREL AND RELATED SERVICES	**1,881**	**1,207**	**1,328**	**1,692**	**2,878**
Men and boys	**435**	**295**	**302**	**385**	**670**
Men, aged 16 or older	351	228	238	294	566
Boys, aged 2 to 15	84	67	63	92	104
Women and girls	**749**	**379**	**519**	**712**	**1,161**
Women, aged 16 or older	627	314	422	585	996
Girls, aged 2 to 15	122	65	97	127	165
Children under age 2	**93**	**94**	**81**	**97**	**101**
Footwear	**327**	**276**	**269**	**276**	**453**
Other apparel products and services	**276**	**163**	**157**	**223**	**493**
TRANSPORTATION	**8,758**	**5,655**	**7,614**	**9,074**	**11,031**
Vehicle purchases	**3,244**	**2,112**	**2,761**	**3,432**	**4,060**
Cars and trucks, new	1,572	847	1,088	1,604	2,338
Cars and trucks, used	1,567	1,246	1,568	1,643	1,654
Other vehicles	105	19	105	184	67
Gasoline and motor oil	**2,384**	**1,785**	**2,269**	**2,519**	**2,654**
Other vehicle expenses	**2,592**	**1,550**	**2,368**	**2,732**	**3,171**
Vehicle finance charges	305	154	289	369	331
Maintenance and repairs	738	425	615	756	987
Vehicle insurance	1,071	766	1,123	1,177	1,062
Vehicle rentals, leases, licenses, other charges	478	204	340	430	792
Public transportation	**538**	**209**	**216**	**391**	**1,146**
HEALTH CARE	**2,853**	**2,003**	**2,594**	**2,754**	**3,625**
Health insurance	1,545	1,136	1,502	1,457	1,889
Medical services	709	391	533	727	1,011
Drugs	481	411	466	460	550
Medical supplies	118	65	92	109	175
ENTERTAINMENT	**2,698**	**1,295**	**1,966**	**2,619**	**4,130**
Fees and admissions	658	131	288	572	1,342
Audio and visual equipment and services	987	638	854	1,009	1,261
Pets, toys, and playground equipment	560	274	485	581	742
Other entertainment products and services	493	252	338	458	786
PERSONAL CARE PRODUCTS AND SERVICES	**588**	**312**	**462**	**564**	**858**
READING	**118**	**40**	**80**	**103**	**207**
EDUCATION	**945**	**145**	**405**	**965**	**1,813**
TOBACCO PRODUCTS AND SMOKING SUPPLIES	**323**	**374**	**457**	**347**	**154**
MISCELLANEOUS	**808**	**386**	**591**	**833**	**1,192**
CASH CONTRIBUTIONS	**1,821**	**757**	**1,333**	**1,390**	**3,263**
PERSONAL INSURANCE AND PENSIONS	**5,336**	**2,415**	**3,749**	**4,973**	**8,635**
Life and other personal insurance	309	136	257	286	471
Pensions and Social Security	5,027	2,278	3,492	4,687	8,164
PERSONAL TAXES	**2,233**	**526**	**1,041**	**1,880**	**4,542**
Federal income taxes	1,569	274	650	1,267	3,369
State and local income taxes	468	166	265	431	843
Other taxes	196	86	127	183	329
GIFTS FOR PEOPLE IN OTHER HOUSEHOLDS	**1,198**	**391**	**705**	**1,084**	**2,157**

Note: Spending by category does not add to total spending because gift spending is also included in the preceding product and service categories and personal taxes are not included in the total.
Source: Bureau of Labor Statistics, 2007 Consumer Expenditure Survey, Internet site http://www.bls.gov/cex/

Table 47. Indexed spending by education of householder, 2007

(indexed average annual spending of consumer units by product and service category and educational attainment of consumer unit reference person, 2007; index definition: an index of 100 is the average for all consumer units; an index of 132 means that spending by consumer units in that group is 32 percent above the average for all consumer units; an index of 68 indicates spending that is 32 percent below the average for all consumer units)

	total consumer units	not a high school graduate	high school graduate	some college or associate's degree	college degree or more
Average spending of consumer units, total	$49,638	$30,201	$39,164	$47,860	$70,605
Average spending of consumer units, index	100	61	79	96	142
FOOD	100	73	85	97	128
Food at home	100	87	92	96	117
Cereals and bakery products	100	86	93	96	116
Cereals and cereal products	100	94	90	96	115
Bakery products	100	82	94	96	117
Meats, poultry, fish, and eggs	100	99	100	96	105
Beef	100	104	105	95	100
Pork	100	108	112	94	91
Other meats	100	87	104	99	105
Poultry	100	101	95	98	106
Fish and seafood	100	88	83	92	129
Eggs	100	105	98	96	102
Dairy products	100	80	90	98	121
Fresh milk and cream	100	95	95	99	106
Other dairy products	100	71	86	96	129
Fruits and vegetables	100	86	84	90	130
Fresh fruits	100	83	78	87	140
Fresh vegetables	100	89	83	89	132
Processed fruits	100	82	88	93	127
Processed vegetables	100	89	93	98	111
Other food at home	100	83	92	98	118
Sugar and other sweets	100	80	92	97	121
Fats and oils	100	89	93	101	111
Miscellaneous foods	100	82	90	98	119
Nonalcoholic beverages	100	92	98	97	109
Food prepared by consumer unit on trips	100	35	65	93	172
Food away from home	100	55	76	99	143
ALCOHOLIC BEVERAGES	100	38	72	94	160
HOUSING	100	65	77	96	143
Shelter	100	63	75	95	147
Owned dwellings	100	47	71	93	161
Mortgage interest and charges	100	47	67	95	162
Property taxes	100	46	73	88	164
Maintenance, repair, insurance, other expenses	100	52	78	93	152
Rented dwellings	100	115	95	105	92
Other lodging	100	17	46	73	219
Utilities, fuels, and public services	100	84	95	98	115
Natural gas	100	78	91	90	130
Electricity	100	91	99	98	108
Fuel oil and other fuels	100	83	104	94	112
Telephone services	100	82	94	101	113
Water and other public services	100	78	89	96	125
Household services	100	35	59	92	178
Personal services	100	33	55	94	181
Other household services	100	36	62	91	177
Housekeeping supplies	100	66	78	90	145
Laundry and cleaning supplies	100	91	91	105	106
Other household products	100	53	77	84	158
Postage and stationery	100	72	68	92	149

	total consumer units	not a high school graduate	high school graduate	some college or associate's degree	college degree or more
Household furnishings and equipment	**100**	**53**	**61**	**101**	**157**
Household textiles	100	38	62	106	156
Furniture	100	45	62	96	165
Floor coverings	100	46	61	87	180
Major appliances	100	58	77	107	135
Small appliances and miscellaneous housewares	100	65	53	113	145
Miscellaneous household equipment	100	56	58	99	159
APPAREL AND RELATED SERVICES	**100**	**64**	**71**	**90**	**153**
Men and boys	**100**	**68**	**69**	**89**	**154**
Men, aged 16 or older	100	65	68	84	161
Boys, aged 2 to 15	100	80	75	109	124
Women and girls	**100**	**51**	**69**	**95**	**155**
Women, aged 16 or older	100	50	67	93	159
Girls, aged 2 to 15	100	53	80	104	135
Children under age 2	**100**	**101**	**87**	**104**	**109**
Footwear	**100**	**84**	**82**	**84**	**139**
Other apparel products and services	**100**	**59**	**57**	**81**	**179**
TRANSPORTATION	**100**	**65**	**87**	**104**	**126**
Vehicle purchases	**100**	**65**	**85**	**106**	**125**
Cars and trucks, new	100	54	69	102	149
Cars and trucks, used	100	80	100	105	106
Other vehicles	100	18	100	176	64
Gasoline and motor oil	**100**	**75**	**95**	**106**	**111**
Other vehicle expenses	**100**	**60**	**91**	**105**	**122**
Vehicle finance charges	100	50	95	121	109
Maintenance and repairs	100	58	83	102	134
Vehicle insurance	100	72	105	110	99
Vehicle rentals, leases, licenses, other charges	100	43	71	90	166
Public transportation	**100**	**39**	**40**	**73**	**213**
HEALTH CARE	**100**	**70**	**91**	**97**	**127**
Health insurance	100	74	97	94	122
Medical services	100	55	75	102	143
Drugs	100	85	97	96	114
Medical supplies	100	55	78	92	148
ENTERTAINMENT	**100**	**48**	**73**	**97**	**153**
Fees and admissions	100	20	44	87	204
Audio and visual equipment and services	100	65	87	102	128
Pets, toys, and playground equipment	100	49	87	104	133
Other entertainment products and services	100	51	69	93	159
PERSONAL CARE PRODUCTS AND SERVICES	**100**	**53**	**79**	**96**	**146**
READING	**100**	**34**	**68**	**87**	**175**
EDUCATION	**100**	**15**	**43**	**102**	**192**
TOBACCO PRODUCTS AND SMOKING SUPPLIES	**100**	**116**	**141**	**107**	**48**
MISCELLANEOUS	**100**	**48**	**73**	**103**	**148**
CASH CONTRIBUTIONS	**100**	**42**	**73**	**76**	**179**
PERSONAL INSURANCE AND PENSIONS	**100**	**45**	**70**	**93**	**162**
Life and other personal insurance	100	44	83	93	152
Pensions and Social Security	100	45	69	93	162
PERSONAL TAXES	**100**	**24**	**47**	**84**	**203**
Federal income taxes	100	17	41	81	215
State and local income taxes	100	35	57	92	180
Other taxes	100	44	65	93	168
GIFTS FOR PEOPLE IN OTHER HOUSEHOLDS	**100**	**33**	**59**	**90**	**180**

Source: Calculations by New Strategist based on the Bureau of Labor Statistics' 2007 Consumer Expenditure Survey

Spending by Household Size, 2007

Spending tends to increase with household size because larger households usually have more earners. The largest households, those including four or more people, have the highest incomes (over $83,000 in 2007). Spending is highest for these households as well, at over $65,000—about one-third more than average household spending. Only 23 percent of the nation's households are home to four or more people, however.

Two-person households are most common. They account for 32 percent of all households. Two-person households spent an average of $53,091 in 2007—or 7 percent more than the average household. Households with two people (many of them empty-nesters) spend more than other households on alcoholic beverages, other lodging (primarily hotel and motel expenses on trips), and reading material among other categories.

Households with five or more people have slightly lower incomes and slightly lower spending than those with just four people. Both household types spend more than other households on many nondiscretionary items such as food at home, laundry and cleaning supplies, utilities, and clothing.

Single-person households are almost as numerous as two-person households, accounting for 30 percent of the total in 2007. Single-person households spend less than the average household on every item except rent.

Table 48. Average spending by size of household, 2007

(average annual spending of consumer units by product and service category, by number of people in consumer unit, 2007)

	total consumer units	one person	two or more people total	two people	three people	four people	five or more people
Number of consumer units (in 000s)	120,171	35,740	84,431	38,260	18,175	16,496	11,499
Average number of persons per consumer unit	2.5	1.0	3.1	2.0	3.0	4.0	5.6
Average before-tax income of consumer units	$63,091	$31,962	$76,269	$70,095	$74,809	$86,902	$83,866
Average annual spending of consumer units	49,638	29,285	58,209	53,091	57,326	66,476	65,042
FOOD	**6,133**	**3,328**	**7,298**	**6,209**	**7,251**	**8,671**	**9,220**
Food at home	**3,465**	**1,814**	**4,150**	**3,375**	**4,227**	**4,967**	**5,564**
Cereals and bakery products	460	238	551	437	563	654	783
Cereals and cereal products	143	72	172	130	174	210	262
Bakery products	317	166	379	308	389	444	521
Meats, poultry, fish, and eggs	777	390	937	744	940	1,146	1,310
Beef	216	104	263	202	272	325	370
Pork	150	69	183	149	190	221	236
Other meats	104	54	125	96	125	164	174
Poultry	142	70	172	128	158	225	270
Fish and seafood	122	67	145	128	146	151	188
Eggs	43	24	50	41	48	59	73
Dairy products	387	201	465	385	449	562	628
Fresh milk and cream	154	80	184	140	180	235	272
Other dairy products	234	121	281	245	270	327	356
Fruits and vegetables	600	322	715	616	708	832	903
Fresh fruits	202	111	239	209	240	268	302
Fresh vegetables	190	100	228	202	229	258	271
Processed fruits	112	62	133	110	122	170	177
Processed vegetables	96	49	115	94	117	136	152
Other food at home	1,241	662	1,482	1,193	1,567	1,775	1,939
Sugar and other sweets	124	66	149	127	148	171	195
Fats and oils	91	47	109	97	107	120	142
Miscellaneous foods	650	346	775	594	861	948	1,029
Nonalcoholic beverages	333	180	396	321	406	482	523
Food prepared by consumer unit on trips	43	23	52	54	45	54	50
Food away from home	**2,668**	**1,514**	**3,149**	**2,834**	**3,024**	**3,704**	**3,656**
ALCOHOLIC BEVERAGES	**457**	**428**	**469**	**528**	**448**	**429**	**353**
HOUSING	**16,920**	**11,269**	**19,307**	**17,248**	**19,035**	**22,635**	**21,789**
Shelter	**10,023**	**7,212**	**11,212**	**9,923**	**11,116**	**13,123**	**12,914**
Owned dwellings	6,730	3,628	8,043	6,730	7,879	10,134	9,541
Mortgage interest and charges	3,890	1,818	4,767	3,470	4,812	6,633	6,334
Property taxes	1,709	1,030	1,996	1,908	1,846	2,330	2,050
Maintenance, repair, insurance, other expenses	1,131	780	1,280	1,392	1,221	1,170	1,157
Rented dwellings	2,602	3,228	2,337	2,153	2,559	2,258	2,710
Other lodging	691	356	832	1,001	678	731	663
Utilities, fuels, and public services	**3,477**	**2,206**	**4,015**	**3,577**	**4,068**	**4,481**	**4,722**
Natural gas	480	325	546	497	528	616	639
Electricity	1,303	804	1,514	1,349	1,532	1,670	1,811
Fuel oil and other fuels	151	107	169	175	172	155	167
Telephone services	1,110	706	1,280	1,104	1,341	1,459	1,514
Water and other public services	434	264	505	452	495	582	591
Household services	**984**	**486**	**1,195**	**823**	**1,361**	**1,800**	**1,303**
Personal services	415	92	552	154	755	1,098	776
Other household services	569	394	643	669	607	702	527
Housekeeping supplies	**639**	**316**	**773**	**825**	**647**	**775**	**780**
Laundry and cleaning supplies	140	69	169	137	180	197	227
Other household products	347	156	426	488	324	393	412
Postage and stationery	152	91	178	200	144	185	141

	total consumer units	one person	two or more people total	two people	three people	four people	five or more people
Household furnishings and equipment	**$1,797**	**$1,049**	**$2,111**	**$2,100**	**$1,842**	**$2,456**	**$2,070**
Household textiles	133	88	152	146	118	210	147
Furniture	446	228	538	512	521	640	507
Floor coverings	46	24	56	48	45	74	74
Major appliances	231	112	282	294	239	309	268
Small appliances, miscellaneous housewares	101	72	113	109	107	126	118
Miscellaneous household equipment	840	525	971	992	812	1,096	955
APPAREL AND RELATED SERVICES	**1,881**	**971**	**2,260**	**1,848**	**2,330**	**2,859**	**2,719**
Men and boys	**435**	**267**	**506**	**397**	**510**	**631**	**692**
Men, aged 16 or older	351	253	392	370	409	411	412
Boys, aged 2 to 15	84	14	114	27	102	220	280
Women and girls	**749**	**352**	**914**	**801**	**924**	**1,109**	**1,014**
Women, aged 16 or older	627	334	749	747	755	786	695
Girls, aged 2 to 15	122	18	165	53	169	322	319
Children under age 2	**93**	**20**	**124**	**49**	**171**	**174**	**240**
Footwear	**327**	**158**	**397**	**292**	**413**	**548**	**529**
Other apparel products and services	**276**	**175**	**319**	**310**	**312**	**398**	**243**
TRANSPORTATION	**8,758**	**4,539**	**10,539**	**9,274**	**10,801**	**11,655**	**12,754**
Vehicle purchases	**3,244**	**1,478**	**3,991**	**3,361**	**4,121**	**4,338**	**5,388**
Cars and trucks, new	1,572	743	1,923	1,908	1,717	1,891	2,344
Cars and trucks, used	1,567	683	1,941	1,324	2,266	2,283	2,989
Other vehicles	105	53	128	129	138	164	55
Gasoline and motor oil	**2,384**	**1,276**	**2,853**	**2,452**	**2,804**	**3,364**	**3,531**
Other vehicle expenses	**2,592**	**1,461**	**3,067**	**2,740**	**3,330**	**3,329**	**3,382**
Vehicle finance charges	305	122	383	323	383	468	458
Maintenance and repairs	738	471	850	796	848	924	927
Vehicle insurance	1,071	621	1,258	1,127	1,461	1,211	1,463
Vehicle rentals, leases, licenses, other charges	478	247	576	494	638	726	534
Public transportation	**538**	**324**	**628**	**722**	**546**	**624**	**453**
HEALTH CARE	**2,853**	**1,790**	**3,302**	**3,709**	**2,876**	**3,147**	**2,840**
Health insurance	1,545	994	1,778	2,005	1,564	1,684	1,498
Medical services	709	403	839	872	697	935	819
Drugs	481	325	547	677	484	418	393
Medical supplies	118	69	138	156	132	111	130
ENTERTAINMENT	**2,698**	**1,413**	**3,238**	**3,079**	**3,009**	**3,785**	**3,373**
Fees and admissions	658	323	799	708	646	1,079	942
Audio and visual equipment and services	987	642	1,132	1,032	1,141	1,296	1,227
Pets, toys, and playground equipment	560	291	672	649	671	770	620
Other entertainment products and services	493	157	634	690	550	640	584
PERSONAL CARE PRODUCTS AND SERVICES	**588**	**364**	**681**	**650**	**653**	**756**	**725**
READING	**118**	**97**	**127**	**140**	**114**	**131**	**94**
EDUCATION	**945**	**621**	**1,082**	**777**	**1,242**	**1,483**	**1,277**
TOBACCO PRODUCTS AND SMOKING SUPPLIES	**323**	**223**	**365**	**350**	**417**	**335**	**378**
MISCELLANEOUS	**808**	**533**	**923**	**977**	**836**	**935**	**863**
CASH CONTRIBUTIONS	**1,821**	**1,219**	**2,076**	**2,512**	**1,655**	**1,819**	**1,663**
PERSONAL INSURANCE AND PENSIONS	**5,336**	**2,491**	**6,540**	**5,789**	**6,659**	**7,835**	**6,994**
Life and other personal insurance	309	146	379	349	394	432	378
Pensions and Social Security	5,027	2,345	6,162	5,441	6,265	7,403	6,616
PERSONAL TAXES	**2,233**	**1,423**	**2,577**	**3,070**	**2,332**	**2,309**	**1,707**
Federal income taxes	1,569	1,033	1,796	2,242	1,607	1,523	1,002
State and local income taxes	468	269	553	588	516	552	495
Other taxes	196	121	228	240	210	234	210
GIFTS FOR PEOPLE IN OTHER HOUSEHOLDS	**1,198**	**837**	**1,350**	**1,805**	**1,300**	**833**	**639**

Note: Spending by category does not add to total spending because gift spending is also included in the preceding product and service categories and personal taxes are not included in the total.
Source: Bureau of Labor Statistics, 2007 Consumer Expenditure Survey, Internet site http://www.bls.gov/cex/

Table 49. Indexed spending by size of household, 2007

(indexed annual spending of consumer units by product and service category and by number of people in consumer unit, 2007; index definition: an index of 100 is the average for all consumer units; an index of 132 means that spending by consumer units in that group is 32 percent above the average for all consumer units; an index of 68 indicates spending that is 32 percent below the average for all consumer units)

	total consumer units	one person	two or more people				
			total	two people	three people	four people	five or more people
Average spending of consumer unit, total	$49,638	$29,285	$58,209	$53,091	$57,326	$66,476	$65,042
Average spending of consumer unit, index	100	59	117	107	115	134	131
FOOD	100	54	119	101	118	141	150
Food at home	100	52	120	97	122	143	161
Cereals and bakery products	100	52	120	95	122	142	170
Cereals and cereal products	100	50	120	91	122	147	183
Bakery products	100	52	120	97	123	140	164
Meats, poultry, fish, and eggs	100	50	121	96	121	147	169
Beef	100	48	122	94	126	150	171
Pork	100	46	122	99	127	147	157
Other meats	100	52	120	92	120	158	167
Poultry	100	49	121	90	111	158	190
Fish and seafood	100	55	119	105	120	124	154
Eggs	100	56	116	95	112	137	170
Dairy products	100	52	120	99	116	145	162
Fresh milk and cream	100	52	119	91	117	153	177
Other dairy products	100	52	120	105	115	140	152
Fruits and vegetables	100	54	119	103	118	139	151
Fresh fruits	100	55	118	103	119	133	150
Fresh vegetables	100	53	120	106	121	136	143
Processed fruits	100	55	119	98	109	152	158
Processed vegetables	100	51	120	98	122	142	158
Other food at home	100	53	119	96	126	143	156
Sugar and other sweets	100	53	120	102	119	138	157
Fats and oils	100	52	120	107	118	132	156
Miscellaneous foods	100	53	119	91	132	146	158
Nonalcoholic beverages	100	54	119	96	122	145	157
Food prepared by consumer unit on trips	100	53	121	126	105	126	116
Food away from home	100	57	118	106	113	139	137
ALCOHOLIC BEVERAGES	100	94	103	116	98	94	77
HOUSING	100	67	114	102	113	134	129
Shelter	100	72	112	99	111	131	129
Owned dwellings	100	54	120	101	117	151	142
Mortgage interest and charges	100	47	123	89	124	171	163
Property taxes	100	60	117	112	108	136	120
Maintenance, repair, insurance, other expenses	100	69	113	123	108	103	102
Rented dwellings	100	124	90	83	98	87	104
Other lodging	100	52	120	145	98	106	96
Utilities, fuels, and public services	100	63	115	103	117	129	136
Natural gas	100	68	114	104	110	128	133
Electricity	100	62	116	104	118	128	139
Fuel oil and other fuels	100	71	112	116	114	103	111
Telephone services	100	64	115	99	121	131	136
Water and other public services	100	61	116	104	114	134	136
Household services	100	49	121	84	138	183	132
Personal services	100	22	133	37	182	265	187
Other household services	100	69	113	118	107	123	93
Housekeeping supplies	100	49	121	129	101	121	122
Laundry and cleaning supplies	100	49	121	98	129	141	162
Other household products	100	45	123	141	93	113	119
Postage and stationery	100	60	117	132	95	122	93

	total consumer units	one person	two or more people total	two people	three people	four people	five or more people
Household furnishings and equipment	100	58	117	117	103	137	115
Household textiles	100	66	114	110	89	158	111
Furniture	100	51	121	115	117	143	114
Floor coverings	100	52	122	104	98	161	161
Major appliances	100	48	122	127	103	134	116
Small appliances, miscellaneous housewares	100	71	112	108	106	125	117
Miscellaneous household equipment	100	63	116	118	97	130	114
APPAREL AND RELATED SERVICES	100	52	120	98	124	152	145
Men and boys	100	61	116	91	117	145	159
Men, aged 16 or older	100	72	112	105	117	117	117
Boys, aged 2 to 15	100	17	136	32	121	262	333
Women and girls	100	47	122	107	123	148	135
Women, aged 16 or older	100	53	119	119	120	125	111
Girls, aged 2 to 15	100	15	135	43	139	264	261
Children under age 2	100	22	133	53	184	187	258
Footwear	100	48	121	89	126	168	162
Other apparel products and services	100	63	116	112	113	144	88
TRANSPORTATION	100	52	120	106	123	133	146
Vehicle purchases	100	46	123	104	127	134	166
Cars and trucks, new	100	47	122	121	109	120	149
Cars and trucks, used	100	44	124	84	145	146	191
Other vehicles	100	50	122	123	131	156	52
Gasoline and motor oil	100	54	120	103	118	141	148
Other vehicle expenses	100	56	118	106	128	128	130
Vehicle finance charges	100	40	126	106	126	153	150
Maintenance and repairs	100	64	115	108	115	125	126
Vehicle insurance	100	58	117	105	136	113	137
Vehicle rentals, leases, licenses, other charges	100	52	121	103	133	152	112
Public transportation	100	60	117	134	101	116	84
HEALTH CARE	100	63	116	130	101	110	100
Health insurance	100	64	115	130	101	109	97
Medical services	100	57	118	123	98	132	116
Drugs	100	68	114	141	101	87	82
Medical supplies	100	58	117	132	112	94	110
ENTERTAINMENT	100	52	120	114	112	140	125
Fees and admissions	100	49	121	108	98	164	143
Audio and visual equipment and services	100	65	115	105	116	131	124
Pets, toys, and playground equipment	100	52	120	116	120	138	111
Other entertainment products and services	100	32	129	140	112	130	118
PERSONAL CARE PRODUCTS AND SERVICES	100	62	116	111	111	129	123
READING	100	82	108	119	97	111	80
EDUCATION	100	66	114	82	131	157	135
TOBACCO PRODUCTS AND SMOKING SUPPLIES	100	69	113	108	129	104	117
MISCELLANEOUS	100	66	114	121	103	116	107
CASH CONTRIBUTIONS	100	67	114	138	91	100	91
PERSONAL INSURANCE AND PENSIONS	100	47	123	108	125	147	131
Life and other personal insurance	100	47	123	113	128	140	122
Pensions and Social Security	100	47	123	108	125	147	132
PERSONAL TAXES	100	64	115	137	104	103	76
Federal income taxes	100	66	114	143	102	97	64
State and local income taxes	100	57	118	126	110	118	106
Other taxes	100	62	116	122	107	119	107
GIFTS FOR PEOPLE IN OTHER HOUSEHOLDS	100	70	113	151	109	70	53

Source: Calculations by New Strategist based on the Bureau of Labor Statistics' 2007 Consumer Expenditure Survey

Spending by Homeowners and Renters, 2007

Homeowners spend far more than renters because their incomes are higher. Homeowners had an average income of $76,875 in 2007, and they spent $57,997—17 percent more than the average household. In contrast, the average income of renters was just $35,390 and they spent $32,829—34 percent less than the average household.

Renters spend less than homeowners on every product and service category except rent, infants' clothes, and tobacco. They spend 17 percent more than the average household on tobacco.

Table 50. Average spending by homeowners and renters, 2007

(average annual spending of consumer units by product and service category and by homeownership status, 2007)

	total consumer units	homeowners	renters
Number of consumer units (in 000s)	120,171	80,244	39,927
Average number of persons per consumer unit	2.5	2.6	2.2
Average before-tax income of consumer units	$63,091	$76,875	$35,390
Average annual spending of consumer units	49,638	57,997	32,829
FOOD	**6,133**	**6,908**	**4,573**
Food at home	**3,465**	**3,856**	**2,678**
Cereals and bakery products	460	520	337
Cereals and cereal products	143	157	115
Bakery products	317	364	222
Meats, poultry, fish, and eggs	777	846	637
Beef	216	237	174
Pork	150	162	125
Other meats	104	116	82
Poultry	142	152	121
Fish and seafood	122	134	98
Eggs	43	45	38
Dairy products	387	435	290
Fresh milk and cream	154	169	124
Other dairy products	234	267	167
Fruits and vegetables	600	670	459
Fresh fruits	202	227	150
Fresh vegetables	190	211	149
Processed fruits	112	126	86
Processed vegetables	96	106	75
Other food at home	1,241	1,384	954
Sugar and other sweets	124	144	86
Fats and oils	91	101	71
Miscellaneous foods	650	719	510
Nonalcoholic beverages	333	365	269
Food prepared by consumer unit on trips	43	55	19
Food away from home	**2,668**	**3,052**	**1,895**
ALCOHOLIC BEVERAGES	**457**	**507**	**355**
HOUSING	**16,920**	**19,297**	**12,141**
Shelter	**10,023**	**11,025**	**8,009**
Owned dwellings	6,730	10,029	100
Mortgage interest and charges	3,890	5,799	54
Property taxes	1,709	2,544	30
Maintenance, repair, insurance, other expenses	1,131	1,686	17
Rented dwellings	2,602	49	7,732
Other lodging	691	947	176
Utilities, fuels, and public services	**3,477**	**4,107**	**2,211**
Natural gas	480	600	239
Electricity	1,303	1,525	857
Fuel oil and other fuels	151	207	38
Telephone services	1,110	1,218	892
Water and other public services	434	558	184
Household services	**984**	**1,212**	**526**
Personal services	415	484	277
Other household services	569	728	249
Housekeeping supplies	**639**	**776**	**363**
Laundry and cleaning supplies	140	155	109
Other household products	347	439	161
Postage and stationery	152	182	93

	total consumer units	homeowners	renters
Household furnishings and equipment	**$1,797**	**$2,177**	**$1,033**
Household textiles	133	160	80
Furniture	446	538	260
Floor coverings	46	64	11
Major appliances	231	306	82
Small appliances, miscellaneous housewares	101	115	72
Miscellaneous household equipment	840	994	529
APPAREL AND RELATED SERVICES	**1,881**	**2,100**	**1,438**
Men and boys	**435**	**476**	**354**
Men, aged 16 or older	351	380	293
Boys, aged 2 to 15	84	96	61
Women and girls	**749**	**871**	**504**
Women, aged 16 or older	627	735	410
Girls, aged 2 to 15	122	136	93
Children under age 2	**93**	**93**	**95**
Footwear	**327**	**362**	**257**
Other apparel products and services	**276**	**300**	**228**
TRANSPORTATION	**8,758**	**10,324**	**5,608**
Vehicle purchases	**3,244**	**3,846**	**2,034**
Cars and trucks, new	1,572	2,046	620
Cars and trucks, used	1,567	1,669	1,361
Other vehicles	105	131	54
Gasoline and motor oil	**2,384**	**2,746**	**1,655**
Other vehicle expenses	**2,592**	**3,092**	**1,587**
Vehicle finance charges	305	361	194
Maintenance and repairs	738	866	480
Vehicle insurance	1,071	1,281	649
Vehicle rentals, leases, licenses, other charges	478	584	265
Public transportation	**538**	**640**	**333**
HEALTH CARE	**2,853**	**3,555**	**1,441**
Health insurance	1,545	1,924	783
Medical services	709	887	352
Drugs	481	595	251
Medical supplies	118	149	56
ENTERTAINMENT	**2,698**	**3,318**	**1,452**
Fees and admissions	658	853	267
Audio and visual equipment and services	987	1,121	718
Pets, toys, and playground equipment	560	706	267
Other entertainment products and services	493	639	200
PERSONAL CARE PRODUCTS AND SERVICES	**588**	**681**	**399**
READING	**118**	**144**	**65**
EDUCATION	**945**	**1,068**	**699**
TOBACCO PRODUCTS AND SMOKING SUPPLIES	**323**	**296**	**377**
MISCELLANEOUS	**808**	**981**	**458**
CASH CONTRIBUTIONS	**1,821**	**2,256**	**948**
PERSONAL INSURANCE AND PENSIONS	**5,336**	**6,562**	**2,873**
Life and other personal insurance	309	415	97
Pensions and Social Security	5,027	6,147	2,775
PERSONAL TAXES	**2,233**	**2,944**	**806**
Federal income taxes	1,569	2,078	547
State and local income taxes	468	582	240
Other taxes	196	284	20
GIFTS FOR PEOPLE IN OTHER HOUSEHOLDS	**1,198**	**1,517**	**556**

Note: Spending by category does not add to total spending because gift spending is also included in the preceding product and service categories and personal taxes are not included in the total.
Source: Bureau of Labor Statistics, 2007 Consumer Expenditure Survey, Internet site http://www.bls.gov/cex/

Table 51. Indexed spending by homeowners and renters, 2007

(indexed annual spending of consumer units by product and service category and by homeownership status, 2007; index definition: an index of 100 is the average for all consumer units; an index of 132 means that spending by consumer units in that group is 32 percent above the average for all consumer units; an index of 68 indicates spending that is 32 percent below the average for all consumer units)

	total consumer units	homeowners	renters
Average spending of consumer units, total	$49,638	$57,997	$32,829
Average spending of consumer units, index	100	117	66
FOOD	100	113	75
Food at home	100	111	77
Cereals and bakery products	100	113	73
Cereals and cereal products	100	110	80
Bakery products	100	115	70
Meats, poultry, fish, and eggs	100	109	82
Beef	100	110	81
Pork	100	108	83
Other meats	100	112	79
Poultry	100	107	85
Fish and seafood	100	110	80
Eggs	100	105	88
Dairy products	100	112	75
Fresh milk and cream	100	110	81
Other dairy products	100	114	71
Fruits and vegetables	100	112	77
Fresh fruits	100	112	74
Fresh vegetables	100	111	78
Processed fruits	100	113	77
Processed vegetables	100	110	78
Other food at home	100	112	77
Sugar and other sweets	100	116	69
Fats and oils	100	111	78
Miscellaneous foods	100	111	78
Nonalcoholic beverages	100	110	81
Food prepared by consumer unit on trips	100	128	44
Food away from home	100	114	71
ALCOHOLIC BEVERAGES	100	111	78
HOUSING	100	114	72
Shelter	100	110	80
Owned dwellings	100	149	1
Mortgage interest and charges	100	149	1
Property taxes	100	149	2
Maintenance, repair, insurance, other expenses	100	149	2
Rented dwellings	100	2	297
Other lodging	100	137	25
Utilities, fuels, and public services	100	118	64
Natural gas	100	125	50
Electricity	100	117	66
Fuel oil and other fuels	100	137	25
Telephone services	100	110	80
Water and other public services	100	129	42
Household services	100	123	53
Personal services	100	117	67
Other household services	100	128	44
Housekeeping supplies	100	121	57
Laundry and cleaning supplies	100	111	78
Other household products	100	127	46
Postage and stationery	100	120	61

	total consumer units	homeowners	renters
Household furnishings and equipment	100	121	57
Household textiles	100	120	60
Furniture	100	121	58
Floor coverings	100	139	24
Major appliances	100	132	35
Small appliances, miscellaneous housewares	100	114	71
Miscellaneous household equipment	100	118	63
APPAREL AND RELATED SERVICES	100	112	76
Men and boys	100	109	81
Men, aged 16 or older	100	108	83
Boys, aged 2 to 15	100	114	73
Women and girls	100	116	67
Women, aged 16 or older	100	117	65
Girls, aged 2 to 15	100	111	76
Children under age 2	100	100	102
Footwear	100	111	79
Other apparel products and services	100	109	83
TRANSPORTATION	100	118	64
Vehicle purchases	100	119	63
Cars and trucks, new	100	130	39
Cars and trucks, used	100	107	87
Other vehicles	100	125	51
Gasoline and motor oil	100	115	69
Other vehicle expenses	100	119	61
Vehicle finance charges	100	118	64
Maintenance and repairs	100	117	65
Vehicle insurance	100	120	61
Vehicle rentals, leases, licenses, other charges	100	122	55
Public transportation	100	119	62
HEALTH CARE	100	125	51
Health insurance	100	125	51
Medical services	100	125	50
Drugs	100	124	52
Medical supplies	100	126	47
ENTERTAINMENT	100	123	54
Fees and admissions	100	130	41
Audio and visual equipment and services	100	114	73
Pets, toys, and playground equipment	100	126	48
Other entertainment products and services	100	130	41
PERSONAL CARE PRODUCTS AND SERVICES	100	116	68
READING	100	122	55
EDUCATION	100	113	74
TOBACCO PRODUCTS AND SMOKING SUPPLIES	100	92	117
MISCELLANEOUS	100	121	57
CASH CONTRIBUTIONS	100	124	52
PERSONAL INSURANCE AND PENSIONS	100	123	54
Life and other personal insurance	100	134	31
Pensions and Social Security	100	122	55
PERSONAL TAXES	100	132	36
Federal income taxes	100	132	35
State and local income taxes	100	124	51
Other taxes	100	145	10
GIFTS FOR PEOPLE IN OTHER HOUSEHOLDS	100	127	46

Source: Calculations by New Strategist based on the Bureau of Labor Statistics' 2007 Consumer Expenditure Survey

Spending by Number of Earners, 2007

Dual-earners account for 33 percent of the nation's households, and they outspend the average household by 28 percent. In 2007, the average two-earner household spent $63,676. Households with three or more earners spend even more ($72,821), but they account for a much smaller share of households—just 9 percent in 2007.

By category, spending does not always rise with the number of earners in a household. Single-person households with one earner (many of them young adults) spend more than other households on rent and alcoholic beverages. Two-or-more-person households with no earners (many of them elderly) spend twice the average on drugs. In general, however, three-earner households outspend the others on many products and services because they are the largest households, averaging 4.3 people.

The needs of two-earner households are readily apparent in these tables. This household type spends 34 percent more than the average household on food away from home, 84 percent more than average on personal household services (primarily day care), and 31 percent more on vehicle purchases.

Table 52. Average spending by number of earners in household, 2007

(average annual spending of consumer units (CU) by product and service category, by consumer unit size and number of earners in consumer unit, 2007)

	total consumer units	single-person CUs		CUs with two or more people			
		no earner	one earner	no earner	one earner	two earners	three+ earners
Number of consumer units (in 000s)	120,171	13,210	22,531	10,133	23,945	40,006	10,346
Average number of persons per consumer unit	2.5	1.0	1.0	2.3	3.0	3.0	4.3
Average before-tax income of consumer units	$63,091	$17,986	$40,156	$33,176	$60,069	$90,315	$101,654
Average annual spending of consumer units	49,638	21,046	34,135	39,020	51,092	63,676	72,821
FOOD	**6,133**	**2,409**	**3,875**	**5,486**	**6,511**	**7,647**	**9,777**
Food at home	**3,465**	**1,630**	**1,923**	**3,535**	**3,971**	**4,085**	**5,570**
Cereals and bakery products	460	228	244	490	537	536	721
Cereals and cereal products	143	68	74	147	170	167	228
Bakery products	317	160	170	344	367	369	493
Meats, poultry, fish, and eggs	777	354	411	788	909	909	1,298
Beef	216	102	106	209	253	264	340
Pork	150	70	69	180	183	172	233
Other meats	104	47	59	100	122	121	179
Poultry	142	60	76	137	161	161	282
Fish and seafood	122	50	78	113	139	144	195
Eggs	43	25	24	50	50	46	69
Dairy products	387	178	214	397	448	462	595
Fresh milk and cream	154	76	83	164	179	182	229
Other dairy products	234	102	131	233	269	280	365
Fruits and vegetables	600	311	330	628	703	696	926
Fresh fruits	202	106	115	222	237	233	290
Fresh vegetables	190	95	103	190	221	233	297
Processed fruits	112	63	62	122	129	126	188
Processed vegetables	96	47	50	94	116	111	151
Other food at home	1,241	559	723	1,232	1,374	1,482	2,029
Sugar and other sweets	124	64	67	127	146	148	187
Fats and oils	91	44	49	116	103	102	149
Miscellaneous foods	650	284	383	620	721	780	1,068
Nonalcoholic beverages	333	155	196	331	357	394	580
Food prepared by consumer unit on trips	43	13	28	39	48	58	45
Food away from home	**2,668**	**779**	**1,952**	**1,951**	**2,539**	**3,562**	**4,207**
ALCOHOLIC BEVERAGES	**457**	**154**	**591**	**305**	**373**	**548**	**546**
HOUSING	**16,920**	**9,048**	**12,573**	**13,506**	**17,771**	**21,201**	**21,264**
Shelter	**10,023**	**5,370**	**8,292**	**6,657**	**10,446**	**12,576**	**12,176**
Owned dwellings	6,730	2,559	4,254	4,450	6,791	9,406	9,192
Mortgage interest and charges	3,890	629	2,515	1,292	3,803	5,961	5,789
Property taxes	1,709	1,032	1,029	1,542	1,816	2,161	2,224
Maintenance, repair, insurance, other expenses	1,131	898	711	1,617	1,173	1,284	1,180
Rented dwellings	2,602	2,647	3,569	1,571	2,773	2,315	2,159
Other lodging	691	163	469	636	882	854	825
Utilities, fuels, and public services	**3,477**	**2,153**	**2,237**	**3,371**	**3,746**	**4,101**	**4,940**
Natural gas	480	342	314	481	503	564	641
Electricity	1,303	806	803	1,357	1,451	1,528	1,760
Fuel oil and other fuels	151	140	88	170	158	171	187
Telephone services	1,110	582	779	886	1,164	1,331	1,741
Water and other public services	434	283	253	477	469	507	611
Household services	**984**	**502**	**476**	**768**	**1,076**	**1,458**	**871**
Personal services	415	135	67	172	485	762	269
Other household services	569	367	409	596	591	696	602
Housekeeping supplies	**639**	**312**	**318**	**1,128**	**684**	**716**	**861**
Laundry and cleaning supplies	140	67	70	161	156	166	227
Other household products	347	152	158	775	360	375	436
Postage and stationery	152	93	90	191	167	176	198

	total consumer units	single-person CUs		CUs with two or more people			
		no earner	one earner	no earner	one earner	two earners	three+ earners
Household furnishings and equipment	**$1,797**	**$711**	**$1,249**	**$1,583**	**$1,819**	**$2,350**	**$2,416**
Household textiles	133	66	101	116	128	173	161
Furniture	446	141	279	271	495	639	513
Floor coverings	46	12	31	46	78	50	36
Major appliances	231	92	125	212	231	327	293
Small appliances, miscellaneous housewares	101	57	81	90	108	121	119
Miscellaneous household equipment	840	343	633	848	780	1,039	1,294
APPAREL AND RELATED SERVICES	**1,881**	**549**	**1,222**	**1,255**	**1,992**	**2,497**	**3,015**
Men and boys	**435**	**86**	**375**	**299**	**405**	**553**	**784**
Men, aged 16 or older	351	80	357	261	261	442	652
Boys, aged 2 to 15	84	6	18	38	144	111	132
Women and girls	**749**	**247**	**415**	**531**	**822**	**987**	**1,249**
Women, aged 16 or older	627	240	390	467	649	806	1,067
Girls, aged 2 to 15	122	7	24	63	173	182	182
Children under age 2	**93**	**12**	**24**	**49**	**142**	**132**	**126**
Footwear	**327**	**116**	**183**	**218**	**374**	**429**	**515**
Other apparel products and services	**276**	**87**	**226**	**158**	**249**	**396**	**341**
TRANSPORTATION	**8,758**	**2,850**	**5,531**	**6,665**	**9,134**	**11,248**	**14,940**
Vehicle purchases	**3,244**	**955**	**1,785**	**2,289**	**3,523**	**4,251**	**5,741**
Cars and trucks, new	1,572	455	911	1,424	1,760	2,043	2,325
Cars and trucks, used	1,567	500	790	813	1,713	2,031	3,223
Other vehicles	105	–	84	52	49	177	193
Gasoline and motor oil	**2,384**	**735**	**1,592**	**1,659**	**2,405**	**3,117**	**4,035**
Other vehicle expenses	**2,592**	**996**	**1,735**	**2,243**	**2,588**	**3,200**	**4,562**
Vehicle finance charges	305	30	176	137	283	462	549
Maintenance and repairs	738	309	567	521	739	906	1,215
Vehicle insurance	1,071	512	686	1,303	1,044	1,190	2,064
Vehicle rentals, leases, licenses, other charges	478	145	307	282	523	641	734
Public transportation	**538**	**164**	**418**	**473**	**618**	**680**	**602**
HEALTH CARE	**2,853**	**2,358**	**1,456**	**5,069**	**3,019**	**3,018**	**3,329**
Health insurance	1,545	1,434	735	3,022	1,594	1,597	1,686
Medical services	709	410	398	880	769	827	1,009
Drugs	481	462	244	966	539	461	484
Medical supplies	118	51	79	201	117	132	150
ENTERTAINMENT	**2,698**	**903**	**1,713**	**2,116**	**2,828**	**3,656**	**3,696**
Fees and admissions	658	162	418	495	790	853	913
Audio and visual equipment and services	987	502	724	766	1,019	1,254	1,287
Pets, toys, and playground equipment	560	188	352	350	600	740	912
Other entertainment products and services	493	51	219	504	419	808	585
PERSONAL CARE PRODUCTS AND SERVICES	**588**	**322**	**389**	**519**	**574**	**733**	**904**
READING	**118**	**94**	**98**	**125**	**114**	**131**	**141**
EDUCATION	**945**	**268**	**828**	**204**	**755**	**1,257**	**2,025**
TOBACCO PRODUCTS AND SMOKING SUPPLIES	**323**	**169**	**255**	**242**	**338**	**383**	**482**
MISCELLANEOUS	**808**	**393**	**616**	**674**	**914**	**990**	**933**
CASH CONTRIBUTIONS	**1,821**	**1,298**	**1,173**	**2,305**	**2,105**	**1,961**	**2,233**
PERSONAL INSURANCE AND PENSIONS	**5,336**	**231**	**3,816**	**549**	**4,663**	**8,408**	**9,534**
Life and other personal insurance	309	180	126	280	315	407	513
Pensions and Social Security	5,027	52	3,690	268	4,348	8,001	9,021
PERSONAL TAXES	**2,233**	**552**	**1,933**	**425**	**1,609**	**3,589**	**3,010**
Federal income taxes	1,569	334	1,443	166	1,043	2,592	2,059
State and local income taxes	468	96	370	67	343	762	703
Other taxes	196	121	121	192	223	235	248
GIFTS FOR PEOPLE IN OTHER HOUSEHOLDS	**1,198**	**576**	**991**	**894**	**1,224**	**1,531**	**1,395**

Note: Spending by category does not add to total spending because gift spending is also included in the preceding product and service categories and personal taxes are not included in the total. "–" means sample is too small to make a reliable estimate.
Source: Bureau of Labor Statistics, 2007 Consumer Expenditure Survey, Internet site http://www.bls.gov/cex/

Table 53. Indexed spending by number of earners in household, 2007

(indexed average annual spending of consumer units by product and service category, consumer unit size, and number of earners in consumer unit, 2007; index definition: an index of 100 is the average for all consumer units; an index of 132 means that spending by consumer units in that group is 32 percent above the average for all consumer units; an index of 68 indicates spending that is 32 percent below the average for all consumer units)

| | total consumer units | single-person CUs | | CUs with two or more people | | | |
		no earner	one earner	no earner	one earner	two earners	three+ earners
Average spending of consumer units, total	$49,638	$21,046	$34,135	$39,020	$51,092	$63,676	$72,821
Average spending of consumer units, index	100	42	69	79	103	128	147
FOOD	100	39	63	89	106	125	159
Food at home	100	47	55	102	115	118	161
Cereals and bakery products	100	50	53	107	117	117	157
Cereals and cereal products	100	48	52	103	119	117	159
Bakery products	100	50	54	109	116	116	156
Meats, poultry, fish, and eggs	100	46	53	101	117	117	167
Beef	100	47	49	97	117	122	157
Pork	100	47	46	120	122	115	155
Other meats	100	45	57	96	117	116	172
Poultry	100	42	54	96	113	113	199
Fish and seafood	100	41	64	93	114	118	160
Eggs	100	58	56	116	116	107	160
Dairy products	100	46	55	103	116	119	154
Fresh milk and cream	100	49	54	106	116	118	149
Other dairy products	100	44	56	100	115	120	156
Fruits and vegetables	100	52	55	105	117	116	154
Fresh fruits	100	52	57	110	117	115	144
Fresh vegetables	100	50	54	100	116	118	156
Processed fruits	100	56	55	109	115	113	168
Processed vegetables	100	49	52	98	121	116	157
Other food at home	100	45	58	99	111	119	163
Sugar and other sweets	100	52	54	102	118	119	151
Fats and oils	100	48	54	127	113	112	164
Miscellaneous foods	100	44	59	95	111	120	164
Nonalcoholic beverages	100	47	59	99	107	118	174
Food prepared by consumer unit on trips	100	30	65	91	112	135	105
Food away from home	100	29	73	73	95	134	158
ALCOHOLIC BEVERAGES	100	34	129	67	82	120	119
HOUSING	100	53	74	80	105	125	126
Shelter	100	54	83	66	104	125	121
Owned dwellings	100	38	63	66	101	140	137
Mortgage interest and charges	100	16	65	33	98	153	149
Property taxes	100	60	60	90	106	126	130
Maintenance, repair, insurance, other expenses	100	79	63	143	104	114	104
Rented dwellings	100	102	137	60	107	89	83
Other lodging	100	24	68	92	128	124	119
Utilities, fuels, and public services	100	62	64	97	108	118	142
Natural gas	100	71	65	100	105	118	134
Electricity	100	62	62	104	111	117	135
Fuel oil and other fuels	100	93	58	113	105	113	124
Telephone services	100	52	70	80	105	120	157
Water and other public services	100	65	58	110	108	117	141
Household services	100	51	48	78	109	148	89
Personal services	100	33	16	41	117	184	65
Other household services	100	64	72	105	104	122	106
Housekeeping supplies	100	49	50	177	107	112	135
Laundry and cleaning supplies	100	48	50	115	111	119	162
Other household products	100	44	46	223	104	108	126
Postage and stationery	100	61	59	126	110	116	130

	total consumer units	single-person CUs		CUs with two or more people			
		no earner	one earner	no earner	one earner	two earners	three+ earners
Household furnishings and equipment	**100**	**40**	**70**	**88**	**101**	**131**	**134**
Household textiles	100	50	76	87	96	130	121
Furniture	100	32	63	61	111	143	115
Floor coverings	100	26	67	100	170	109	78
Major appliances	100	40	54	92	100	142	127
Small appliances, miscellaneous housewares	100	56	80	89	107	120	118
Miscellaneous household equipment	100	41	75	101	93	124	154
APPAREL AND RELATED SERVICES	**100**	**29**	**65**	**67**	**106**	**133**	**160**
Men and boys	**100**	**20**	**86**	**69**	**93**	**127**	**180**
Men, aged 16 or older	100	23	102	74	74	126	186
Boys, aged 2 to 15	100	7	21	45	171	132	157
Women and girls	**100**	**33**	**55**	**71**	**110**	**132**	**167**
Women, aged 16 or older	100	38	62	74	104	129	170
Girls, aged 2 to 15	100	6	20	52	142	149	149
Children under age 2	**100**	**13**	**26**	**53**	**153**	**142**	**135**
Footwear	**100**	**35**	**56**	**67**	**114**	**131**	**157**
Other apparel products and services	**100**	**32**	**82**	**57**	**90**	**143**	**124**
TRANSPORTATION	**100**	**33**	**63**	**76**	**104**	**128**	**171**
Vehicle purchases	**100**	**29**	**55**	**71**	**109**	**131**	**177**
Cars and trucks, new	100	29	58	91	112	130	148
Cars and trucks, used	100	32	50	52	109	130	206
Other vehicles	100	–	80	50	47	169	184
Gasoline and motor oil	**100**	**31**	**67**	**70**	**101**	**131**	**169**
Other vehicle expenses	**100**	**38**	**67**	**87**	**100**	**123**	**176**
Vehicle finance charges	100	10	58	45	93	151	180
Maintenance and repairs	100	42	77	71	100	123	165
Vehicle insurance	100	48	64	122	97	111	193
Vehicle rentals, leases, licenses, other charges	100	30	64	59	109	134	154
Public transportation	**100**	**30**	**78**	**88**	**115**	**126**	**112**
HEALTH CARE	**100**	**83**	**51**	**178**	**106**	**106**	**117**
Health insurance	100	93	48	196	103	103	109
Medical services	100	58	56	124	108	117	142
Drugs	100	96	51	201	112	96	101
Medical supplies	100	43	67	170	99	112	127
ENTERTAINMENT	**100**	**33**	**63**	**78**	**105**	**136**	**137**
Fees and admissions	100	25	64	75	120	130	139
Audio and visual equipment and services	100	51	73	78	103	127	130
Pets, toys, and playground equipment	100	34	63	63	107	132	163
Other entertainment products and services	100	10	44	102	85	164	119
PERSONAL CARE PRODUCTS AND SERVICES	**100**	**55**	**66**	**88**	**98**	**125**	**154**
READING	**100**	**80**	**83**	**106**	**97**	**111**	**119**
EDUCATION	**100**	**28**	**88**	**22**	**80**	**133**	**214**
TOBACCO PRODUCTS AND SMOKING SUPPLIES	**100**	**52**	**79**	**75**	**105**	**119**	**149**
MISCELLANEOUS	**100**	**49**	**76**	**83**	**113**	**123**	**115**
CASH CONTRIBUTIONS	**100**	**71**	**64**	**127**	**116**	**108**	**123**
PERSONAL INSURANCE AND PENSIONS	**100**	**4**	**72**	**10**	**87**	**158**	**179**
Life and other personal insurance	100	58	41	91	102	132	166
Pensions and Social Security	100	1	73	5	86	159	179
PERSONAL TAXES	**100**	**25**	**87**	**19**	**72**	**161**	**135**
Federal income taxes	100	21	92	11	66	165	131
State and local income taxes	100	21	79	14	73	163	150
Other taxes	100	62	62	98	114	120	127
GIFTS FOR PEOPLE IN OTHER HOUSEHOLDS	**100**	**48**	**83**	**75**	**102**	**128**	**116**

Note: "–" means sample is too small to make a reliable estimate.
Source: Calculations by New Strategist based on the Bureau of Labor Statistics' 2007 Consumer Expenditure Survey

Spending by Occupation, 2007

Households headed by managers and professionals spent $69,510 in 2007, 40 percent more than the average household. Behind the higher level of spending are their higher incomes, which averaged $99,577 in 2007. Among all wage and salary workers, average household income was $71,518 and their spending was only 9 percent above average. Households headed by retirees spend 29 percent less than the average household, while the self-employed spend 28 percent more than average.

Households headed by managers and professionals spend more than average on many of the products and services associated with the income elite. They spend 46 percent more than the average household on food away from home, 43 percent more on alcoholic beverages, 86 percent more on other lodging (which includes vacation homes as well as hotels and motels), 40 percent more on men's clothes, 47 percent more on women's clothes, 41 percent more on new cars and trucks, 73 percent more on fees and admissions to entertainment events, and 68 percent more on gifts for people in other households.

The self-employed are big spenders on products and services needed by people who are likely to work at home. They spend more than average on electricity and out-of-pocket health insurance expenses. Their spending is below average on only rent, floor coverings, and tobacco.

The retired spend more than the average household on health care, home maintenance and repairs, heating fuels, reading material, and cash contributions among others.

Table 54. Average spending by occupation of householder, 2007

(average annual spending of consumer units by product and service category and by selected occupation of consumer unit reference person, 2007)

| | total consumer units | self-employed | wage and salary workers | | | | | | retired |
			total	managers and professionals	technical, sales, admin. support	service workers	construction workers, mechanics	operators, fabricators, laborers	
Number of consumer units (in 000s)	120,171	5,471	79,622	30,543	21,668	13,178	4,663	9,570	20,658
Average number of persons per consumer unit	2.5	2.6	2.6	2.6	2.6	2.6	2.7	2.6	1.7
Average before-tax income of consumer units	$63,091	$90,530	$71,518	$99,577	$60,210	$47,797	$56,150	$47,715	$35,040
Average annual spending of consumer units	49,638	63,455	53,873	69,510	48,509	40,246	44,100	39,377	35,424
FOOD	6,133	7,236	6,614	7,988	6,222	5,321	5,610	5,276	4,420
Food at home	3,465	4,039	3,582	4,090	3,394	3,110	3,382	3,082	2,813
Cereals and bakery products	460	502	477	548	450	418	435	403	382
Cereals and cereal products	143	158	149	173	131	134	136	133	110
Bakery products	317	344	328	375	319	284	299	271	272
Meats, poultry, fish, and eggs	777	881	796	833	790	732	846	753	629
Beef	216	230	221	215	231	193	263	231	171
Pork	150	176	149	148	149	137	164	159	138
Other meats	104	113	109	115	108	108	108	91	79
Poultry	142	166	146	158	144	132	143	130	101
Fish and seafood	122	143	129	151	118	121	122	99	100
Eggs	43	52	43	44	41	40	45	44	39
Dairy products	387	457	401	463	377	350	373	342	315
Fresh milk and cream	154	181	158	170	153	142	155	147	123
Other dairy products	234	276	244	292	223	208	218	195	192
Fruits and vegetables	600	728	612	753	531	531	529	486	537
Fresh fruits	202	227	206	266	172	173	155	158	187
Fresh vegetables	190	228	194	239	168	171	173	148	170
Processed fruits	112	154	113	137	103	97	103	89	101
Processed vegetables	96	119	98	112	87	90	98	91	80
Other food at home	1,241	1,472	1,295	1,494	1,246	1,079	1,199	1,099	950
Sugar and other sweets	124	133	129	143	128	118	111	107	105
Fats and oils	91	104	91	99	89	82	87	85	88
Miscellaneous foods	650	783	685	804	657	549	630	568	470
Nonalcoholic beverages	333	395	347	384	334	301	349	314	251
Food prepared by consumer unit on trips	43	56	44	64	37	30	22	25	37
Food away from home	2,668	3,197	3,033	3,898	2,827	2,212	2,227	2,194	1,607
ALCOHOLIC BEVERAGES	457	508	525	653	503	351	602	359	303
HOUSING	16,920	20,678	18,187	23,295	16,579	13,869	15,107	12,932	12,274
Shelter	10,023	12,326	10,985	14,337	9,966	8,246	8,886	7,391	6,455
Owned dwellings	6,730	9,088	7,434	10,635	6,379	4,596	5,667	4,371	4,277
Mortgage interest and charges	3,890	5,476	4,636	6,561	3,998	2,952	3,755	2,688	1,179
Property taxes	1,709	2,232	1,752	2,565	1,451	1,069	1,317	990	1,622
Maintenance, repair, insurance, other expenses	1,131	1,380	1,045	1,510	929	576	594	693	1,476
Rented dwellings	2,602	2,335	2,817	2,419	3,070	3,310	2,958	2,765	1,635
Other lodging	691	903	735	1,282	517	340	261	255	543
Utilities, fuels, and public services	3,477	3,964	3,587	4,077	3,432	3,097	3,449	3,115	3,022
Natural gas	480	515	491	601	464	385	444	371	476
Electricity	1,303	1,472	1,327	1,460	1,282	1,209	1,307	1,174	1,142
Fuel oil and other fuels	151	204	138	171	116	87	142	150	182
Telephone services	1,110	1,225	1,200	1,326	1,161	1,081	1,153	1,071	791
Water and other public services	434	548	432	520	409	335	403	348	431
Household services	984	1,261	1,085	1,588	1,039	572	618	519	726
Personal services	415	459	520	724	561	240	331	255	143
Other household services	569	802	565	864	479	332	287	265	583
Housekeeping supplies	639	833	597	707	601	444	539	468	791
Laundry and cleaning supplies	140	147	142	154	132	125	114	160	118
Other household products	347	374	312	365	330	221	309	222	510
Postage and stationery	152	312	144	188	139	98	115	86	163

	total consumer units	self-employed	wage and salary workers						retired
			total	managers and professionals	technical, sales, admin. support	service workers	construction workers, mechanics	operators, fabricators, laborers	
Household furnishings and equipment	**$1,797**	**$2,294**	**$1,932**	**$2,586**	**$1,540**	**$1,510**	**$1,615**	**$1,439**	**$1,280**
Household textiles	133	183	145	193	137	102	102	87	111
Furniture	446	589	490	699	389	376	360	269	272
Floor coverings	46	40	48	72	37	47	7	13	34
Major appliances	231	317	247	311	246	162	207	181	161
Small appliances, miscellaneous housewares	101	162	104	146	77	103	54	54	88
Miscellaneous household equipment	840	1,002	899	1,164	653	720	886	835	614
APPAREL AND RELATED SERVICES	**1,881**	**2,366**	**2,116**	**2,740**	**1,901**	**1,646**	**1,402**	**1,569**	**1,044**
Men and boys	**435**	**628**	**485**	**611**	**431**	**378**	**326**	**418**	**208**
Men, aged 16 or older	351	508	389	508	337	278	243	336	193
Boys, aged 2 to 15	84	120	96	103	94	100	83	82	16
Women and girls	**749**	**940**	**847**	**1,103**	**812**	**650**	**474**	**546**	**473**
Women, aged 16 or older	627	772	702	928	679	518	368	429	446
Girls, aged 2 to 15	122	168	145	174	133	132	106	117	26
Children under age 2	**93**	**116**	**104**	**108**	**101**	**109**	**80**	**102**	**28**
Footwear	**327**	**355**	**361**	**441**	**305**	**311**	**308**	**320**	**188**
Other apparel products and services	**276**	**327**	**319**	**477**	**251**	**198**	**213**	**184**	**146**
TRANSPORTATION	**8,758**	**10,139**	**9,609**	**11,448**	**8,881**	**7,989**	**8,586**	**8,102**	**5,970**
Vehicle purchases	**3,244**	**3,416**	**3,553**	**4,189**	**3,263**	**3,096**	**3,363**	**2,899**	**2,169**
Cars and trucks, new	1,572	1,599	1,668	2,215	1,337	1,253	1,681	1,237	1,319
Cars and trucks, used	1,567	1,701	1,750	1,893	1,734	1,689	1,423	1,568	826
Other vehicles	105	116	135	81	191	153	259	95	25
Gasoline and motor oil	**2,384**	**2,784**	**2,662**	**2,896**	**2,589**	**2,288**	**2,780**	**2,542**	**1,432**
Other vehicle expenses	**2,592**	**3,139**	**2,822**	**3,431**	**2,621**	**2,263**	**2,145**	**2,424**	**1,969**
Vehicle finance charges	305	309	371	424	355	303	368	334	115
Maintenance and repairs	738	924	806	994	760	584	655	688	549
Vehicle insurance	1,071	1,173	1,115	1,214	1,082	1,055	848	1,073	1,052
Vehicle rentals, leases, licenses, other charges	478	733	530	798	424	321	274	329	253
Public transportation	**538**	**801**	**571**	**932**	**408**	**343**	**298**	**236**	**399**
HEALTH CARE	**2,853**	**3,566**	**2,486**	**3,097**	**2,398**	**1,827**	**1,974**	**1,887**	**4,380**
Health insurance	1,545	1,709	1,306	1,626	1,268	940	989	1,026	2,664
Medical services	709	1,209	676	839	662	483	612	487	751
Drugs	481	510	390	486	366	308	292	292	823
Medical supplies	118	138	114	147	102	95	80	81	143
ENTERTAINMENT	**2,698**	**4,389**	**2,884**	**3,992**	**2,445**	**1,932**	**2,310**	**1,907**	**1,852**
Fees and admissions	658	929	696	1,138	545	365	338	256	441
Audio and visual equipment and services	987	1,247	1,065	1,287	999	900	948	784	716
Pets, toys, and playground equipment	560	676	630	753	576	497	638	530	333
Other entertainment products and services	493	1,537	493	815	324	169	386	337	361
PERSONAL CARE PRODUCTS AND SERVICES	**588**	**700**	**627**	**847**	**574**	**446**	**448**	**374**	**514**
READING	**118**	**151**	**116**	**175**	**100**	**62**	**62**	**62**	**141**
EDUCATION	**945**	**1,139**	**1,154**	**1,821**	**909**	**691**	**479**	**545**	**279**
TOBACCO PRODUCTS AND SMOKING SUPPLIES	**323**	**283**	**345**	**262**	**334**	**346**	**598**	**514**	**187**
MISCELLANEOUS	**808**	**919**	**874**	**1,145**	**882**	**562**	**665**	**520**	**647**
CASH CONTRIBUTIONS	**1,821**	**2,369**	**1,772**	**2,686**	**1,254**	**1,178**	**1,196**	**1,122**	**2,167**
PERSONAL INSURANCE AND PENSIONS	**5,336**	**9,011**	**6,563**	**9,359**	**5,529**	**4,026**	**5,063**	**4,209**	**1,246**
Life and other personal insurance	309	398	317	444	276	177	272	219	305
Pensions and Social Security	5,027	8,612	6,246	8,915	5,253	3,849	4,791	3,990	941
PERSONAL TAXES	**2,233**	**2,684**	**2,776**	**4,835**	**1,859**	**804**	**1,820**	**1,463**	**1,029**
Federal income taxes	1,569	1,940	1,981	3,571	1,265	494	1,242	932	687
State and local income taxes	468	384	607	984	425	222	466	416	144
Other taxes	196	360	188	280	168	88	113	115	198
GIFTS FOR PEOPLE IN OTHER HOUSEHOLDS	**1,198**	**1,423**	**1,291**	**2,015**	**942**	**722**	**850**	**766**	**1,039**

Note: Spending by category does not add to total spending because gift spending is also included in the preceding product and service categories and personal taxes are not included in the total.

Source: Bureau of Labor Statistics, 2007 Consumer Expenditure Survey, Internet site http://www.bls.gov/cex/

Table 55. Indexed spending by occupation of householder, 2007

(indexed average annual spending of consumer units by product and service category and selected occupation of consumer unit reference person, 2007; index definition: an index of 100 is the average for all consumer units; an index of 132 means that spending by consumer units in that group is 32 percent above the average for all consumer units; an index of 68 indicates spending that is 32 percent below the average for all consumer units)

| | total consumer units | self-employed | wage and salary workers | | | | | | retired |
			total	managers and professionals	technical, sales, admin. support	service workers	construction workers, mechanics	operators, fabricators, laborers	
Average spending of consumer units, total	$49,638	$63,455	$53,873	$69,510	$48,509	$40,246	$44,100	$39,377	$35,424
Average spending of consumer units, index	100	128	109	140	98	81	89	79	71
FOOD	100	118	108	130	101	87	91	86	72
Food at home	100	117	103	118	98	90	98	89	81
Cereals and bakery products	100	109	104	119	98	91	95	88	83
Cereals and cereal products	100	110	104	121	92	94	95	93	77
Bakery products	100	109	103	118	101	90	94	85	86
Meats, poultry, fish, and eggs	100	113	102	107	102	94	109	97	81
Beef	100	106	102	100	107	89	122	107	79
Pork	100	117	99	99	99	91	109	106	92
Other meats	100	109	105	111	104	104	104	88	76
Poultry	100	117	103	111	101	93	101	92	71
Fish and seafood	100	117	106	124	97	99	100	81	82
Eggs	100	121	100	102	95	93	105	102	91
Dairy products	100	118	104	120	97	90	96	88	81
Fresh milk and cream	100	118	103	110	99	92	101	95	80
Other dairy products	100	118	104	125	95	89	93	83	82
Fruits and vegetables	100	121	102	126	89	89	88	81	90
Fresh fruits	100	112	102	132	85	86	77	78	93
Fresh vegetables	100	120	102	126	88	90	91	78	89
Processed fruits	100	138	101	122	92	87	92	79	90
Processed vegetables	100	124	102	117	91	94	102	95	83
Other food at home	100	119	104	120	100	87	97	89	77
Sugar and other sweets	100	107	104	115	103	95	90	86	85
Fats and oils	100	114	100	109	98	90	96	93	97
Miscellaneous foods	100	120	105	124	101	84	97	87	72
Nonalcoholic beverages	100	119	104	115	100	90	105	94	75
Food prepared by consumer unit on trips	100	130	102	149	86	70	51	58	86
Food away from home	100	120	114	146	106	83	83	82	60
ALCOHOLIC BEVERAGES	100	111	115	143	110	77	132	79	66
HOUSING	100	122	107	138	98	82	89	76	73
Shelter	100	123	110	143	99	82	89	74	64
Owned dwellings	100	135	110	158	95	68	84	65	64
Mortgage interest and charges	100	141	119	169	103	76	97	69	30
Property taxes	100	131	103	150	85	63	77	58	95
Maintenance, repair, insurance, other expenses	100	122	92	134	82	51	53	61	131
Rented dwellings	100	90	108	93	118	127	114	106	63
Other lodging	100	131	106	186	75	49	38	37	79
Utilities, fuels, and public services	100	114	103	117	99	89	99	90	87
Natural gas	100	107	102	125	97	80	93	77	99
Electricity	100	113	102	112	98	93	100	90	88
Fuel oil and other fuels	100	135	91	113	77	58	94	99	121
Telephone services	100	110	108	119	105	97	104	96	71
Water and other public services	100	126	100	120	94	77	93	80	99
Household services	100	128	110	161	106	58	63	53	74
Personal services	100	111	125	174	135	58	80	61	34
Other household services	100	141	99	152	84	58	50	47	102
Housekeeping supplies	100	130	93	111	94	69	84	73	124
Laundry and cleaning supplies	100	105	101	110	94	89	81	114	84
Other household products	100	108	90	105	95	64	89	64	147
Postage and stationery	100	205	95	124	91	64	76	57	107

	total consumer units	self-employed	wage and salary workers						retired
			total	managers and professionals	technical, sales, admin. support	service workers	construction workers, mechanics	operators, fabricators, laborers	
Household furnishings and equipment	100	128	108	144	86	84	90	80	71
Household textiles	100	138	109	145	103	77	77	65	83
Furniture	100	132	110	157	87	84	81	60	61
Floor coverings	100	87	104	157	80	102	15	28	74
Major appliances	100	137	107	135	106	70	90	78	70
Small appliances, miscellaneous housewares	100	160	103	145	76	102	53	53	87
Miscellaneous household equipment	100	119	107	139	78	86	105	99	73
APPAREL AND RELATED SERVICES	100	126	112	146	101	88	75	83	56
Men and boys	100	144	111	140	99	87	75	96	48
Men, aged 16 or older	100	145	111	145	96	79	69	96	55
Boys, aged 2 to 15	100	143	114	123	112	119	99	98	19
Women and girls	100	126	113	147	108	87	63	73	63
Women, aged 16 or older	100	123	112	148	108	83	59	68	71
Girls, aged 2 to 15	100	138	119	143	109	108	87	96	21
Children under age 2	100	125	112	116	109	117	86	110	30
Footwear	100	109	110	135	93	95	94	98	57
Other apparel products and services	100	118	116	173	91	72	77	67	53
TRANSPORTATION	100	116	110	131	101	91	98	93	68
Vehicle purchases	100	105	110	129	101	95	104	89	67
Cars and trucks, new	100	102	106	141	85	80	107	79	84
Cars and trucks, used	100	109	112	121	111	108	91	100	53
Other vehicles	100	110	129	77	182	146	247	90	24
Gasoline and motor oil	100	117	112	121	109	96	117	107	60
Other vehicle expenses	100	121	109	132	101	87	83	94	76
Vehicle finance charges	100	101	122	139	116	99	121	110	38
Maintenance and repairs	100	125	109	135	103	79	89	93	74
Vehicle insurance	100	110	104	113	101	99	79	100	98
Vehicle rentals, leases, licenses, other charges	100	153	111	167	89	67	57	69	53
Public transportation	100	149	106	173	76	64	55	44	74
HEALTH CARE	100	125	87	109	84	64	69	66	154
Health insurance	100	111	85	105	82	61	64	66	172
Medical services	100	171	95	118	93	68	86	69	106
Drugs	100	106	81	101	76	64	61	61	171
Medical supplies	100	117	97	125	86	81	68	69	121
ENTERTAINMENT	100	163	107	148	91	72	86	71	69
Fees and admissions	100	141	106	173	83	55	51	39	67
Audio and visual equipment and services	100	126	108	130	101	91	96	79	73
Pets, toys, and playground equipment	100	121	113	134	103	89	114	95	59
Other entertainment products and services	100	312	100	165	66	34	78	68	73
PERSONAL CARE PRODUCTS AND SERVICES	100	119	107	144	98	76	76	64	87
READING	100	128	98	148	85	53	53	53	119
EDUCATION	100	121	122	193	96	73	51	58	30
TOBACCO PRODUCTS AND SMOKING SUPPLIES	100	88	107	81	103	107	185	159	58
MISCELLANEOUS	100	114	108	142	109	70	82	64	80
CASH CONTRIBUTIONS	100	130	97	148	69	65	66	62	119
PERSONAL INSURANCE AND PENSIONS	100	169	123	175	104	75	95	79	23
Life and other personal insurance	100	129	103	144	89	57	88	71	99
Pensions and Social Security	100	171	124	177	104	77	95	79	19
PERSONAL TAXES	100	120	124	217	83	36	82	66	46
Federal income taxes	100	124	126	228	81	31	79	59	44
State and local income taxes	100	82	130	210	91	47	100	89	31
Other taxes	100	184	96	143	86	45	58	59	101
GIFTS FOR PEOPLE IN OTHER HOUSEHOLDS	100	119	108	168	79	60	71	64	87

Source: Calculations by New Strategist based on the Bureau of Labor Statistics' 2007 Consumer Expenditure Survey

Appendix: About the Consumer Expenditure Survey

History

The Consumer Expenditure Survey is an ongoing study of the day-to-day spending of American households. In taking the survey, government interviewers collect spending data on products and services as well as data on the amount and sources of household income, changes in saving and debt, and demographic and economic characteristics of household members. The Bureau of the Census collects data for the survey under contract with the Bureau of Labor Statistics, which is responsible for analysis and release of the data.

Since the late 19th century, the federal government has conducted expenditure surveys about every 10 years. Although the results have been used for a variety of purposes, their primary application is to track consumer prices. Beginning in 1980, the Consumer Expenditure Survey became a continuous survey with annual release of data (and a lag time of about two years between data collection and release). The survey is used to update prices for the market basket of products and services used in calculating the consumer price index.

Description of the Consumer Expenditure Survey

The Consumer Expenditure Survey comprises two components: an interview survey and a diary survey. In the interview portion of the survey, respondents are asked each quarter for five consecutive quarters to report their expenditures for the previous three months. The interview survey records purchases of big-ticket items such as houses, cars, and major appliances, and recurring expenses such as insurance premiums, utility payments, and rent. The interview component covers about 95 percent of all expenditures.

The diary survey records expenditures on small, frequently purchased items during a two-week period. These detailed records include expenses for food and beverages purchased in grocery stores and at restaurants, as well as other items such as tobacco, housekeeping supplies, nonprescription drugs, and personal care products and services. The diary survey is intended to capture expenditures respondents are likely to forget or recall incorrectly over longer periods of time.

Average spending figures shown in this report represent integrated data from both the diary and interview components of the survey. Integrated data provide a more complete accounting of consumer expenditures than either component of the survey is designed to do alone.

Data collection and processing

Interview and diary surveys use two separate, nationally representative samples. For the interview survey, about 7,000 consumer units are interviewed on a rotating panel basis each quarter for five consecutive quarters. Another 7,000 consumer units kept weekly diaries of spending for two consecutive weeks. Data collection is carried out in 91 areas of the country.

The Bureau of Labor Statistics reviews, audits, and cleanses the data, then weights them to reflect the number and characteristics of all U.S. consumer units. Like any sample survey, the Consumer Expenditure Survey is subject to two major types of error. Nonsampling error occurs when respondents misinterpret questions or interviewers are inconsistent in the way they ask questions or record answers. Respondents may forget items, recall expenses incorrectly, or deliberately give wrong answers. A respondent may remember how much he or she spent at the grocery store but forget the items picked up at a local convenience store. Most surveys of alcohol consumption or spending on alcohol suffer from this type of underreporting, for example. Mistakes during the various stages of data processing and refinement can also cause nonsampling error.

Sampling error occurs when a sample does not accurately represent the population it is supposed to represent. This kind of error is present in every sample-based survey and is minimized by using a proper sampling procedure. Standard error tables documenting the extent of sampling error in the Consumer Expenditure Survey are available from the Bureau of Labor Statistics at http://www.bls.gov/cex/csxstnderror.htm.

Although the Consumer Expenditure Survey is the best source of information about the spending behavior of American households, it should be treated with caution because of the above problems. Comparisons with consumption data from other sources show that Consumer Expenditure Survey data tend to underestimate expenditures except for rent, fuel, telephone service, furniture, transportation, and personal care services. Despite these problems, the data reveal important spending patterns by demographic segment that can be used to better understand consumer behavior.

Definition of consumer unit

The Consumer Expenditure Survey uses the consumer unit as the sampling unit instead of the household, the sampling unit used by the Census Bureau. The term household is used interchangeably with the term consumer unit in this book for convenience, although they are not exactly the same. Some households contain more than one consumer unit.

The Bureau of Labor Statistics defines consumer unit as (1) members of a household who are related by blood, marriage, adoption, or other legal arrangements; (2) a person living alone or sharing a household with others or living as a roomer in a private home or lodging house or in permanent living quarters in a hotel or motel, but who is financially independent; or (3) two or more persons living together who pool their income to make joint expenditure decisions. The bureau defines financial independence in terms of the three major expenses categories: housing, food, and other living expenses. To be considered financially independent, at least two of the three major expense categories have to be provided by the respondent.

The Census Bureau uses household as its sampling unit in the decennial census and in the monthly Current Population Survey. The Census Bureau's household consists of all persons who occupy a housing unit. A house, an apartment or other groups of rooms, or a single room is regarded as a housing unit when it is occupied or intended for occupancy as separate living quarters; that is, when the occupants do not live and eat with any other persons in the structure and there is direct access from the outside or through a common hall.

The definition goes on to specify that a household includes the related family members and all the unrelated persons, if any, such as lodgers, foster children, wards, or employees who share the housing unit. A person living alone in a housing unit or a group of unrelated persons sharing a housing unit as partners is also counted as a household. The count of households excludes group quarters.

Because there can be more than one consumer unit in a household, consumer units outnumber households by several million. Young adults under age 25 head most of the additional consumer units.

For more information

To find out more about the Consumer Expenditure Survey, contact the specialists at the Bureau of Labor Statistics at (202) 691-6900, or visit the Consumer Expenditure Survey home page at http://www.bls.gov/cex/. The web site includes news releases, technical documentation, and current and historical summary-level data. The detailed average spending data shown in this report are available from the Bureau of Labor Statistics only by special request.

For a comprehensive look at detailed household spending data for all products and services, see the 14th edition of *Household Spending: Who Spends How Much on What*. New Strategist's books are available in hardcopy or as downloads with links to the Excel version of each table. Find out more by visiting http://www.newstrategist.com or by calling 1-800-848-0842.

Glossary

age The age of the reference person.

alcoholic beverages Includes beer and ale, wine, whiskey, gin, vodka, rum, and other alcoholic beverages.

annual spending The annual amount spent per household. The Bureau of Labor Statistics calculates the annual average for all households in a segment, not just for those that purchased an item. The averages are calculated by integrating the results of the diary (weekly) and interview (quarterly) portions of the Consumer Expenditure Survey. For items purchased by most households—such as bread—average annual spending figures are a fairly accurate account of actual spending. For products and services purchased by few households during a year's time—such as cars—the average annual amount spent is much less than what purchasers spend.

apparel, accessories, and related services Includes the following:

• *men's and boys' apparel* Includes coats, jackets, sweaters, vests, sport coats, tailored jackets, slacks, shorts and short sets, sportswear, shirts, underwear, nightwear, hosiery, uniforms, and other accessories.

• *women's and girls' apparel* Includes coats, jackets, furs, sport coats, tailored jackets, sweaters, vests, blouses, shirts, dresses, dungarees, culottes, slacks, shorts, sportswear, underwear, nightwear, uniforms, hosiery, and other accessories.

• *infants' apparel* Includes coats, jackets, snowsuits, underwear, diapers, dresses, crawlers, sleeping garments, hosiery, footwear, and other accessories for children.

• *footwear* Includes articles such as shoes, slippers, boots, and other similar items. It excludes footwear for babies and footwear used for sports such as bowling or golf shoes.

• *other apparel products and services* Includes material for making clothes, shoe repair, alterations and sewing patterns and notions, clothing rental, clothing storage, dry cleaning, sent-out laundry, watches, jewelry, and repairs to watches and jewelry.

baby boom Americans born between 1946 and 1964.

cash contributions Includes cash contributed to persons or organizations outside the consumer unit including court-ordered alimony, child support payments, and support for college students, and contributions to religious, educational, charitable, or political organizations.

consumer unit (1) All members of a household who are related by blood, marriage, adoption, or other legal arrangements; (2) a person living alone or sharing a household with others or living as a roomer in a private home or lodging house or in permanent living quarters in a hotel or motel, but who is financially independent; or (3) two or more persons living together who pool their income to make joint expenditure decisions. Financial independence is determined by the three major expense categories: housing, food, and other living expenses. To be considered financially independent, at least two of the three major expense categories have to be provided by the respondent. For convenience, called household in the text of this report.

consumer unit, composition of The classification of interview households by type according to (1) relationship of other household members to the reference person; (2) age of the children of the reference person; and (3) combination of relationship to the reference person and age of the children. Stepchildren and adopted children are included with the reference person's own children.

earner A consumer unit member aged 14 or older who worked at least one week during the twelve months prior to the interview date.

education Includes tuition, fees, books, supplies, and equipment for public and private nursery schools, elementary and high schools, colleges and universities, and other schools.

entertainment Includes the following:

• *fees and admissions* Includes fees for participant sports; admissions to sporting events, movies, concerts, plays; health, swimming, tennis, and country club memberships, and other social recreational and fraternal organizations; recreational lessons or instructions; and recreational expenses on trips.

• *audio and visual equipment and services* Includes television sets; radios; cable TV; tape recorders and players; video cassettes, tapes, and discs; video cassette recorders and video disc players; video game hardware and software; personal digital audio players; streaming and downloading audio and video; sound components; CDs, records, and tapes; musical instruments; and rental and repair of TV and sound equipment.

• *pets, toys, hobbies, and playground equipment* Includes pet food, pet services, veterinary expenses, toys, games, hobbies, and playground equipment.

• *other entertainment equipment and services* Includes indoor exercise equipment, athletic shoes, bicycles, trailers, campers, camping equipment, rental of cameras and trailers, hunting and fishing equipment, sports equipment, winter sports equipment, water sports equipment, boats, boat motors and boat trailers, rental of boats, landing and docking fees, rental and repair of sports equipment, photographic equipment, film, photo processing, photographer fees, repair and rental of photo equipment, fireworks, pinball and electronic video games.

expenditure The transaction cost including excise and sales taxes of goods and services acquired during the survey period. The full cost of each purchase is recorded even though full payment may not have been made at the date of purchase. Expenditure estimates include gifts. Excluded from expenditures are purchases or portions of purchases directly assignable to business purposes and periodic credit or installment payments on goods and services already acquired.

federal income tax Includes federal income tax withheld in the survey year to pay for income earned in survey year plus additional tax paid in survey year to cover any underpayment or underwithholding of tax in the year prior to the survey.

financial products and services Includes accounting fees, legal fees, union dues, professional dues and fees, other occupational expenses, funerals, cemetery lots, dating services, shopping club memberships, and unclassified fees and personal services.

food Includes the following:

• *food at home* Refers to the total expenditures for food at grocery stores or other food stores during the interview period. It is calculated by multiplying the number of visits to a grocery or other food store by the average amount spent per visit. It excludes the purchase of nonfood items.

• *food away from home* Includes all meals (breakfast, lunch, brunch, and dinner) at restaurants, carry-outs, and vending machines, including tips, plus meals as pay, special catered affairs such as weddings, bar mitzvahs, and confirmations, and meals away from home on trips.

generation X Americans born between 1965 and 1976; also known as the baby-bust generation.

gifts for people in other households Includes gift expenditures for people living in other consumer units. The amount spent on gifts is also included in individual product and service categories.

health care Includes the following:

• *health insurance* Includes health maintenance plans (HMOs), Blue Cross/Blue Shield, commercial health insurance, Medicare, Medicare supplemental insurance, long-term care insurance, and other health insurance.

• *medical services* Includes hospital room and services, physicians' services, services of a practitioner other than a physician, eye and dental care, lab tests, X-rays, nursing, therapy services, care in convalescent or nursing home, and other medical care.

• *drugs* Includes prescription and nonprescription drugs, internal and respiratory over-the-counter drugs.

• *medical supplies* Includes eyeglasses and contact lenses, topicals and dressings, antiseptics, bandages, cotton, first aid kits, contraceptives; medical equipment for general use such as syringes, ice bags, thermometers, vaporizers, heating pads; supportive or convalescent medical equipment such as hearing aids, braces, canes, crutches, and walkers.

Hispanic origin The self-identified Hispanic origin of the consumer unit reference person. All consumer units are included in one of two Hispanic origin groups based on the reference person's Hispanic origin: Hispanic or non-Hispanic. Hispanics may be of any race.

household According to the Census Bureau, all the people who occupy a household. A group of unrelated people who share a housing unit as roommates or unmarried partners is also counted as a household. Households do not include group quarters such as college dormitories, prisons, or nursing homes. A household may contain more than one consumer unit. The terms household and consumer unit are used interchangeably in this report.

household furnishings and equipment Includes the following:

• *household textiles* Includes bathroom, kitchen, dining room, and other linens, curtains and drapes, slipcovers and decorative pillows, and sewing materials.

• *furniture* Includes living room, dining room, kitchen, bedroom, nursery, porch, lawn, and other outdoor furniture.

• *carpet, rugs, and other floor coverings* Includes installation and replacement of wall-to-wall carpets, room-size rugs, and other soft floor coverings.

• *major appliances* Includes refrigerators, freezers, dishwashers, stoves, ovens, garbage disposals, vacuum cleaners, microwave ovens, air-conditioners, sewing machines, washing machines, clothes dryers, and floor-cleaning equipment.

• *small appliances and miscellaneous housewares* Includes small electrical kitchen appliances, portable heating and cooling equipment, china and other dinnerware, flatware, glassware, silver and other serving pieces, nonelectric cookware, and plastic dinnerware. Excludes personal care appliances.

• *miscellaneous household equipment* Includes computer hardware and software, luggage, lamps and other lighting fixtures, window coverings, clocks, lawn mowers and gardening equipment, hand and power tools, telephone answering devices, personal digital assistants, Internet services away from home, office equipment for home use, fresh flowers and house plants, rental of furniture, closet and storage items, household decorative items, infants' equipment, outdoor equipment, smoke alarms, other household appliances, and small miscellaneous furnishing.

household services Includes the following:

• *personal services* Includes baby sitting, day care, and care of elderly and handicapped persons.

• *other household services* Includes computer information services; housekeeping services; gardening and lawn care services; coin-operated laundry and dry-cleaning of household textiles; termite and pest control products; moving, storage, and freight expenses; repair of household appliances and other household equipment; reupholstering and furniture repair; rental and repair of lawn and gardening tools; and rental of other household equipment.

housekeeping supplies Includes soaps, detergents, other laundry cleaning products, cleansing and toilet tissue, paper towels, napkins, and miscellaneous household products; lawn and garden supplies, postage, stationery, stationery supplies, and gift wrap.

housing tenure Owner includes households living in their own homes, cooperatives, condominiums, or townhouses. Renter includes households paying rent as well as families living rent free in lieu of wages.

income before taxes The total money earnings and selected money receipts accruing to a consumer unit during the 12 months prior to the interview date. Income includes the following components:

• *wages and salaries* Includes total money earnings for all members of the consumer unit aged 14 or older from all jobs, including civilian wages and salaries, Armed Forces pay and allowances, piece-rate payments, commissions, tips, National Guard or Reserve pay (received for training periods), and cash bonuses before deductions for taxes, pensions, union dues, etc.

• *self-employment income* Includes net business and farm income, which consists of net income (gross receipts minus operating expenses) from a profession or unincorporated business or from the operation of a farm by an owner, tenant, or sharecropper. If the business or farm is a partnership, only an appropriate share of net income is recorded. Losses are also recorded.

• *Social Security, private and government retirement* Includes payments by the federal government made under retirement, survivor, and disability insurance programs to retired persons, dependents of deceased insured workers, or to disabled workers; and private pensions or retirement benefits received by retired persons or their survivors, either directly or through an insurance company.

• *interest, dividends, rental income, and other property income* Includes interest income on savings or bonds; payments made by a corporation to its stockholders, periodic receipts from estates or trust funds; net income or loss from the rental of property, real estate, or farms, and net income or loss from roomers or boarders.

• *unemployment and workers' compensation and veterans' benefits* Includes income from unemployment compensation and workers' compensation, and veterans' payments including educational benefits, but excluding military retirement.

• *public assistance, supplemental security income, and food stamps* Includes public assistance or welfare, including money received from job training grants; supplemental security income paid by federal, state, and local welfare agencies to low-income persons who are aged 65 or older, blind, or disabled; and the value of food stamps obtained.

• *regular contributions for support* Includes alimony and child support as well as any regular contributions from persons outside the consumer unit.

• *other income* Includes money income from care of foster children, cash scholarships, fellowships, or stipends not based on working; and meals and rent as pay.

indexed spending Indexed spending figures compare the spending of particular demographic segments with that of the average household. To compute an index, the amount spent on an item by a demographic segment is divided by the amount spent on the item by the average household. That figure is then multiplied by 100. An index of 100 is the average for all households. An index of 132 means average spending by households in a segment is 32 percent above average (100 plus 32). An index of 75 means average spending by households in a segment is 25 percent below average (100 minus 25). Indexed spending figures identify the consumer units that spend the most on a product or service.

life and other personal insurance Includes premiums from whole life and term insurance; endowments; income and other life insurance; mortgage guarantee insurance; mortgage life insurance; premiums for personal life liability, accident and disability; and other non–health insurance other than homes and vehicles.

market share The market share is the percentage of total household spending on an item that is accounted for by a demographic segment. Market shares are calculated by dividing a demographic segment's total spending on an item by the total spending of all households on the item. Total spending on an item for all households is calculated by multiplying average spending by the total number of households. Total spending on an item for each demographic segment is calculated by multiplying the segment's average spending by the number of households in the segment. Market shares reveal the demographic segments that account for the largest share of spending on a product or service.

millennial generation Americans born between 1977 and 1994.

occupation The occupation in which the reference person received the most earnings during the survey period. The occupational categories follow those of the Census of Population. Categories shown in the tables include the following:

• *self-employed* Includes all occupational categories; the reference person is self-employed in own business, professional practice, or farm.

• *wage and salary earners, managers and professionals* Includes executives, administrators, managers, and professional specialties such as architects, engineers, natural and social scientists, lawyers, teachers, writers, health diagnosis and treatment workers, entertainers, and athletes.

• *wage and salary earners, technical, sales, and clerical workers* Includes technicians and related support workers; sales representatives, sales workers, cashiers, and sales-related occupations; and administrative support, including clerical.

• *retired* People who did not work either full- or part-time during the survey period.

owner See housing tenure.

pensions and Social Security Includes all Social Security contributions paid by employees; employees' contributions to railroad retirement, government retirement and private pensions programs; retirement programs for self-employed.

personal care Includes products for the hair, oral hygiene products, shaving needs, cosmetics, bath products, suntan lotions, hand creams, electric personal care appliances, incontinence products, other personal care products, personal care services such as hair care services (haircuts, bleaching, tinting, coloring, conditioning treatments, permanents, press, and curls), styling and other services for wigs and hairpieces, body massages or slenderizing treatments, facials, manicures, pedicures, shaves, electrolysis.

quarterly spending Quarterly spending data are collected in the interview portion of the Consumer Expenditure Survey. The quarterly spending tables show the percentage of households that purchased an item during an average quarter, and the amount spent during the quarter on the item by purchasers. Not all items are included in the interview portion of the Consumer Expenditure Survey.

reading Includes subscriptions for newspapers, magazines, and books through book clubs; purchase of single-copy newspapers and magazines, books, and encyclopedias and other reference books.

reference person The first member mentioned by the respondent when asked to Start with the name of the person or one of the persons who owns or rents the home. It is with respect to this person that the relationship of other consumer unit members is determined. Also called the householder or head of household.

region Consumer units are classified according to their address at the time of their participation in the survey. The four major census regions of the United States are the following state groupings:

• *Northeast* Connecticut, Maine, Massachusetts, New Hampshire, New Jersey, New York, Pennsylvania, Rhode Island, and Vermont.

• *Midwest* Illinois, Indiana, Iowa, Kansas, Michigan, Minnesota, Mississippi, Nebraska, North Dakota, Ohio, South Dakota, and Wisconsin.

• *South* Alabama, Arkansas, Delaware, District of Columbia, Florida, Georgia, Kentucky, Louisiana, Maryland, Mississippi, North Carolina, Oklahoma, South Carolina, Tennessee, Texas, Virginia, and West Virginia.

• *West* Alaska, Arizona, California, Colorado, Hawaii, Idaho, Minnesota, Nevada, New Mexico, Oregon, Utah, Washington, and Wyoming.

renter See housing tenure.

shelter Includes the following:

• *owned dwellings* Includes interest on mortgages, property taxes and insurance, refinancing and prepayment charges, ground rent, expenses for property management and security, homeowner's insurance, fire insurance and extended coverage, landscaping expenses for repairs and maintenance contracted out (including periodic maintenance and service contracts), and expenses of materials for owner-performed repairs and maintenance for dwellings used or maintained by the consumer unit, but not dwellings maintained for business or rent.

• *rented dwellings* Includes rent paid for dwellings, rent received as pay, parking fees, maintenance, and other expenses.

• *otherlodging* Includes all expenses for vacation homes, school, college, hotels, motels, cottages, trailer camps, and other lodging while out of town.

• *utilities, fuels, and public services* Includes natural gas, electricity, fuel oil, coal, bottled gas, wood, other fuels; residential telephone service, cell phone service, phone cards; water, garbage, trash collection; sewerage maintenance, septic tank cleaning; and other public services.

size of consumer unit The number of people whose usual place of residence at the time of the interview is in the consumer unit.

state and local income taxes Includes state and local income taxes withheld in the survey year to pay for income earned in survey year plus additional taxes paid in the survey year to cover any underpayment or underwithholding of taxes in the year prior to the survey.

tobacco and smoking supplies Includes cigarettes, cigars, snuff, loose smoking tobacco, chewing tobacco, and smoking accessories such as cigarette or cigar holders, pipes, flints, lighters, pipe cleaners, and other smoking products and accessories.

transportation Includes the following:

• *vehicle purchases (net outlay)* Includes the net outlay (purchase price minus trade-in value) on new and used domestic and imported cars and trucks and other vehicles, including motorcycles and private planes.

• *gasoline and motor oil* Includes gasoline, diesel fuel, and motor oil.

• *other vehicle expenses* Includes vehicle finance charges, maintenance and repairs, vehicle insurance, and vehicle rental licenses and other charges.

• *vehicle finance charges* Includes the dollar amount of interest paid for a loan contracted for the purchase of vehicles described above.

• *maintenance and repairs* Includes tires, batteries, tubes, lubrication, filters, coolant, additives, brake and transmission fluids, oil change, brake adjustment and repair, front-end alignment, wheel balancing, steering repair, shock absorber replacement, clutch and transmission repair, electrical system repair, repair to cooling system, drive train repair, drive shaft and rear-end repair, tire repair, vehicle video equipment, other maintenance and services, and auto repair policies.

• *vehicle insurance* Includes the premium paid for insuring cars, trucks, and other vehicles.

• *vehicle rental, licenses, and other charges* Includes leased and rented cars, trucks, motorcycles, and aircraft, inspection fees, state and local registration, drivers' license fees, parking fees, towing charges, tolls on trips, and global positioning services.

• *public transportation* Includes fares for mass transit, buses, trains, airlines, taxis, private school buses, and fares paid on trips for trains, boats, taxis, buses, and trains.

weekly spending Weekly spending data are collected in the diary portion of the Consumer Expenditure Survey. The data show the percentage of households that purchased an item during the average week, and the amount spent per week on the item by purchasers. Not all items are included in the diary portion of the Consumer Expenditure Survey.